Issues in Higher Education
and the Professions in the 1980s

Issues in Higher Education and the Professions in the 1980s

Martha Boaz

Libraries Unlimited, Inc.
Littleton, Colorado
1981

Copyright © 1981 Libraries Unlimited, Inc.
All Rights Reserved
Printed in the United States of America

LIBRARIES UNLIMITED, INC.
P.O. Box 263
Littleton, Colorado 80160

Library of Congress Cataloging in Publication Data

Main entry under title:

Issues in higher education and the professions in
the 1980s.

Includes index.
1. Education, Higher--United States--Addresses,
essays, lectures. 2. Professional education--United
States--Addresses, essays, lectures. I. Boaz,
Martha Terosse, 1913-   .
LB2325.I84   378.73   81-12357
ISBN 0-87287-260-2   AACR2

PREFACE

This book is concerned, as its title indicates, with issues in higher education and the professions in the 1980s. The first article deals with general problems, issues, trends, and prospects in higher education. Among the problems are skyrocketing tuition, declining enrollments, financial pressures, friction within the academic community, and a downward trend in educational quality and research capability. Among the issues are education for minorities, women, and the older population, a trend toward vocational training, and a changing sense of values among the younger generation. Questions are raised about how to maintain educational programs and change them to meet the present and future needs of society.

Other articles in the book deal with trends, issues, problems and prospects in education for the professions. A selected group of representative professions have been chosen for inclusion and recognized authorities in each field have written on the following topics: medicine (general medicine and pharmacy), law, architecture, business administration, public administration, engineering, library and information science, higher education, continuing education, and gerontology. There is also a section on liberal education and careers and a concluding section containing a brief summary and recommendations. Each author has followed his or her own style of writing and point of view in the material presented. The hope is that aggressive concerned steps will be taken to meet current and future challenges, to strengthen higher education and professional education, and to meet the needs of an *interdependent* society.

Martha Boaz

TABLE OF CONTENTS

HIGHER EDUCATION IN THE 1980s:
TRENDS, ISSUES, PROBLEMS, PROSPECTS

by
Martha Boaz

Research Associate, Center for Study of the American Experience
Dean Emeritus, Graduate Library School
University of Southern California

INTRODUCTION

Higher education in America has made great progress in the last 100 years. The period of the golden years in higher education in the United States was the decade of the 1960s when there was a prevailing spirit of optimism. Enrollments, faculty, and the number of graduates doubled and government support for education made the decade one of affluence. Federal and state financial support was provided for student aid, construction, equipment, libraries, research, and other special projects. The investments paid off as was proved by the advances in science and technology—the most spectacular achievement being the landing of men on the moon.

Higher education has long been respected for its contributions to human advancement, to improved quality of life, to individual and group fulfillment, and to a highly significant role in society. Yet in recent years there has been much criticism of the educational system.

Following is a summary of some of the general trends, issues, problems, and prospects for higher education in the 1980s. This paper is intended to serve as a general background for the papers that follow on professional and graduate education.

Some Public Perceptions of Higher Education

General public disillusionment with higher education began in the late 1960s and has continued into the 1980s. Employers were often disappointed in the graduates who did not meet anticipated educational competencies, and graduates, involved in intense job competition, were disenchanted with the benefits of the educational degree. Because of the diminishing number of jobs, employers have had more applicants from which to choose, and as a consequence applicants are now more concerned about their abilities and educational qualifications. Higher education is no longer an elitist system, due to social changes, minority and sexist problems, the economic recession, and many other allied factors.

A decline in the standards of American colleges has been noticeable for some time and the educational degree has already become tainted by instructional shoddiness and institutional fraud. Signs of moral deterioration are found in shabby student recruiting techniques, guilt-driven allowances for minority status, lowering of admission standards, grade inflation, instructional laziness, lowered academic requirements, and other laxities.

Contrary to the former expectation of a collegial atmosphere on the college and university campus, one now finds faculty jealousy and dissension, backbiting, and maneuvering for power. Stories of these and other problems have decreased the public's confidence in educational institutions. Rivalry between institutions, as well as dissension on individual campuses and public disillusionment with education in general portend unfortunate effects on university fund-raising efforts in the future.

Unions and collective bargaining also produce adversary relationships in educational institutions. The struggle for power between faculty/staff and administration produces a climate devoid of trust and respect, leads to lowered standards and to personal aggrandizement rather than to professional and institutional progress. Perhaps it is a healthy trend that educators are being challenged by the public.

The time has come for recognizing our problems and attempting to solve them. Kenneth Ashworth, commissioner for the Coordinating Board of the Texas College and University System, says, "It is ironic that our colleges and universities . . . give so little attention to the study of their own past and the social processes at work upon them. The colleges and universities equally neglect consideration of their alternate futures. The university community probably spends less time studying itself than it does almost any other topic for scholars to contemplate."[1] And, "Despite the influence of educational reformers," says Herbert London, dean of the Gallatin Division at New York University, "the educational system generally is not organized to change society so much as to reflect changes. It is also not adept at revitalizing itself."[2] London notes that educational innovations come in various guises, but they are all supported by present cultural values. Because the future of education is closely related to other social developments, it must be considered as a vital element in the total environment. Speaking of future planning, Herman Kahn, director of Hudson Institute, asks the question, "How does one go about making useful statements about the future in a climate of uncertainty and disorientation?"[3] He answers himself by saying, "In the final analysis, all one can say is that the importance of the subject justifies the effort."[4]

SOCIAL AND DEMOGRAPHIC TRENDS

A significant fact influencing education and the work world is the demographic change that prevails. Studies made by the Organization for Economic Cooperation and Development (OECD)[5] show a universal decline in the member countries. The birthrate of the future is uncertain but projections for working-age people for the immediate future (the next ten years) are more reliable, since these people have already been born; these figures predict a continuing rise in the working-age population up to 1990.

Major demographic and geographical changes will be serious matters, says Waldman A. Nielson, a fellow of the Aspen Institute:

Because of a steep decline in the birthrate which began in the 1960s, the number of college-age students from now until the end of the century will decrease, which in turn will require great program and financial adjustments by institutions of higher education. The increasing proportion of the population which is elderly will impose costly new demands on health-related

institutions. Most important of all perhaps in terms of future capital requirements of the private nonprofit sector is the huge population movement out
of the central cities to the suburbs, and regionally from the Northeast to
the so-called Sunbelt. These shifts mean a drain of higher income families
away from locations where the bulk of private cultural, educational, religious,
and welfare institutions have historically been located into areas in which
they are relatively lacking.[6]

Aging

The aging of our society and its impact on the educational system is a subject
that is receiving wide attention. John Naisbitt, president of Yankelovich, Skelly
and White, publisher of the *Trend Report*, says that agism has replaced racism and
sexism as society's major anti-discrimination preoccupation.[7] Projections for the
year 2000 indicate that there will be 30 million persons in our population who are
65 or older and that the middle-aged group will be a dominant one in the United
States. Projections for future learning for the middle-aged adult suggest a great
demand for educational opportunities for this group and a resultant great impact
on society because of the power and influence of these people in the social structure.

Changing Values

Trends indicate that families will undergo social change, exhibited in part by
permissive parental attitudes and less home guidance. Contributing to such changes
is the fact that many mothers are now working, that parents are less ambitious, and
that many of them do not push their children academically. The changing role of
women is another important trend. The need for continuing education for women
throughout their lives is receiving a great deal of attention. In addition, people are
now more interested in the quality of life than in former years and they are no
longer thinking in terms of early education and preparation for a job, then of a job,
and finally of retirement. Rather, they are opting for a blended life plan that permits learning, work, and leisure to go on concurrently.

Inflation and Tuition

If present trends continue, inflation will become a more serious problem in the
future. Harold Shane, professor of education at Indiana University, gives a frightening
forecast of what might happen as to increases in college tuition, over a four-year
period, to a child who is three years old today: "By the time the child reaches 18,
the cost of tuition will have increased from $16,000 to more than $42,000 even if
the inflation rate averages no more than a conservative 6 percent each year."[8]

Enrollment

Decreased enrollment has become a serious problem for universities due to the
financial importance of tuition. Many universities, particularly private ones, must
have income from tuition to survive. It is generally recognized that higher education
is no longer a growth industry. The Carnegie Council on Policy Studies in Higher
Education predicts that college enrollments will shrink 5% to 15% during the next
20 years, producing a Golden Age for students as colleges scramble to attract them
and tailor courses to their tastes. The council said that it was quite likely, though

not inevitable, that the nation's 3,000 colleges and universities would suffer a downward drift in quality, integrity, diversity, and research capability.[9]

Predicting future enrollment is easy in so far as age distribution data are available for those already born, but mobility and "flight from the cities" as well as interest in going to school at all are less predictable issues. Tentative projections imply that during the next two generations the fastest growing geographical areas for education in the United States will be the southern states, Texas, and California. The birthrate may rise or fall and the movement out of cities may intensify; nobody can give a definite answer on these matters.

Enrollment trends indicate that more "nontraditional" students are attending school. Such students include nondegree candidates, women returning to school after raising their families as well as more women in general, minority students, older students changing careers, elderly and retired students, and part-time students. With the enrollment of the more nontraditional students, universities will need to accommodate them by adjusting programs and services to include more flexible course offerings, intensive courses, independent study, more flexible hours for admissions and financial aid services, commuting and parking conveniences, and child care services.

Unemployment and Labor Force Problems

Many people who currently hold degrees are unemployed or cannot find the type of professional positions they want. Harold Shane quotes a U.S. Bureau of Labor report that "foresees a 'surplus' of 2.7 million graduates with the B.A. by 1985, and a Mellon Foundation inquiry which says that by 1990 there will be a 'surplus' of 60,000 Ph.D. recipients in the humanities."[10] According to Shane, other labor studies indicate that blacks are twice as likely as whites to be unemployed and that employment plans will need to be established for the several million immigrants who have entered this country.

Competition for jobs will increase in the 1980s and 1990s as the baby boom children move into their adult years, but there may be positive forces that will help this situation. Changes in life-style may initiate "shift work," encourage one worker to work six months of the year and another the other six months, urge workers already on the job to return to school for additional or updated education, or allow more travel and more use of vacation time. These practices would enable beginning workers to have the vacated jobs on a part-time basis.

Different Educational Patterns

Varied types of educational programs should be planned, including general, professional, paraprofessional, continuing education, and education for special groups. Different time slots should be considered for special programs. Programs could be available at Christmas or during vacation periods, during the summer, and on weekends. Many programs are already under way at these times. The nontraditional programs should be geared to the needs of the people who need the services. Author Alvin Toffler predicts that the years of compulsory schooling will grow shorter, not longer. "Instead of rigid age segregation, young and old will mingle. Education will become more interspersed and interwoven with work and more spread out over a lifetime."[11]

Changes in Locale and Time

Toffler notes that education does not necessarily take place in a classroom as it has in the past, and that in the future more learning will occur outside rather than inside the classroom. He asserts that "Today we need to combine learning with work, political struggle, community service, and even play. All our conventional assumptions about education need to be re-examined both in the rich countries and in the poor."[12]

More and more, courses are being offered "off campus" in extension settings and by nontraditional technological delivery systems so that many people are earning college degrees without ever going to a campus. Certain programs may move from college and university settings to large business companies, research institutes, or other specialized settings. In some cases, companies want specialized or research education for their own immediate company work and there are instances when they have highly qualified staff to serve as faculty members. This is true of the Rand Corporation in Santa Monica, California, which offers Ph.D. courses to qualified employees of the company. Programs such as this should stimulate universities to seek more cooperative research arrangements with industry.

More Practical Programs

Owing to many factors, college and university administrators are becoming more and more concerned with the content, the practicality, and the quality of academic programs. Managers, with a business point of view, emphasize the concept that would require "institutions to base decisions about their programs on realistic assessments of market trends and their own strengths and weaknesses."[13] As survival becomes more crucial, academic administrators are becoming keenly interested in aggressive marketing techniques. Part of the overall concept is the philosophy that strong academic programs are essential to a college's success and that a buyer's market prevails— people will pay for quality. The connotation is that tuition rates might vary according to the market value of the programs. "For example, the rate for a course in business might be higher than the rate for one in English or history . . ."[14]

Technological Trends

The accelerated rate of change in technology indicates mandatory and frequent changes in education. It is estimated that the body of information in the exact sciences doubles every 8 to 10 years. There is also greater specialization in occupations. Technology is related to the growth of occupational obsolescence and the need for frequent retraining and recertification in certain fields, such as medicine. Comments about technology are made by the vice president and one of the chief scientists of the International Business Machines (IBM) Lewis M. Branscomb: "In education, computers are currently useful but limited tools, yet they hold the potential of altering the role of educational institutions. Today universities are not just generators of knowledge but also distributors. Electronic media—television in our time and interactive home video computers in the future—will provide even more effective mechanisms for education than the classroom because of the personalized nature of the educational processing."[15]

Because of advances in computer and communication technology since 1950, the size and cost of computers has decreased greatly while the efficiency, speed, and access to large pools of knowledge through telecommunications satellites transmission have improved dramatically.

The world is going from a mass industrial to a postindustrial society and from a material world to an information-based age. There is a noticeable growth in knowledge-intensive industries and a specific direction toward an information-based society. The educational world should work closely with these developments as it looks to the future. Instead of being afraid of new technological developments, education should reach out and "use" them to advantage, without disadvantage to the software. In coming years each home may serve as a learning center for persons of all ages and for different purposes such as degree attainment, retraining, professional development, recreation, and hobbies.

FINANCIAL PROBLEMS

The current budgetary struggle in Washington and a downward trend towards a necessary American austerity will impose new financial and political restraints on education. The budgetary cutbacks do not augur well for public institutions, which rely heavily on government support for future academic quality. As a result, the elite private universities may come into even greater prominence than they now have, but they too will be in a stressful situation with high inflation and reduced student enrollments. Higher education faces a serious question. Will it be able to address and cope with the austere economic situation that has evolved? Will certain institutions be able to survive? Someone has said that there comes a time when public service institutions are best dismantled rather than providing marginal services. Certainly academic institutions are already confronted with the possibility of being forced to close. According to information reported by Logan Wilson, former chancellor of the University of Texas and president emeritus of the American Council on Education, "the fiscal crunch that began around 1970 caused about fifty small colleges to close by 1974, and even some public universities with enrollment drops and/or decreased funding had to take drastic actions."[16] Other dramatic cuts occurred. One major university "gave notice a year in advance to 88 tenured faculty members and to 200 non-tenured faculty and staff members that effective July 1, 1974, they would be terminated."[17] The officials at another university anticipated a future in which nine out of ten junior academics would have to go out rather than up. In still other institutions entire schools and programs have been eliminated. This has not been a matter of preference, but a fact of life in a time of diminishing returns.

Financial problems are not singular to the United States. A case in England involves the University of London: "The University of London, Great Britain's largest conventional university, may shut down two of its medical schools and several institutes as a result of declining enrollment, and declining government support."[18] According to David Walker, London Correspondent for *The Chronicle of Higher Education*, the closing of the financially strapped university's two medical schools "has been proposed by Lord Annan, the university's vice-chancellor. The committee also proposed that 34 separate medical training facilities associated with the university be merged into 6 units."[19] Although this is cold comfort, it is interesting to know that other than American institutions are having to make changes in midstream. Postmortems are unpleasant, but can serve as preventives for the deaths of other institutions.

With the competition for students and with senior colleges working harder to attract them, the number of people attending two-year colleges will drop even lower and communities will question the practicality of supporting them. Arthur Cohen, professor of higher education at the University of California, Los Angeles, and John Lombardi, former president of Los Angeles City College, comment on the financial side, saying, "The most significant development of the 1980s may be the abandonment of the no-tuition policy. The public will be less disturbed about anything the community college does as long as the students are paying for part of their education."[20]

Use of Vouchers

Reform methods in education have been under way for several years in the secondary schools. One of these is called the voucher system, a federally supported program for parents to purchase educational services for their children. Distribution of state funds is related to the institutions' ability to attract students.

Decline in Scholarships and Student Aid

Statistics presented by Richard E. Anderson, associate professor of higher education, Teachers College, Columbia University, indicate that student aid has remained fairly stable, but the method of allocation has shifted from that of strictly need to a combination of need and merit and to both scholarships and tuition discounts.[21] In reality the result is a decrease in actual student aid and a continuing decline in student scholarships.

Expenditures for Physical Plant Operations

The budget item for plant operations and maintenance has seemed to remain comparatively stable but, in reality, with the increased cost of energy and all materials there has been a decreased amount for overall maintenance, and depreciation has been ignored. This deferred maintenance figure will eventually run into billions of dollars. These facts indicate an underestimation of capital consumption, and this is a serious matter, especially for private institutions.

Another building-related problem may develop, if whole schools or departments are closed for financial reasons. In this event, educational institutions may have to rent or sell buildings to businesses or other agencies.

As school construction slows down or stops, it may be necessary to make use of the "double session" type of schedule. This is for two or more day and night sessions as well as weekend and vacation times. The space in buildings is worth thousands of dollars per square foot and buildings that are empty for several weeks at Christmas or during the summer may be considered as great financial drains.

Cooperative Programs

One answer to fiscal shortages is to establish inter-university/inter-school programs. This is easy to manage if universities are geographically close to each other and it is not difficult even if long distances separate them. In the latter case, a student may attend another university for a summer, a semester, or a year and receive credit at the home institution. Thus, universities/schools could specialize without duplicating programs offered elsewhere. In so doing they could save money as well as foster friendly cooperative relationships instead of the current (often bitter) rivalries that exist. A case of one joint effort that has been noted exists in the medical schools of Brown University and Dartmouth College. The colleges, finding that one was weak where the other was strong, have agreed to a cooperative program to increase their enrollments. "Starting in the fall of 1981, 20 students, each year, will be admitted jointly by the two institutions. Those students will get their first two years of medical education at Dartmouth, their second two years at Brown."[22] Another cooperative effort is being made by 20 liberal arts colleges in the northeastern part of the United States. They are working together on their energy expenses and a study of their common energy problems. The University of Southern California and the University of California at Los Angeles Library Schools have an option for a cooperative program. This was set up several years ago under the auspices of the USC Graduate School. It is regrettable that this consortium type of agreement is little observed, however. Perhaps more cooperative projects will develop in the future—by mutual desire or by fiscal necessity. In organizing such programs, of course, it will be necessary to provide built-in protection for the maintenance of quality in each program.

Retrenchment

Institutions should be practical and realistic about retrenchment. If a department or school has insufficient enrollment, or, if there is no active demand for its continued existence, the unit should be closed or merged with some other division of the university. Financial problems have already caused several professional schools to be eliminated and, in some cases, as noted above, whole colleges have been closed. Educational institutions can no longer sit as ivory towers in an intellectual dream world. True, it is difficult to produce evidence, as the business world does, of the value of the products. In comparison with an industry such as General Motors that can measure its output and judge the efficiency of its management, it is difficult to measure education in areas such as critical thinking. It is also difficult to measure it in relation to cost. This fact is not restricted to education alone, but is characteristic of most service-oriented professions. Perhaps the time has come when higher education will have to present convincing evidence of its value in order to survive.

Government, Foundations, and Private Support

Government support for higher education increased noticeably in the 1960s but by the mid-1970s interest in university-based research began to decline and funding decreased. This situation caused changes in universities, with some faculty members being dismissed and others transferred to different assignments within the university. These losses brought the attention of state legislatures back to tuition and fees as primary sources of revenue.

It seems likely that government financing in the future will be much more limited than at present. This will stimulate intense competition for the money that will be available.

The funding of higher education differs greatly from the public to the private sector. Public institutions receive three-fourths of their funds for instruction from public sources whereas private institutions receive more than half of their resources from tuition and only about 5% from government aid.

Private foundations usually provide funding only to requests that are geared to the interests and objectives of the particular foundation. However, some foundations finance programs for a university that are of especial interest to the university.

With government support goes government control and this is unfortunate, for legislators are not usually attuned to the objectives of educational programs and are not qualified to judge them. In addition, they impose demands and require elaborate reporting minutiae so that thousands of hours of faculty and administrative time are spend in preparing reports for the government. This use of time is costly and becomes a tedious chore.

Government Control

Hence, while in the beginning government was a major ben⸱factor to education, it has now become something of a deterrent to progress and a control over the advancement of free study and enlightened inquiry. In the future there may be even more government control due to the separate Department of Education that has recently been established. An aggressive department may attempt to impose restrictions or to demand control over directions. It is hoped that the opposite will be true. The university's autonomy is important and for this reason it should guard its integrity in any dealings with government or foundations or other agencies by adhering to the purposes and objectives of the university, even to the point of not requesting or accepting outside funding.

Gifts and Endowments

Most colleges and universities now have active vigorous fund-raising programs employing full-time fund raisers and, in some cases, full-time lobbyists in state capitols and in Washington. Although gifts and endowments are not vital to public institutions, they are very important to most private universities and may even serve as measures of survival.

Endowment income is a "safe" type of gift, provided it is set up for that purpose and principles of the agreement are strictly maintained. With the current inflation increases, it is difficult to maintain the levels of purchasing power of endowments that were established some years ago. For this reason, gifts and additions to endowments are often necessary, depending on the annual expenditures from the funds. Endowment income declined in the 1970s and there is now more competition for it, in both public and private institutions.

ADMINISTRATION, FACULTY, AND WORKING CONDITIONS OF THE UNIVERSITY

The administration of a university requires organization and is similar to the management of other organizations and businesses. Fiscal responsibility, in legal terms, is usually the responsibility of the members of the Board of Trustees, who donate their time to the institution. But the president and other administrative officers are the people who carry out the fiscal directives of the trustees. In today's educational world, the trend toward leveling and participatory management makes it difficult to know who actually has the authority to make decisions.

Administration

As a result of public criticism, there is more demand today for good governance, good management, and an accompanying accountability in educational institutions. These functions exist at three levels: department, school or college, and the university. Each administrator and manager in these groups is or should be held strictly accountable for the allocation and use of budgets and for the quality of programs.

The President

The "giant" presidents such as Hutchins at Chicago and Eliot at Harvard were leaders and scholars. Today the president has to be a fund raiser and a public relations expert. It has been said that college and university presidents think of themselves as practitioners of the world's roughest profession. The office of president in a university has become a thankless job. Reasons for this are the fiscal problems, the faculty/staff problems (salaries, unionization, tenure), student problems (enrollment, tuition, campus discontent), and program development problems. All of these are parts of the package that a president must handle. The power of the president is, in part, a matter of his or her own personality and strength, but because of the many problems that are now prevalent in universities, the tenure of a president is often five years or less.

The president works with other academic, financial and business officers of the university in planning and implementing the goals, objectives, and policies of the university. This requires close cooperation within the group. The allocation of resources is an important activity and demands well-defined objectives and clear-cut priorities for the institution's programs.

There are sometimes problems in the various administrative areas, such as professional schools; each school is usually more concerned with its own needs and advantages than with the total university welfare. Participation in cooperative inter-disciplinary programs is not as prevalent as it should be. On the contrary, each school works independently for its own funding, for grants, and for its individual needs.

Faculty

There is a rather universal agreement that the quality of higher education has declined in recent years. How can this trend be changed, moved to an upward direction? One of the most evident ways lies in faculty activity and commitment. The quality of faculty, their standards, their requirements, and their dedication to teaching, learning, and research are vital to quality education. Some faculty take unfair advantage of benefits. Traditionally they have been expected to do productive research, to assist students in their studies, and to work for overall university programs. Many are now abandoning most of these responsibilities, meeting classes only a minimum number of hours, and working as off-campus "consultants" or in other regular outside jobs. Scholarship, intellectual activity, and research suffer.

Unionization

Unionization has been a topic of interest to a number of faculty members in recent years. A. H. Raskin, a labor editor with the *New York Times*, says there is mounting evidence of the decreasing power and division within the unionized section of the work force. Raskin makes one nondebatable point when he says "none of us will have a future worth the struggle unless we can restructure our institutions in a way that convinces us they are deserving of trust."[2][3] Educational institutions should note this admonition.

POSSIBLE SOLUTIONS TO PROBLEMS

How to do as much or more with the same or less is a management problem that requires attention in academic circles. Living in a rarefied educational "ivory tower" atmosphere is a thing of the past. Low enrollments, deficit budgets, continuing inflation, cuts in faculty and staff, and accompanying union activities, plus depreciation and closing of physical facilities are facts of life that must be faced. They require efficient management and tough administrative decisions. Educators who are not willing to sink into a slough of depression will think of countervailing forces and innovative plans.

New and Innovative Programs

Action is required to solve these problems. Educational institutions may offer new and innovative programs designed to attract new clienteles. These may involve senior citizens, who have the time and interest to go back to school, as well as other groups—more mid-career people, more minority, more female, and more part-time students, more foreign students, and those with more specialized interests. Institutions may capitalize on career and vocational needs of persons who are in technological fields that change rapidly and require frequent re-education in order for employees to hold their jobs. Speaking to this point, Beverly Watkins, assistant editor of *The Chronicle of Higher Education*, urges the new Department of Education to promote more communication between educational institutions and business on manpower issues and to identify occupational education and training needs for skilled workers. Included in this plan is the philosophy that sees education and training as a lifelong "absolutely necessary national investment." Such a program would not only fill the gap for skilled workers but would also remove millions of people from unemployment lines. These people could then be contributing to society instead of being recipients of doles and food coupons.[24]

Changes in the traditional locale, format, and time for offering courses present other opportunities for educational institutions to cope with their financial problems and to attract students.

Unmet Learning Needs

There are unmet learning needs that are "targets of opportunity." George W. Bonham, editor-in-chief of *Change* magazine, lists the following:

- 60 million Americans now find themselves in some form of instructional setting, with 46 million of them outside our formal school and college systems.
- 40 million Americans regard themselves at any moment in time as undergoing some form of career transition.
- Over $17 billion in educational benefits is available, of which only a small fraction is being utilized.
- Business and industry alone spend $10 billion annually on training and upgrading. And the needs for learning seem equally impressive.
- 65 million Americans lack basic competency skills.
- 15 million Americans lack college degrees.
- 12 million professionals require regular in-service education.[25]

Today's Adult Learner

George Bonham presents a profile of today's adult learner based on a pilot study using a representative sampling of 1,500 adults. The study, prepared by the College Board—The Future Directions for a Learning Society and funded by the Exxon Education Foundation, includes, in abbreviated form, the following characteristics of today's adult learner:

- Learners are slightly more likely to live in urbanized areas . . .
- Learners are considerably younger than nonlearners . . . Half of all adult learners are under 40.
- Blacks supply considerably less than their proportionate share of learners; Hispanics supply their share; whites supply a bit more than their share; other groups supply considerably more than their share.
- Learners are considerably better educated than nonlearners. Adults who have gone beyond high school are twice as likely to learn as those who have not . . .
- Adults with high incomes are more likely to learn.
- Employed adults are far more likely to engage in learning than unemployed adults . . . In short, the more work a person is doing, the more likely he or she is to engage in learning.
- Of all occupational groups, adults in professional and technical work are more likely to engage in learning . . .
- Participation in learning drops sharply among adults who have five or more children.
- Females with children under 18 are considerably more likely to engage in learning than females with children over 18.
- Adults in the Pacific Coast states are more likely to engage in learning than those in any other region . . .
- Single adults who have never married and divorced adults are more likely to engage in learning than others . . .[26]

The profile of the adult learner and the lists of unmet learning needs provide data for the development of programs to educate potential students.

Newer Trends in Teaching

Self-paced instruction is an alternate to traditional regular class meetings with students and a teacher in a classroon setting. This approach is based on the idea that topics can be divided into units or modules and a set of objectives and assignments for each unit can be measured by an examination; when the student passes the exam he or she continues to the next unit. Another departure in self-instruction from the regular classroom meeting is television programming.

Still another change that has been tried in public education is that of alternative schools. These are experimental laboratories that concentrate on certain fundamental questions in education and provide a type of career education that students do not get in conventional schools.

Technology

George Bonham says that education will need the new telecommunications in the decades ahead, and that telecommunications will require the best educationally-based "software" to provide the widest possible spectrum of services.[27]

There have been a number of trial runs using open television for education, but past experiments using television have not been well adapted to learning. Significant opportunities lie ahead, however. Bonham quotes James Loper, head of public television station KCET in Los Angeles, who recently predicted some of these changes and said that they will be influenced by different modes of distribution. Loper thinks the satellite will cause the most radical changes.[28]

Bonham explains that there is no longer any technical reason that would prohibit any one of the major universities from beaming instructional offerings into 30,000,000 cable-connected homes.[29] As another editorial writer noted recently, the next great leap forward beyond the schools is teleducation abetted by extraordinary new capabilities to deliver education to class-size audiences at per-student costs strikingly similar to those in traditional schools and colleges.

Coinciding with rapid technological change is the rapid growth and change in knowledge. "The belief that knowledge is stable is a myth,"[30] declares Arthur Combs, professor of psychology and education at Miami-Dade College in Florida. He gives reasons for this statement: "Two things are happening in the world we live in that guarantee we can never again base our thinking on the concept of a stable society or the certainty of a body of knowledge. These are: (1) the information explosion, and (2) the ever accelerating pace of change!"[31]

Combs thinks that schools, because of the explosion of information, can never again devise a program required of everyone. The reason for this lies in the fact that the knowledge is so voluminous that any sample selected could not prepare students for effective living in our modern complex society. In addition to the volume of knowledge there is frequent and rapid change so that "what is 'so' today may be 'not so' tomorrow."[32]

A postindustrial society will be heavily dependent on information, knowledge, and service. But this society will still be dependent upon the production industries of the industrial soceity and these will be characterized as no-growth. Higher education will be expected to deal with growth and limitations of growth in a number of areas. How to cope with a lower supply of resources and higher prices for them as well as with climbing environmental costs is a problem.

In line with these thoughts, Kenneth Ashworth points out that higher education will have two overriding tasks, both of which are intensifications of activities already under way. "The first will be to focus science and technology on ways to continue our growth despite the undeniable constraints on resources and the low tolerance of the environment to additional abuse."[33] Ashworth says that both applied and basic research are needed to solve these problems and that funding must be secured. He emphasizes the need for basic research "in a society as dependent as ours upon scientific and technological advances to save us from economic and social collapse . . ."[34] The second task listed for the universities is that of serving as "the central mind for modeling, theorizing, and discussing the impact of no-growth on economic systems and how we must prepare for adjustments and accommodations . . . discover how a stable, good, and improving society can be built and sustained in the face of the problems the world is certain to encounter within this generation or the next."[35]

CONCLUSIONS AND RECOMMENDATIONS

A well-educated society is vital to the future of the world. If this generalization is valid, it follows that each citizen should have an opportunity for quality education. This quality education should focus on the mastery of basic skills, on development of individual talent, and on the social role of every person.

Education suffers from a general lack of leadership. It is no longer an elitist enterprise or a growth industry. The prospects for improvement in the next 10 years are bleak, for we are facing problems that we should have anticipated 15 years ago. Since we have not done much to get ready for the future there may be a return, 5 to 10 years hence, to the militant social conflict that existed in the 1960s. Or, we may have the opposite—universal inertia and a lazy acceptance of whatever conditions exist. Certainly the economy may compel action that might not be first choice, if there is a choice.

Taking into account our international problems and the dependence on other countries for energy and other material supplies, it becomes increasingly important to drive toward excellence in education. The international aspects of each curriculum should be studied and changed from nineteenth century concepts to handle twentieth century problems. No longer are we living in a separate independent, national environment. On the contrary, nations are "dependent" on each other for industrial products, for food, and for other necessities in a civilized world. Because of this *interdependence*, schools should include in their curricula courses that will provide for communication (language), international relations, and world understanding. The need for solutions to social problems will increase. The logical place for solving these problems is the educational institution. But colleges and universities will have to do some careful planning, make changes, set priorities, and make hard choices. This may mean refusing to accept federal/state grants, for education must resist government control, plan and execute its own programs, and remain autonomous if it is to fulfill its role and responsibility to society.

There should be more quality control in education and more realistic planning for a system designed for the needs of a postindustrial society in a highly competitive world. To some extent, Alvin Toffler addresses this issue when he comments on the back-to-basics movement in education. He says: "Legitimately outraged by the disaster in mass education, it (the movement) does not recognize that a de-massified society calls for new educational strategies . . . the thrust of Third Wave change is toward increased diversity, not toward the further standardization of life."[36]

Although we are unable to control all circumstances, the chances for directing our own progress are better if decisions are made and choices based on valid information and careful direction. Each institution should examine its *raison d'etre* and either reaffirm current goals and objectives or develop new ones.

Education should not only be responsive to change but should be a leader in the field. The question is not *whether* to cope with the problems and challenges but *how* to do it. A large part of procedure is attitudinal. Higher education will be expected to do more with less, but educators can turn a losing proposition into a winning one. Let us say that this age anticipates. Other ages have reacted.

Within the Institution

Plans should be established for regular reports and for measuring results against the goals. Each institution should reexamine its official policies for trustees, faculty, staff, and students and issue, in written form, statements relating to expectations of job performance, service, responsibility, and conduct. This will involve administration, teaching, research, public service, and other duties.

For purposes of evaluation and future planning, each department and division should have periodic reviews and a meeting of the entire university family should be held at least once a year. Elected representatives should be present, but the meeting should be open to anyone from the university who wishes to attend. The matter of tenure should be reviewed and perhaps abolished, but this decision should be made after all constituents have voted on retention or abolishment.

As for the curriculum, the undergraduate program could become, in the interest of time and economy, a more intense study period with year-round attendance ending in graduation after three years. In an effort to raise standards, each division of a university could have complete and intensive written comprehensive examinations administered after completion of the undergraduate program. The same policy should be used for graduate and professional schools.

Accreditation

Accreditation has become an expensive and time-consuming process. Instead of having multiple specialized accreditation visits, each institution could have only one periodic visitation by a regional accrediting association. This group would, of course, have very high standards and would involve persons qualified to examine each of the institution's specialized programs.

Certification and Recertification

In order to ensure competence in a field, it is suggested that each profession and vocation require state or national certification in the field. In addition to the original certification, these certificate renewals should be required periodically to ensure that the individual maintains an awareness of current knowledge.

Licensing

Licensing of professional people supposedly protects the public from malpractice in the particular profession. The state of New York is in the process of making teaching a licensed profession similar to medicine and engineering. Each profession would be strengthened by requiring its practitioners to be licensed and to have periodic reviews for relicensing.

Interdependent Work

In the future, in a world that is becoming increasingly interdependent, it would seem that institutions of higher learning should work together in more cooperative endeavors. A step in this direction has been taken by Gene Budig, president of West Virginia University. In a study of 20 major institutions of higher education, several of the administrators who were involved in the survey "favor the creation of a network of economic centers on university campuses which would be charged with the responsibility for developing regional economic plans and policies. These university officials envision the centers as meeting places for the best economic minds, as places where new and effective ideas can be debated, tested, and disseminated."[37]

General Guidelines

Some of the general guidelines for meeting the needs of the 1980s are:

- Plan for a period of years ahead, not on a month-to-month or year-to-year basis.
- Establish goals and objectives that are visionary and at the same time achievable.
- View the schools and departments within a university as whole, with all parts working and interacting with each other; work with other similar institutions in cooperative programs.

- Establish high expectations of performance and excellence from everyone: administrators, faculty, staff, students, and all other persons who
  are involved. As a part of this, plan for regular and periodic educational/
  training programs to assist growth and improvement for these people.
- Plan for regular assessment procedures and for accountability of results.

School systems should have alternative ways for achieving results so that if one
method is not as successful as another, other methods may be tried.

It is generally recognized that lifetime learning will become more necessary in the
future, that occupational change for each individual may take place several times
within a lifetime, and that a high technology society and changing labor needs will
require frequent reeducation. Learners should be motivated to seek satisfying personal
and professional/vocational aspirations and to allocate education, work, and leisure
in a more flexible pattern.

In its final report, *Three Thousand Futures*, the Carnegie Council on Policy Studies
in Higher Education expresses general optimism about the future of education. The
editor of *Change* magazine quotes from the report:

> . . . A downward drift in quality, balance, integrity, dynamism, diversity,
> private initiative, research capability is not only possible—it is quite
> likely. But it is not required by external events. It is a matter of choice
> and not just of fate. The emphasis should be on "managing of excellence."[38]

Great colleges and universities have been conceived from dreams, built by hard
work, and maintained through dedicated people who had visions of intellectual
and educational greatness for a people or a nation. To bring about change in education will require entrepreneurship, imagination, marketing skills, courage, and concern. Whatever changes and reforms are envisioned should be based on universal
standards of excellence and should be directed not only to immediate reforms but
to timeless enduring concepts.

In order to survive and to move forward, universities will need to be willing and
able to move boldly. Do we have the interest, imagination, courage, and commitment
to meet these challenges?

NOTES

1. Kenneth H. Ashworth, *American Higher Education in Decline* (College Station,
TX: Texas A & M University Press, c1979), [p. 19].

2. Herbert London, "Innovations in Public Education: Failures and Prospects,"
in *Future Trends in Education Policy*, ed. by Jane Newitt (Lexington, MA: D. C.
Heath and Co., 1979), p. 51.

3. Herman Kahn, "Introduction," in *Future Trends in Education Policy*, ed. by
Jane Newitt (Lexington, MA: D. C. Heath and Co., 1979), p. VII.

4. Ibid.

5. Jane Bengtsson, "The Shape of Work to Come—Prospects," *Change* (July-August
1979), p. 18.

6.   Waldemar A. Nielsen, "The Crisis of the Nonprofits," *Change* (January 1980), p. 23.

7.   John Naisbitt, Remarks made in a lecture given at the University of Southern California, February 21, 1980.

8.   Harold G. Shane, "Forecast for the 80's," *Today's Education*, vol. 68, no. 2 (April-May 1979), pp. 63-64.

9.   "College Enrollment," *Los Angeles Times* (January 23, 1980), Part I, p. 2.

10.   Shane, "Forecast," pp. 63-64.

11.   Alvin Toffler, *The Third Wave* (New York: William Morrow and Co., Inc., 1980), p. 400.

12.   Ibid., p. 364.

13.   Robert L. Jacobson, "Campus Managers Shift Focus to Academic Quality," *The Chronicle of Higher Education*, XX (March 10, 1980), p. 9.

14.   Ibid.

15.   Lewis M. Branscomb, "The Ultimate Frontier," *Data Processor*, XXIII (March 1980), p. 9.

16.   Logan Wilson, *American Academics Then and Now* (New York: Oxford University Press, 1979), p. 79.

17.   Ibid.

18.   David Walker, "Financially Strapped University of London May Close Institutes and 2 Medical Schools," *The Chronicle of Higher Education*, XX, no. 4 (March 24, 1980), p. 17.

19.   Ibid.

20.   Arthur M. Cohen and John Lombardi, "Can the Community College Survive Success?" *Change* (November-December 1979), p. 27.

21.   Richard E. Anderson, "The Money Crunch," in *Disorders in Higher Education* (Englewood Cliffs, NJ: Prentice-Hall, 1979), p. 27.

22.   *The Chronicle of Higher Education*, XX (March 10, 1980), p. 11.

23.   A. H. Raskin, "The Shape of Work to Come: Perils," *Change* (July-August 1979), p. 22.

24.   Beverly T. Watkins, "Drive to End Shortage of Skilled Workers Proposed by Educators and Industrialists," *The Chronicle of Higher Education*, XX (March 24, 1980), p. 1.

25.   George W. Bonham, "Inching Toward the Learning Society," *Change* (July-August 1979), p. 4.

26.   Ibid.

27.   George W. Bonham, "Education and the Telefuture," *Change* (November-December 1979), p. 12.

28.   Ibid.

29.   Ibid.

30.   Arthur W. Combs, *Myths in Education* (Boston: Allyn and Bacon, c1974), p. 77.

31.   Ibid.

32.   Ibid.

33.   Ashworth, *American Higher Education*, p. 97.

34.   Ibid.

35.   Ibid.

36.   Toffler, *Third Wave*, pp. 273-74.

37.   Gene A. Budig, "Realities and Opportunities for Higher Education," *The College Review Board*, no. 112 (Summer 1974), p. 12.

38.   George W. Bonham, "Three Thousand Futures" [editorial] *Change* (February-March 1980), p. 13.

TRENDS AND CHOICES IN LEGAL EDUCATION

by
Martin Lyon Levine

Professor of Law
Professor of Psychiatry and Behavioral Sciences
University of Southern California

The choices law schools face in the decade ahead must be made in the context of trends external to individual schools—trends in society, the legal profession, and higher education—that define both constraints and opportunities. This paper discusses both issues affecting the substance of legal education in the 1980s and institutional issues, as well as the need for creative planning and leadership on the part of law school decision makers.

SUBSTANTIVE ISSUES

Each school, by decision or drift, continually chooses its goals. Traditionally, the fundamental goal of a law school is the education of future lawyers. Schools vary in how they balance this professional school role with the graduate school role of conducting research and fostering scholarship.[1] Schools also differ in their goals as to style of leadership,[2] student-faculty interaction,[3] and quality level.

There are also differences in the extent to which various law schools embrace the wider definition of teaching and service embraced in the concept of "Law Center."[4] Such a center might, for example, train court administrators, paraprofessionals, judges, practicing lawyers, college and graduate students, as well as law students.

Some law schools may define their goals more broadly: to contribute to the achievement of justice in the community, through the effects of their graduates' practice, faculty scholarship, and public service activities.[5] Each law school in the decade ahead must take into account the changing needs of the community it serves, as well as the possibility of serving a wider community. Schools that formerly drew students from the local region, returned graduates to the region, and engaged in research concerning local problems may find themselves increasingly serving a wider community. The local community may also change, as an agricultural region becomes industrialized, new populations groups emerge, or a parochial home town becomes a base for international business transactions. The school may have to respond to the community's need for fewer lawyers, or better trained ones, or lawyers of wider perspectives.[6]

Changes in Society

An image of a certain state of society underlies much of traditional law school teaching. Individual persons of means have disputes with other such individuals. They turn for assistance in resolving the dispute to a lawyer likely to be in solo practice, who applies knowledge of the common law.

Graduates of local law schools may still find themselves engaged in such a small town practice. The continuing modernization of society, however, renders that image less relevant for many law school graduates.[7] Much legal business in the 1980s will involve relations between the individual and large organizations or bureaucracies, or relationships among government agencies, large corporations, labor unions, and so on. Those who need legal assistance may be involved in an ongoing relationship rather than a single dispute, such as in labor-management negotiations or transactions with a regular business supplier. Preventive law, or planning by lawyers to avoid disputes, will have increased importance.[8] Government increasingly regulates our affairs with multiplying complexities. Lawyers and courts are not only consulted for solutions to individual disputes; large-scale problems such as school desegregation, environmental impact, and conditions in prisons and mental hospitals are dealt with as well.

These continuing trends in society create curriculum issues for law schools in the decade ahead.[9] For example, private law and judge-made common law will increasingly be challenged to share room with public law involving government regulation, whose source is legislation and the administrative process. Traditionally there has been concern for due process and individual rights against the government; in the years ahead, when industry, unions, universities, and other large organizations often function as "private governments,"[10] lawyers and law schools will be concerned with protection of fairness and liberty in a bureaucratic civilization.

The growing interdependence of the world will also affect legal education. Many lawyers deal with business problems: as businesses increasingly engage in international transactions or organize their own corporations multinationally, their lawyers must take into account the laws of other nations. Public international law and the law of multinational organizations like the EEOC (Equal Employment Opportunity Commission) may also increase in importance to American lawyers. Just as Virginia and California law schools teach the legal system of the United States as a whole, so too American law schools will increasingly perceive the need for their students to be knowledgeable about the legal systems of the world.

Administration of Justice

Other social trends in the decade ahead will raise issues for the law schools. From the time of Roscoe Pound's seminal criticisms at the turn of the century[11] to recent conferences and hearings organized by the Chief Justice and by Congress, there has been widespread "popular dissatisfaction with the administration of justice."

Watergate renewed criticism that too many lawyers are unethical. The Chief Justice and influential committees have declared that many lawyers lack courtroom competence, and that legal education needs reform.[12] Civil disputes handled by lawyers through courts cost too much and take too long to be resolved. Lawyers' activities are thought to obstruct the finding of truth and the achievement of fairness, by exploitation of mere legal technicalities. There is periodic widespread criticism of specific criminal law rules or practices, such as plea-bargaining. There is also widespread criticism of specific types of civil lawsuits, such as malpractice actions against doctors, integration suits involving northern school systems, personal injury cases where a lawyer collects a contingent fee of one-third or more, and divorce actions under laws inviting perjury.

Legislatures have already responded to such popular dissatisfaction, for example, through "no fault" insurance and "no fault" divorce, lessening the need for legal services. Bar and judicial groups have moved to mandate specific law school curriculum offerings—already done, as to legal ethics, and under discussion, as to trial-related courses.

Legal education in the decade ahead can respond to these developments in different ways. It can teach the causes of popular dissatisfaction with the administration of justice, anticipate areas ripe for change, and address its scholarship to reform of abuses.[13] Law schools can emphasize study of the values that justify some of the unpopular rules and practices. They can develop students' abilities to communicate with the public, such as writing and speaking on law for lay audiences. And they can act autonomously to obviate the call for externally mandated curriculum changes.

The Legal Process

While previously legal services were readily accessible only to businesses and persons of means, in recent years there have been moves to increase access to the courts by poor and middle-income persons. Poor persons with civil disputes now can often receive free legal assistance, through federally-funded local legal services programs;[14] poor criminal defendants facing imprisonment now have a right to free legal representation;[15] and other persons of limited means increasingly can obtain legal assistance through prepaid legal insurance, low-cost legal clinics, or similar means.[16] As the delivery system for legal services is reformed, the demand will be modified concomitantly.

More lawyers in the decade ahead are likely to function within the context of large organizations: in private firms numbering hundreds of attorneys, with branch offices in other states or countries; in corporate departments; in government agencies; in legal aid societies or public defender organizations; or through such third-party intermediaries as insurance carriers. Computers will be used increasingly as adjuncts to legal practice, both as aids to research (through systems like WESTLAW and LEXIS)[17] and as necessary means of data management in massive lawsuits, such as antitrust or desegration cases. Lawyers will frequently find that their work overlaps skills traditionally associated with other professionals, such as the accountant, manager, or psychologist, and will find it useful to cultivate new skills, such as in mediation or conflict resolution.

Another ongoing trend in the legal profession concerns the distribution of work between lawyers and others, a trend that is part of larger changes in the division of labor in society. Many work tasks that lawyers historically claimed for their own have in part shifted to other, perhaps cheaper, practitioners. From the position of the organized bar, changes in work allocation raise issues of the unauthorized practice of law, and have led to "treaties" with such groups as real estate brokers, accountants, and title insurance companies. While graduates of leading schools will still find their legal skills much in demand, graduates of local law schools may find that many traditional tasks are performed by these nonlawyers. Local schools must either upgrade or otherwise redefine the roles for which they train their students.

A parallel trend is the rise of the "legal paraprofessional" or "lawyer's assistant." The American Bar Association now accredits paraprofessional programs; several universities and independent institutions are offering such courses. Paraprofessional programs currently train three groups: experienced legal secretaries upgrading their skills and credentials, undergraduate college students seeking marketable skills, and college graduates with the same vocational purpose. College graduates may predominate in future years, and persons so trained may no longer be regarded as "paraprofessional," but as constituting a profession in their own right. In some law firms, these workers already have their own business cards, offices with windows, and secretaries of their own. Some paraprofessionals have formed firms of their own handling such matters as evictions, and hiring attorneys to work for them.

Paraprofessional training programs can be compared with the law schools of the early nineteenth century. Students with or without college degrees receive legal training of a predominantly vocational nature, requiring a few months or a year, primarily in lecture or lecture-textbook form. It might be argued that the Litchfield Law School has been reinvented.

Another trend, toward alternative means of dispute resolution, may dispense with lawyers altogether. Neighborhood justice centers, ombudsmen and patient advocates in hospitals, and organized programs of mediation and conciliation may grow in prevalence.[18] These processes and forums will seek to reconcile adversaries and settle quarrels without the skills, or the expense, of lawyers and judges as we know them. Law schools in the future may either withdraw from these processes or may train persons (whether or not called "lawyers") to work with them.

Intellectual Trends

The issue of the substance of legal education in the coming decade may also be viewed in terms of the underlying jurisprudential approach. Roscoe Pound has identified a series of "movements" in legal education: historical jurisprudence about 1890, economic interpretation at the turn of the century, logical analysis of rights about the time of World War I, then psychological realism, and by 1950 a "rising cult" of natural law.[19] A variety of intellectual trends are currently discernible in the law schools. There is a revival of interest in grand theories of several types:[20] One is a rationalist, utilitarian, scientific approach to legal issues, intellectually related to the call for a "law, science and policy" jurisprudence,[21] and currently typified by law-and-economics analysis. Another is a renewed concern for morality, rights, and theories of justice. There is also new interest in courses dealing with people rather than with business or with intellectual abstractions—an interest exemplified in courses dealing with women, minority racial groups, children, and the elderly.[22]

Law schools will also face issues of teaching methodologies. While the case method is prototypical, there are many available modes: lecture-text, legislative-statutory, historical, problem, conceptual, functional, and transactional. Law courses may emphasize skills training, human relations skill, professional responsibility-values orientation, clinical exposure, integration of law and the social sciences, analysis of the judicial decision making process, use of empirical methods, and use of electronic data processing.[23]

The continued interest in clinical legal education manifests an interrelated set of concerns: skills of trial advocacy, office counseling, and negotiation; realistic teaching of substantive law; early exposure to live clients; and ethical dilemmas experienced in vivo.[24]

The rise of multidisciplinary study of the legal process is reflected in the existence of law teachers with dual training, the appointment of nonlawyers to law faculties and lawyers to other departments, and team teaching.[25] Economics is the most popular "law-and- . . ." subject; psychiatry, philosophy, and accounting are other disciplines frequently represented in law schools. Upwardly mobile schools may seek out areas in which distinction can be achieved, having in mind social need, weakness of competition, and existing strengths.

Students in law schools, like those in colleges, tended in the last decade to stress "relevance," or attention to immediate social significance. And like the college students, today's law students seem to emphasize vocational usefulness. Law schools of the next decade are therefore likely to attempt to combine liberal arts and academic and intellectual goals with those of immediate practical utility; courses and programs recently instituted to deal with social problems, such as poverty law, may find decreased student interest.

Law schools in the 1980s will continue to face the ongoing issue of defining the underlying model of legal education. Five models, in turn, have historically characterized American legal education.[26] In the first, how to *practice* law is learned, typically by apprenticeship. This is historically the oldest form of lawyer training in America. In the second, historically almost as old as the Practice Model, *rules* are learned, whether through textbooks, lectures, or a combination of the two. In the third, cases are studied intensively so that the underlying *principles* of law can be perceived. Law is divided into conceptual fields, each with its own sets of principles; questions of social policy and nonlegal data are generally thought to be excluded from this model. In the fourth, *policy* considerations are integrated into the study of law. Recognizing that lawyers are important decision makers, there is a conscious attempt to cope with issues of what the law should be, often necessitating use of nonlegal data as well as legal. Perhaps a *Fifth Vision* of the law school is coming into being, supplementing the other models, comprehending clinical education stressing lawyer-client responsibility, humanistic and psychological emphases on the individual, and new emphasis on theories of justice and values.[27]

INSTITUTIONAL ISSUES

Demographic Trends

There are variations from period to period in the total pool of potential law school applicants, in the relative attractiveness to college graduates of legal education compared to other professional and graduate schools, as well as in the attractiveness of law school to specific subgroups in the student population. Phenomena of the recent past enabled the national law schools to become extraordinarily selective, enabled many local schools to reach the previous standards of the national law schools, and enabled many new schools to come into existence. The laws on draft deferment encouraged postgraduate education. The "Warren era" of liberal decisions, the War on Poverty, and the civil rights movement attracted to law schools many who were interested in social reform. The women's movement encouraged many women college graduates to seek professional roles.

No such increases in the available student population are foreseeable in the decade ahead. In fact, demographic projections indicate a declining pool in the age group from which university students have traditionally been drawn.[28] While current experience shows that more selective schools are able to keep up their numbers of students in the face of such trends, sometimes by lowering admission standards, schools which are already less selective in admission criteria face decreasing enrollment.

Many schools will therefore search for new student populations, such as older students, women, minorities, and international students. If the participation rate in legal education among these groups approached that of young, white, middle-class, American males, the available student pool would be more than adequate.[29] Women already number one-third of the class in many law schools. Affirmative action programs have been instituted by schools that formerly had few if any minority students, and minorities are present in numbers more nearly approximating their presence in the college population. After the Bakke case, schools must reconsider their stands on affirmative action programs:[30] some schools that had not yet made a meaningful commitment to integrated education may be just beginning to do so. In the next decade, schools may adjust class schedules or full-time requirements, so as to accommodate women with children. Night divisions may flourish, despite academic criticism, because of their attractiveness to older, employed persons. There may be an increase in students from newly-rich countries, as education is a natural American export— though legal education is less transferable to other countries than is, for example, engineering. New substantive programs and special recruitment efforts may be tried. Some of the new student populations may be defined as outside the "central" mission of the law school, in separate units for continuing legal education or undergraduate legal studies.

Some schools will successfully carve out new market shares for themselves, or lower admission standards. Others will face lower student population size, and being largely tuition-dependent, will have to find new revenues or efficiencies. Many schools will reduce or suspend faculty hiring; some will go out of existence.

Other Financial Issues

In addition to the financial issues generated by demographic trends, the overall inflation (driven in part by increased energy costs) is likely to continue and to produce financial exigencies for law schools as well as for other units of education. In times of inflation, it is difficult to cope with financial problems in education by increased investment to improve "productivity."[31] Nor can "productivity" be improved merely by having each teacher deal with an increased number of students, as that would likely decrease the effectiveness of instruction for each student, as well as decrease such other outputs as research. In past generations law schools operated with large lectures, and thus with small faculty-student ratios. With the increase in legal research, seminars, and specialized electives, legal education has become as labor-intensive as other graduate education.

Law school revenues are derived from such sources as state appropriations, the tuition-paying ability of students and their families, and donations by alumni and philanthropists. Law schools may begin to seek more federal contracts and research grants. Federal financial aid for students is a major law school income source, often overlooked. Inflation and taxpayer revolts may limit the availability of these resources, both private and public, and require new economies.[32]

There will, however, continue to be those who can afford private tuition and those who are able to make substantial gifts to both private and public law schools.[33] Private schools, while taking advantage of these sources of funds, will face the issue of continuing to be accessible to students who cannot afford higher tuition rates, and continuing to be responsive to the legal needs of groups that are not wealthy. Federal funds and new donors will be eagerly sought by both private and public schools, but educators will have to battle anew to avoid strings and preserve their integrity and independence.[34]

State and private law schools may both find it increasingly necessary to justify to representatives of a frugal public the high costs per student. Each discipline has its own set of reasons for deserving support, including traditional values, intellectual and cultural importance, and contribution to civilization. Legal educators will point out that law schools make an immediate contribution to the public good: legal research and the work of law school graduates contribute to the achievement of justice in the community and the provision of peaceful means to resolve social disputes. Since less equipment is required than in some other fields, a relatively smaller university investment in a law school is needed to produce noticeable improvements in quality. Many graduates will be successful in practice, and their charity in later years may return to the university, many times over, the money invested in their schooling. And as legal education becomes less parochial, interdisciplinary research and teaching in law schools may benefit the college and other graduate and professional disciplines.

Technology

New technology will affect the law schools. More and more schools will teach the skills of computer-assisted legal research; students will learn to use LEXIS and WESTLAW computers, and office word processors and microcomputers, as well as traditional printed indexes and office files. Law libraries will increasingly use computerized bibliographic data bases, such as RLN and OCLC, and other specialized data bases, as well as new data storage methods involving microforms instead of hard copy for material seldom consulted. There is likely to be continued, but slow, increase in the use of new technology in teaching. A few computer programs to teach specific subjects are now available: students at terminals in the local school can be connected via phone lines to a central computer. Cheaper computers, and satellite transmissions accessible by the consumer, may sharply lower costs of such teaching. Teaching through video cassette, or immediate feedback on student clinical or classroom performance through video taping, may also increase in use as the price of the technology comes down.

Faculty Composition

The makeup of law faculties will be influenced by a number of trends. Compensation of law professors, like that of other university faculty, has lagged behind the increases earned outside the university. With continuing inflation, it may be harder to attract to the career of teaching law new graduates and experienced lawyers, and to retain those who are currently teachers. Some geographical areas have experienced disproportionate increases in the cost of residential housing; schools in such areas may find it particularly difficult to attract faculty, and may increasingly find their pool of teaching applicants limited to local residents, those in dual-career families, and those retiring from successful private practice.

The abolition of mandatory retirement at age 65, already effective for other large employers, will soon extend to tenured university faculty. In law schools, as in other fields, there are predictions of a period of several years in the decade ahead when the decrease in forced retirements, combined with the projected decrease in number of students, may choke off new faculty openings.[35]

Notwithstanding the Supreme Court's decision in the Yeshiva case, the drive toward unionization of faculty in higher education is likely to continue. Law faculties in the decade ahead, however, will probably continue to choose to be excluded from bargaining units of college faculty because of separate traditions, different salary and promotion standards, and a strong history of faculty governance.[36]

THE ROLE OF LAW SCHOOL LEADERSHIP

The leadership of each school will make choices to help determine its direction against the background of the trends discussed above. These choices cannot be made in an abstract way; each school has a unique situation at any given time. Each faculty has its own range of abilities and interests. Students, alumni, university administration, the local bench and bar, donors, state administrators and legislators—each constituency has a sense of the identity of the school and is a bearer of its traditions and hopes. Each school, furthermore, also has its own financial realities,[37] reflecting previous decisions and influencing future ones, on quality, size, and breadth of program.

The leadership of a school cannot define its goals autocratically. Though a dean may be looked to from all sides for decisions, he or she typically has much less power than other managers. An educational leader must deal with a tenured faculty conscious of its own capacities and prerogatives, a relatively fixed plant and product, and the need to rely on philanthropic gifts or government subventions to meet a major portion of the budget. Moreover, achievement of the school's goals requires the enthusiastic cooperation of many persons who should be involved in the ongoing process of planning.

Though a dean has limited power, he or she still has responsibility for leadership. Opportunities for leadership are available through use of available points of leverage, such as influencing decisions at hiring and up-or-out stages, allocation of discretionary funds and merit raises, and the setting of the intellectual agenda. Leadership is also exercisable through encouragement and praise, the provision of opportunities for professional development, the structuring of decision processes, and the identification of measurable objectives. The leader can facilitate change through basic managerial efficiency and fiscal responsibility.[38]

Faculty share with deans many of the responsibilities of leadership, and the central administration has its own role to play. While it will take different forms in each unique school, leadership is required for law schools to successfully deal with the crucial issues they face in the decade ahead.

NOTES

1.   A. Goldstein, "Educational Planning at Yale," *University of Miami Law Review*, 21 (1967), p. 520.

2.   L. Abramson and G. Moss, "Law School Deans: A Self Portrait," *Journal of Legal Education*, 29 (1977), p. 6; A. Astin and R. Scherrei, *Maximizing Leadership Effectiveness: Impact of Administrative Style on Faculty and Students* (San Francisco: Jossey-Bass, 1980); J. Baldridge, "Managerial Innovation: Rules for Successful Implementation," *Journal of Higher Education*, 51 (1980), p. 117.

3.   D. Kennedy, "How the Law School Fails: A Polemic," *Yale Review of Law and Social Action*, 1 (1970), p. 1.

4.   A. Vanderbilt, "The Mission of a Law Center," *New York University Law Review*, 27 (1952), p. 20; "The Vocation of a Law Center," *Oklahoma Law Review*, 29 (1976), p. 651.

5.   J. Auerbach, "What Has the Teaching of Law to do with Justice?," *New York University Law Review*, 53 (1978), p. 457; C. Fried, "The Lawyer as Friend: The Moral Foundations of the Lawyer-Client Relation," *Yale Law Journal*, 85 (1976), p. 1060.

6.   M. Schwartz, "How Can Legal Education Respond to Changes in Legal Profession?," *New York University Law Review*, 53 (1978), p. 440. "Number and Earnings of Lawyers: Some Recent Findings," *American Bar Foundation Research Journal* (Winter 1978), p. 51; R. Spring, "O Where Will the New Lawyers Go?," *Washburn Law Journal*, 16 (1977), p. 623.

7. . Committee on Educational Planning and Development, *Interim Report, October 1980* [unpublished] (Cambridge, MA: Harvard Law School, 1980).

8.   L. Brown and E. A. Dauer, *Planning by Lawyers: Materials on a Nonadversarial Legal Process* (Mineola, NY: Foundation Press, 1978).

9.   Committee on Educational Planning and Development, *Interim Report*.

10.   M. Levine, "Private Government on the Campus: Judicial Review of University Expulsions," *Yale Law Journal*, 72 (1963), p. 1362.

11.   R. Pound. "The Causes of Popular Dissatisfaction with the Administration of Justice," *American Law Review*, 40 (1906), p. 729.

12.   See, for example, W. Burger, "The Future of Legal Education: Address before the American Bar Association, August, 1969" [Reprinted in Council on Legal Education for Professional Responsibility.] *Selected Readings in Clinical Legal Education* (New York: Council on Legal Education for Professional Responsibility and the International Legal Center, 1973).

13.   D. W. Nelson, *Cases and Materials on Judicial Administration and the Administration of Justice* (St. Paul, MN: West Publishing Co., 1974).

14.   Legal Services Corporation Act, *United States Code*, 42: SS2296 and the following.

15.   Gideon v. Wainwright, 372 U.S. 335 (1963).

16.   "Legal Insurance Coverage Growing: Comes to California," *Los Angeles Daily Journal*, 93 (August 12, 1980), p. 1; "State Bar Forms Unit to Support Prepaid Plans," *New York Law Journal*, 183 (January 29, 1980), p. 1.

17.   J. Sprowl, "Westlaw v. Lexis: Computer Assisted Legal Research Comes of Age," *Illinois Bar Journal*, 68 (November 1979), p. 156.

18.   E. Johnson, *Outside the Courts: A Survey of Diversion Alternatives in Civil Cases* (Denver: National Center for State Courts, 1977).

19.   R. Pound, "Some Comments on Law, Teachers and Law Teaching," *Journal of Legal Education*, 3 (1951), p. 519.

20.   I. England, "The System Builders: A Critical Appraisal of Modern American Tort Theory," *Journal of Legal Studies*, 9 (1980), p. 27.

21.   H. Lasswell and M. McDougal, "Legal Education and Public Policy: Professional Training in the Public Interest," *Yale Law Journal*, 52 (1943), p. 203;

M. McDougal, "The Law School of the Future: From Legal Realism to Policy Science in the World Community," *Yale Law Journal*, 56 (1947), p. 1345.

22. V. A. Church, "The Real Business of Law Is People Not Cases: An Argument for Training Counselors," *Learning and the Law*, 2 (Spring 1975), p. 54; M. Levine, "A People-Oriented Law Confronts Problems of the Elderly," *USC Cites*, 1980 (Fall 1980), p. 16.

23. L. Del Duca, "Continuing Evaluation of Law School Curricula: An Initial Survey," *Journal of Legal Education*, 20 (1978), p. 309.

24. Council on Legal Education for Professional Responsibility, *Selected Readings in Clinical Legal Education, supra*; D. Barnhizer, "The Clinical Method of Legal Instruction: Its Theory and Implementation," *Journal of Legal Education*, 30 (1979), p. 67.

25. M. W. Gordon, "Interdisciplinary Teaching and the Law," *American Journal of Comparative Law*, 26 (1978 Supp.), p. 43.

26. M. Levine, "Legal Education and Curriculum Innovation: Law and Aging as a New Legal Field," *Minnesota Law Review*, 64 (1980), p. 501.

27. R. Redmount, "Humanistic Law Through Legal Education," *Connecticut Law Review*, 1 (1968), p. 201; C. Reich, "Toward the Humanistic Study of Law," *Yale Law Journal*, 74 (1965), p. 1402; D. Riesman, "In Memory of Harold Solomon: Comments on Southern California's Flyer in Legal Education," *Southern California Law Review*, 41 (1968), p. 506.

28. J. Centra, "College Enrollment in the 1980's: Projections and Possibilities," *Journal of Higher Education*, 51 (1980), p. 18; "Graduate Enrollment Declines in Most Academic Disciplines," *Chronicle of Higher Education*, 20 (June 23, 1980), p. 7; J. White, "Law School Enrollment Continues to Level," *American Bar Association Journal*, 66 (1980), p. 724.

29. J. Magarrell, "Despite Drop in Number of 18 Year Olds, College Rolls Could Rise During the 1980's," *Chronicle of Higher Education*, 20 (April 21, 1980), p. 1.

30. ACE-AALS Committee on Bakke, *The Bakke Decision: Implications for Higher Education Admissions* (Washington, DC: American Council on Education and Association of American Law Schools, 1978).

31. D. Selden, "The Mystery of Educational Productivity," *Change*, 10 (February 1978), p. 50.

32. "Financing Legal Education," *American Bar Association Journal*, 64 (December 1978), p. 1880; "The Federal Stake in a Learning Society: An Interview with Ernest L. Boyer," *Change*, 10 (May 1978), p. 21; J. Magarrel, "State Appropriations for Higher Education," *Chronicle of Higher Education*, 21 (October 14, 1980), p.71; J. Maysall, "32 Pct. of Public Colleges Found to be Losing Ground Financially," *Chronicle of Higher Education*, 21 (September 15, 1980), p. 11.

33. "Gifts to Higher Education Surpass $3.2 Billion," *Chronicle of Higher Education*, 20 (June 9, 1880), p. 1; "A Long View of Philanthropy, 1920-1990," *Chronicle of Higher Education* (July 7, 1980), p. 4.

34. R. Rosenzweig, "An End to Autonomy: Who Pulls the Strings?," *Change*, 10 (March 1978), p. 28; R. Scott, "More Than Greenbacks and Red Tape: The Hidden Costs of Government Regulations," *Change*, 10 (April 1978), p. 16.

35. C. Nevison, "Effects of Tenure and Retirement Policies on the College Faculty," *Journal of Higher Education*, 51 (1980), p. 150.

36. National Labor Relations Board v. Yeshiva University, 444 U.S. 672 (1980); "AAUP to Fight Yeshiva Ruling," *Chronicle of Higher Education*, 20 (June 30, 1980), p. 4; "Collective Bargaining and Private University Governance: A Look from the Law Schools," *University of Florida Law Review*, 29 (1977), p. 625.

37. C. D. Kelso, "Adding Up the Law Schools: A Tabulation and Rating of Their Resources," *Learning and the Law*, 2 (1975), p. 39.

38. R. Heyns, ed., *Leadership for Higher Education* (Washington, DC: American Council on Education, 1977); R. W. Hostrop, *Managing Education for Results* (Homewood, IL: ETC Publications, 1973).

BIBLIOGRAPHY

"AAUP to Fight Yeshiva Ruling." *Chronicle of Higher Education*, 20 (June 30, 1980), p. 4.

ACE-AALS Committee on Bakke. *The Bakke Decision: Implications for Higher Education Admissions*. Washington, DC: American Council on Education and Association of American Law Schools, 1978.

Abramson, L., and Moss, G. "Law School Deans: A Self Portrait." *Journal of Legal Education*, 29 (1977), p. 6.

Astin, A., and Scherrei, R. *Maximizing Leadership Effectiveness: Impact of Administrative Style on Faculty and Students*. San Francisco: Jossey-Bass, 1980.

Auerbach, J. "What Has the Teaching of Law to do with Justice?" *New York University Law Review*, 53 (1978), p. 457.

Baldridge, J. "Managerial Innovation: Rules for Successful Implementation." *Journal of Higher Education*, 51 (1980), p. 117.

Barnhizer, D. "The Clinical Method of Legal Instruction: Its Theory and Implementation." *Journal of Legal Education*, 30 (1979), p. 67.

Brown, L., and Dauer, E. A. *Planning by Lawyers: Materials on a Nonadversarial Legal Process*. Mineola, NY: Foundation Press, 1978.

Burger, W. "The Future of Legal Education: Address before the American Bar Association, August, 1969." Reprinted in Council on Legal Education for Professional Responsibility. *Selected Readings in Clinical Legal Education*. New York: Council on Legal Education for Professional Responsibility and the International Legal Center, 1973.

Centra, J. "College Enrollment in the 1980's: Projections and Possibilities." *Journal of Higher Education*, 51 (1980), p. 18.

Church, V. A. "The Real Business of Law Is People Not Cases: An Argument for Training Counselors." *Learning and the Law*, 2 (Spring 1975), p. 54.

"Collective Bargaining and Private University Governance: A Look from the Law Schools." *University of Florida Law Review*, 29 (1977), p. 625.

Committee on Educational Planning and Development. *Interim Report, October 1980* [unpublished]. Cambridge, MA: Harvard Law School, 1980.

Council on Legal Education for Professional Responsibility. *Selected Readings in Clinical Legal Education*. New York: Council on Legal Education for Professional Responsibility and the International Legal Center, 1973.

Del Duca, L. "Continuing Evaluation of Law School Curricula: An Initial Survey." *Journal of Legal Education*, 20 (1978): p. 309.

England, I. "The System Builders: A Critical Appraisal of Modern American Tort Theory." *Journal of Legal Studies*, 9 (1980), p. 27.

"The Federal Stake in a Learning Society: An Interview with Ernest L. Boyer." *Change*, 10 (May 1978), p. 21.

"Financing Legal Education." *American Bar Association Journal*, 64 (December 1978), p. 1880.

Fried, C. "The Lawyer as Friend: The Moral Foundations of the Lawyer-Client Relation." *Yale Law Journal*, 85 (1976), p. 1060.

Gideon v. Wainwright, 372 U.S. 335 (1963).

"Gifts to Higher Education Surpass \$3.2 Billion." *Chronicle of Higher Education*, 20 (June 9, 1980), p. 1.

Goldstein, A. "Educational Planning at Yale." *University of Miami Law Review*, 21 (1967), p. 520.

Gordon, M. W. "Interdisciplinary Teaching and the Law." *American Journal of Comparative Law*, 26 (1978 Supp.), p. 43.

"Graduate Enrollment Declines in Most Academic Disciplines." *Chronicle of Higher Education*, 20 (June 23, 1980), p. 7.

Heyns, R., ed. *Leadership for Higher Education*. Washington, DC: American Council on Education, 1977.

Hostrop, R. W. *Managing Education for Results*. Homewood, IL: ETC Publications, 1973.

Johnson, E. *Outside the Courts: A Survey of Diversion Alternatives in Civil Cases*. Denver: National Center for State Courts, 1977.

Kelso, Charles D. "Adding Up the Law Schools: A Tabulation and Rating of Their Resources." *Learning and the Law*, 2 (1975), p. 39.

Kennedy, D. "How the Law School Fails: A Polemic." *Yale Review of Law and Social Action*, 1 (1970), p. 1.

Lasswell, H., and McDougal, M. "Legal Education and Public Policy: Professional Training in the Public Interest." *Yale Law Journal*, 52 (1943), p. 203.

"Legal Insurance Coverage Growing: Comes to California." *Los Angeles Daily Journal*, 93 (August 12, 1980), p. 1.

Legal Services Corporation Act. *United States Code*, 42: SS2296 and the following.

Levine, M. "Legal Education and Curriculum Innovation: Law and Aging as a New Legal Field." *Minnesota Law Review*, 64 (1980), p. 501.

Levine, M. "A People-Oriented Law Confronts Problems of the Elderly." *USC Cites*, 1980 (Fall 1980), p. 16.

Levine, M. "Private Government on the Campus: Judicial Review of University Expulsions." *Yale Law Journal*, 72 (9163), p. 1362.

"A Long View of Philanthropy, 1920-1990." *Chronicle of Higher Education* (July 7, 1980), p. 4.

Magarrell, J. "Despite Drop in Number of 18 Year Olds, College Rolls Could Rise During the 1980's." *Chronicle of Higher Education*, 20 (April 21, 1980), p. 1.

Magarrell, J. "State Appropriations for Higher Education." *Chronicle of Higher Education*, 21 (October 14, 1980), p. 71.

Maysall, J. "32 Pct. of Public Colleges Found to be Losing Ground Financially." *Chronicle of Higher Education*, 21 (September 15, 1980), p. 11.

McDougal, M. "The Law School of the Future: From Legal Realism to Policy Science in the World Community." *Yale Law Journal*, 56 (1947), p. 1345.

National Labor Relations Board v. Yeshiva University, 444 U.S. 672 (1980).

Nelson, D. W. *Cases and Materials on Judicial Administration and the Administration of Justice*. St. Paul, MN: West Publishing Co., 1974).

Nevison, C. "Effects of Tenure and Retirement Policies on the College Faculty." *Journal of Higher Education*, 51 (1980), p. 150.

"Number and Earnings of Lawyers: Some Recent Findings." *American Bar Foundation Research Journal* (Winter 1978), p. 51.

Pound, R. "The Causes of Popular Dissatisfaction with the Administration of Justice." *American Law Review*, 40 (1906), p. 729.

Pound, R. "Some Comments on Law, Teachers and Law Teaching." *Journal of Legal Education*, 3 (1951), p. 519.

Redmount, R. "Humanistic Law Through Legal Education." *Connecticut Law Review*, 1 (1968), p. 201.

Reich, C. "Toward the Humanistic Study of Law." *Yale Law Journal*, 74 (1965), p. 1402.

Riesman, D. "In Memory of Harold Solomon: Comments on Southern California's Flyer in Legal Education." *Southern California Law Review*, 41 (1968), p. 506.

Rosenzweig, R. M. "An End to Autonomy: Who Pulls the Strings?" *Change*, 10 (March 1978), p. 28.

Schwartz, M. "How Can Legal Education Respond to Changes in the Legal Profession?" *New York University Law Review*, 53 (1978), p. 440.

Scott, R. A. "More Than Greenbacks and Red Tape: The Hidden Costs of Government Regulations." *Change*, 10 (April 1978), p. 16.

Selden, D. "The Mystery of Educational Productivity." *Change*, 10 (February 1978), p. 50.

Spring, R. "O Where Will the New Lawyers Go?" *Washburn Law Journal*, 16 (1977), p. 623.

Sprowl, J. "Westlaw v. Lexis: Computer Assisted Legal Research Comes of Age." *Illinois Bar Journal*, 68 (November 1979), p. 156.

"State Bar Forms Unit to Support Prepaid Plans." *New York Law Journal*, 183 (January 29, 1980), p. 1.

Vanderbilt, A. "The Mission of a Law Center." *New York University Law Review*, 27 (1952), p. 20.

"The Vocation of a Law Center." *Oklahoma Law Review*, 29 (1976), p. 651.

White, J. "Law School Enrollment Continues to Level." *American Bar Association Journal*, 66 (1980), p. 724.

EDUCATION FOR HEALTH PROFESSIONS: PROBLEMS AND PROSPECTS

by
Stephen Abrahamson

Professor, School of Medicine
University of Southern California

INTRODUCTION

Consideration of education for health professions today is both a challenging and a frustrating experience. The challenge comes from the fact that the delivery of health care is inexorably changing; thus, the education and training for health care personnel must, of necessity, change in response to those new demands created by the newer health care practices. The frustration comes from the fact that the changes in health care delivery are sweeping and broad and, at the same time, slow and unpredictable. Changes in practice of health professionals are imbedded in the more comprehensive changes in health care. These latter include introduction of technological advances, redistribution of health care tasks among the many health professions, emergence of new health professions, and development of assistant-level, semiprofessional personnel within many of the existing professions.

Even prior to the examination of these changing patterns, however, discussion of education for health professions demands a shared understanding of the definition of a profession and the nature of professional education. In the pages that follow, first there is a review of what a profession is, along with some exploration of the reasons educators should be concerned with the differences between a profession and other occupations. Then, growing out of the definition of a profession, the emphasis shifts to a consideration of universal patterns of education for professions, including speculation about what should be inherent characteristics of that education and training because of the very nature of the concept of a profession.

The treatment of education for health professions starts with a brief overview—almost a listing—of health professions today and then continues with a general description of education for health professions. This general picture is then enhanced by a discussion of the trends and problems that characterize medical education today. Out of that broad general review, there emerge some hints of the future—an era that might be considered encouraging or depressing, depending on the perspective of the individual reader.

WHAT IS A PROFESSION?

pro-fes-sion . . . 4a: a calling requiring specialized knowledge and often long and intensive academic preparation . . .

Thus does *Webster's Seventh New Collegiate Dictionary* contribute to a potentially endless (and fruitless) debate concerning what a profession is and how a profession differs from other occupations. Indeed, Morris L. Cogan may have said it best: "To define 'profession' is to invite controversy."[1] Because an occupation that is considered to be a "profession" accrues to itself more prestige, members of a given occupation are prone to consider themselves "professionals" and their occupations "professions." For students of higher education in general and of professional education in particular, however, understanding what a profession is enables them to analyze problems of education for professions far more easily and facilitates their solving of quite practical educational problems such as how to select students, how to evaluate student progress, and how to plan an appropriate set of learning experiences.

In another article Cogan attempts a definition that illustrates both the difficulty of defining a profession and the danger of the invitation to controversy.[2] He includes essentially four major points in that definition. First, a profession is an occupation based on "an understanding of . . . theoretical structure . . . and upon the abilities accompanying such understanding."

Second, the practice of a profession involves the application of that understanding and of those abilities and skills to "the vital practical affairs of man." Indeed, it seems clear that a practitioner of a profession is primarily engaged in solving problems of others through an ability to apply sciences.

Third, the experience of an individual practitioner and of the collection of practitioners known as "the profession" serve as the basis to modify those practices—perhaps merely illustrative of why we call members of a profession "practitioners" and why we refer to the "practice" of a profession.

Finally, Cogan states that a profession "considers its first ethical imperative to be altruistic service to the client." This last part of his proposed definition appears in almost all of the many definitions that can be found in higher education literature. And once again, *if* one accepts this definition, education for a given profession can be expected to include experiences that are designed to help students develop a value structure that incorporates this affective component at its core.

It is quite clear, however, that any definition will not enable us to draw a line that separates professions from other occupations. Not only can the definition itself invite controversy, but attempts to apply it can lead to argument (not debate) because of the emotional content associated with the prestige of "being a professional." Many students of higher education, therefore, have turned away from strict definitions and have, instead, begun to think of "characteristics" that tend to distinguish professions from other occupations. One of the early statements of this kind was made by Lloyd E. Blauch, who suggested three "principal earmarks of those occupations that are widely and commonly recognized as professions."[3] The first of these is "study and training." A profession is based upon a theoretic structure, a collection of sciences. The learning of these sciences is an obvious prerequisite to becoming a practicing member of a given profession. Moreover, as the bodies of information in each science grow, the time needed for "study and training" grows also. Futhermore, while a profession involves intellectual processes for the most part, there are also skills involved—frequently manipulative. The learning of these demands opportunity for repeated learning trials. Thus, the reference is to "training" as well as to "study" or education.

The second "earmark" Blauch calls "measure of success." Here he points out that while members of a profession are compensated by fees or salary, the true measure of success in the life of a professional is how well he performs the services for his clients. That is, in many occupations, the generally accepted standard of success is financial: "How much money does he make?" In the case of a profession, the question tends to be "how well does he perform his services" and the satisfaction for each professional tends much more to be derived internally (did I serve my client well?) and even the external reward system is professionally oriented (did I earn the esteem of my fellow professionals?).

The final "earmark" is that of "associations." In Blauch's words, ". . . members organize associations through which they act collectively to maintain and improve (the profession's) service." Associations tend to be selective in admission policies and thus serve to raise standards for their respective professions. Furthermore, these associations become the source of codes of conduct and the means of enforcement of high standards of practice.

Perhaps the most useful set of "characteristics" of a profession is presented by Myron Lieberman—"useful" in the sense of providing important implications for planning professional education. After making the point that "there is no authoritative set of criteria by means of which we can distinguish professions from other occupations," he then states, in effect, that an occupation can be considered to be a profession to the extent to which it possesses the following characteristics.[4]

"A unique, definite, and essential social service." For example, the profession of dentistry involves a definite service or collection of services deemed to be essential in our society. Furthermore, only members of the dental profession are considered qualified or eligible to perform those services. Indeed, society has considered this so important that it provides enforcement through legislation.

"An emphasis upon intellectual techniques in performing its service." A profession depends very heavily upon intellectual processes in the provision of its services. Problem solving appears to be a critical ingredient in the service provided by a given profession. The scientific basis for the practice of a profession is usually well defined and somewhat formidable. It is important to interject that some laymen are critical of this concept and protest that a profession is only attempting to make it seem more difficult to become a member—and thus make the profession more exclusive. While there may be some tendency (to be discussed later) to become less selective in what science(s) must be learned by students in preparation for a given profession, for the most part a true profession demands a solid foundation in science(s) for its practice(s) to take place.

"A long period of specialized training." Three concepts are embodied in this "characteristic." In the first place, preparation for a profession involves a long period of time. Preparation for the practice of medicine, for instance, typically includes four years of medical school and a minimum of two years of practice under supervision—after a usual premedical education in a baccalaureate degree program. Dental education and law education are similar. While some professions have a shorter period of preparation, even they require much longer time for education and training than do occupations not considered to be professions.

Secondly, there is reference to "training," as distinguished from education. That is, preparation to enter a profession demands a considerable period of time devoted to practicing—under supervision—performance of the tasks, the skills, and the processes of that profession. Thus, every profession clearly has two major components: intellectual techniques and non-intellectual skills. In other words, ". . . professional training is *primarily*, not *wholly*, intellectual."

Finally, Lieberman emphasizes the "specialized" quality of the "long training," suggesting that many critics feel that "too many professional workers are said to be uneducated outside their field of specialization." But it is an inescapable fact that as a profession develops, its scientific base grows (and in recent years the growth has been described—accurately—as "explosive") and its skills become more complex. Thus, preparation for a profession demands specialization that, in turn, leads to narrowness and that, furthermore, requires more time.

"**A broad range of autonomy for both the individual practitioners and for the occupational group as a whole.**" Throughout each work day, a professional person is required to make a number of important decisions in the ordinary course of providing services to clients. The professional person, therefore, must have autonomy to do so. Obviously, if each decision had to be reviewed by some authority, service could not be efficiently or effectively provided. In addition, through their professional organizations, practitioners set their own standards of performance and requirements for membership. Thus, autonomy is one of the differentiating characteristics of a profession.

"**An acceptance by the practitioners of broad personal responsibility for judgments made and acts performed within the scope of professional autonomy.**" Simply stated, "a large measure of autonomy implies a correspondingly large measure of responsibility." If the professional person acts autonomously and if the actions carry potentially great impact on the lives of others, the practitioner is assuming a grave personal responsibility. The dentist, in recommending corrective procedures and then performing them, is also stating that he or she is willing to assume the responsibility *personally* for those actions. The pharmacist, in counseling patients with regard to drug action and/or drug-drug interaction, is doing likewise. The *personal* responsibility is in stark contrast to the general societal movement in the direction of *corporate* or *institutional* responsibility.

"**An emphasis upon the service to be rendered, rather than the economic gain to the practitioners, as the basis for the organization and performance of the social service delegated to the occupational group.**" Some refer to this characteristic as "altruism." There is no intent here to suggest that members of professions are universally altruistic. Indeed, there is little reason to believe that the population of a given profession does not include a full spectrum of practitioners ranging from those totally dedicated to their clients and their profession to those quite materialistically motivated. But the true impact of this "characteristic" is derived from the earlier definition that included reference to an "ethical imperative" involving "altruistic service to the client."

"**A comprehensive self-governing organization of practitioners.**" Since most professions have membership quite large and scattered throughout the country, they must have some mechanism for collectively conducting the business associated with governance of the profession: setting standards for membership, policing malpractices within the profession, promoting higher quality practices, providing safeguards for society.

"**A code of ethics which has been clarified and interpreted at ambiguous and doubtful points by concrete cases.**" Each profession tends to develop an increasingly specific set of behavioral standards. In the enforcement of this code of behavior, the profession relies on specific cases to help clarify the code and illustrate each ethical principle.

The importance of Lieberman's "characteristics" in the study of education for the professions lies not so much in the ability of that list to differentiate between professions and other occupations as in the implications for the planning of professional education. In other words, if an occupation is clearly seen to be a profession in that it possesses these characteristics to a significant extent, then the educational program should include provisions for helping students both to understand the professional nature of the life work they have chosen and to develop the traits that will enable them to perform better in their chosen professional roles. For example, consider the first characteristic, that a profession provides "a unique, definite, and essential social service." The educational preparation for a given profession should specifically provide experiences that will help students understand both the nature of the professional service *and* the fact that it is "unique, definite and essential." Or, consider the fifth characteristic, that there is grave personal responsibility for the practitioner. Students need learning experiences that will help them know the personal responsibilities, recognize the accompanying consequences, and learn coping mechanisms to help them through periods of stress.

Indeed, with all of what we study about professions, the goal for those charged with responsibility for education for the professions is to learn how to apply that knowledge to the educational planning process and to the educational program, as well. Learning to differentiate between professions and other occupations as an intellectual exercise is hardly worth the effort; learning to do so in order to plan better for the education and training of those entering the profession is quite valuable.

THE NATURE OF EDUCATION FOR THE PROFESSIONS

Education for a given profession seems to have a universal "developmental" pattern regardless of the profession itself. This phenomenon should come as no surprise since the very definition of profession suggests certain similarities that would govern education and training. There are essentially six developmental stages.

Apprenticeship. Since a profession involves providing a service, the earliest form of preparation of novices for membership in a profession involves an apprenticeship system of some kind. The practitioner, in essence, says to the person who wants to become a member of that profession, "Spend time with me; watch what I do; ask me questions about these procedures; I'll let you try them under my supervision. When I think you are ready for independent practice, I'll tell my colleagues and they will receive you as a member." And that approach serves very well during the early stages of the development of a profession—unless, of course, it is a profession that is emerging from the practice of a semiprofession or of another (nonprofession) occupation. As the profession grows in complexity and importance, the apprenticeship system is not sufficient.

Generation of knowledge. As the practitioners conduct their daily activities, as they provide those "essential services," a body of knowledge grows out of their experience. Indeed, concerted efforts at discovery of knowledge in a given profession also contribute to the growth of an information base—and then a science—for that profession. Thus, knowledge grows, at an increasing rate, from two sources: experience and research. That increase in knowledge demands that the preparation of new professionals include some systematic "coverage" of the information and science base. Education for the profession then begins to change.

Classification of the knowledge. Because the knowledge base grows rapidly, those charged with teaching tend to classify and organize it in neat and orderly units for instructional purposes. (Whether this neatness and orderliness serves the needs of the learners or those of the teachers is an interesting question—but one which will not be discussed here.)

Teaching the knowledge and providing the apprenticeship. It is not unexpected that the next developmental step should be that of combining the now insufficient apprenticeship with some means of "teaching" the growing bodies of information. The early developmental forms of this educational combination vary according to the unique qualities of a given profession and the usual influences of tradition, cost considerations, and society's needs. That is, the teaching of the knowledge base *may* precede the apprenticeship or it may accompany it; the time allotted for the purely professional preparation may vary from a minimum of less than a year to as much as four (or more) years.

Formalization of the teaching. No matter what the original intent is with regard to flexibility, inevitably the program becomes highly specific and quite formal. Learning of the knowledge base is promoted through a series of "courses" usually associated with a degree or at least a certificate. The courses themselves are organized around the information bases to be learned and even the sciences tend to be taught as collections of information rather than as concepts and principles to be applied in the practice of the profession. Indeed, in some professional schools the curriculum has become so formalized and ritualized that the educators themselves refer to their own educational programs as "lock-step" curricula.

Improvement of the profession. Finally, there is an attempt on the part of the professionals to improve their profession through research, continuing education, and general expansion of services and of fields of knowledge. Needless to say, this "improvement" leads to lengthening the education and training period and to even further rigidity in the education and training programs.

The development of a simple apprenticeship system into a formal and ritualized education and training program almost always results in the emergence of a professional school. While it is true that some professions provide their preparation programs through a department or other similar administrative unit, generally, one considers the program to be that offered by a "school." And professional schools, for the most part, are found in the context of a university or a system of colleges.

Professional schools have essentially three major functions: 1) recruitment, 2) education and training, and 3) certification. With regard to recruitment, the professional school, acting as an arm of the profession, is expected to locate, attract, and enroll sufficient numbers of qualified and capable students to provide the profession with the numbers needed to continue (and possibly expand) their "essential service to society." The recruitment efforts can be facilitated by actions of strong national professional organizations that serve to publicize the profession and its needs and/or go so far as to provide a standardized, national system of applications—as is the case with the Association of American Medical Colleges through its AMCAS program. But equally important—now more so than ever—is the responsibility of the profession, perhaps through research efforts of the schools, to study the manpower needs of the profession and the society it serves, using the results of such studies to plan the size of classes and the number of schools.

The second function, that of training and education, is the most self-evident of the three. Obviously a professional school has as its major purpose the preparation of students to take their place in that profession. Implicit in this function, however, is the stipulation that the professional school must educate and train its students to meet the competency demands of the profession. That is, the school must train and educate the students to attain the professionally approved levels of scientific, technical, and professional competence. In some instances, this function is shared with another agency in which the students (or recent graduates) are obtaining their apprenticeship training.

Finally, the professional school has as one of its functions graduating—and certifying—its students. The school is expected to produce graduates who have the knowledge, technical abilities, personal character, and social outlook necessary for practice of that profession. The implication is quite clear: the school must know what those attributes are; it must provide for measurement of those attributes; and it must gather the data that permits it to certify that the graduates have met the minimum criteria for practice of that profession. Again, in some cases outside agencies can participate in this process through a form of "external" examination system.

In studying any professional school, one should be concerned with a number of components of professional education:

1. **Prerequisites.** What entry levels of achievement, behavior, personal characteristics, and the like are deemed necessary prior to admission to the professional school?

2. **Selection and admission.** How does the professional school determine which students are to be accepted and how does it conduct the admissions processes?

3. **Curriculum.** What bodies of knowledge are to be learned by students and what learning experiences are provided by the school?

4. **Objectives.** Specifically what are students expected to learn—bodies of knowledge, skills and habits, attitudes and values, etc.?

5. **Certification.** How does the school go about gathering information concerning student achievement and performance?

6. **Continuing education.** What provisions are made by the school for the continuing education of its graduates?

While individual schools may differ somewhat, there are clear patterns of professional education within any single profession. In other words, while one dental school may differ from another somewhat in style or even content, they are basically quite similar in their provision of the above components—with the possible exception of the last one, which is only recently considered universally to be a component of professional education.

Formal professional education consists of a number of components, the aggregate of which encompasses the entire continuum of preparation for a profession from before the student arrives for education and training to after he or she has begun practice.

1. **Prerequisites.** Each professional school describes a set of traits and characteristics necessary for entry level into the particular professional preparation. Also, the school usually provides the measures that are acceptable indications of the satisfactory attainment of the entry-level attributes.

2. **Selection and admission.** Each professional school then applies a standard set of procedures to screen applicants, admitting only those who meet the entry-level criteria. When the number of applicants exceeds the number of "places" available for training and education in that school, procedures also allow for selection of the "best" of the applicant pool through the application of standardized and objective selection procedures.

3. **Curriculum.** The preparation of students in a given profession then involves having them participate in a sequence of learning experiences carefully designed to facilitate the desired learning. Examination of the curriculum should include study of both the *content* (what subjects are involved) and the *learning experiences* (lectures, labs, and clerkships, for example).

4. **Objectives.** For each professional school there should be a statement describing the desired learning outcomes. That is, what information should students acquire? What understanding should they gain? What skills should they achieve? What professional habits should they establish? What attitudes should they develop? These recent years have seen the process of answering the above questions begun in earnest in most professional education areas with significant contributions to improvement of the educational programs.

5. **Certification.** At the conclusion of the formal training and education program conducted within the professional school there is an expectation that the school will—at least implicitly—certify that the students have achieved minimum levels of professional competency in that profession. In some, it is certification that the graduates are "ready" for further training and/or education. In others, it is certification that the graduates are "ready" for beginning practice in that profession. Regardless of whether the certification procedure is formal or implied, it is a significant component of professional education.

6. **Continuing education.** More and more, professional schools are being asked to assume responsibility for the continuing education of practitioners. Once a responsibility of the professional, then the responsibility of the profession, continuing education seems now to be one of the many responsibilities of the school. The evolutionary change in responsibility seems to have accompanied the explosion of knowledge in professions and the increased use of continuing education "credits" for recertification and/or relicensure.

No discussion of professional education is complete without some treatment of the strange response by many educators to one remarkable characteristic of any profession. Every profession consists of two major components. One such component consists of the necessary bodies of science that underlie the practice of that profession. That is, every profession—by any definition or description of the term—is dependent upon sciences, and every practitioner should be well versed in them. The other major component is the collection of techniques, skills, and/or abilities that comprise the practice itself. Since many of the teachers in professional schools are not actively engaged in practice and since many of the teachers are academicians actively engaged in research in one of the sciences, a schism appears between these two "camps," often approaching a kind of internecine warfare—in which, incidentally, only the students are losers and there are no "winners." Then, as the struggle finds an arena in the curriculum, attempts to strengthen the program in the "clinical" area and/or attempts to increase emphasis in that area are met with the cry, "Do you want to change us into a 'trade school'?" In other words, many teachers in professional schools see the school as one branch of a dichotomy and the "trade school" as the other. Figure 1 summarizes that dichotomy rather neatly.

Figure 1. The (False) Dichotomy of Professional Education

The reason for labeling the dichotomy as "false" is that the pejorative comparison assumes that graduates must become one or the other: a scientist or a technician. In fact, those rabid defenders of science often tend to lose sight of the fact that the "product" of their professional schools is expected to be something different entirely—yet include parts of both of those. Thus, it is more useful to look at professional education as one branch of a *trichotomy* (Fig. 2).

Figure 2. The (True) Trichotomy of Professional Education

In other words, *the practice of a profession involves the application of sciences to the solution of problems.* The student in a professional school must learn the sciences that are the basis for the profession; the student must also learn how to apply these to solve problems for the "first ethical imperative": the client. Thus, the student in a professional school is obliged to master the sciences, often to the same criterion level as a graduate school. At the same time the student must master the requisite technical skills, again often to the same criterion level as a technician. But it is this characteristic of *application* of the scientific base that separates the professional from both the scientist and the technician.

With that much of a brief review of the nature of a profession and of professional education, attention can now be turned to a rather important collection of professions—the health professions—and problems of education and training in preparation for them.

EDUCATION FOR HEALTH PROFESSIONS

With the remarkable explosion of knowledge in biological and chemical sciences and with the equally remarkable expansion of health services both provided for and promised to Americans, there has been an accompanying proliferation of professions whose members are engaged in providing health care services. No longer is there just the physician and the nurse; now there are so many different professionals as to make one exhaustive list virtually impossible. Including the older, established professions and the newer, still developing professions, the list would certainly include at least the following:

> Dentistry
> Dietetics
> Hospital Administration
> Medical Social Work
> Medical Technology
> Medicine
> Nursing
> Nurse Practitioner
> Occupational Therapy
> Optometry
> Osteopathy
> Pharmacy
> Physician Assistant
> Physical Therapy
> Podiatry
> Public Health
> Rehabilitation Counseling

The list is not all-inclusive; there are undoubtedly many omissions, not counting the proliferation of specialists within many of those professions. For instance, it is fair to point out that medicine includes at least 20-odd formally established specialties and many more "subspecialties." But the aim here is not to attempt to prepare a definitive listing of health professions; rather, it is to present a reminder that there are many, many health professions, and many other health occupations that approach being professions and may indeed already be in that developmental pattern.

What is also important is to note that preparation for any of those professions essentially has an important basic structure. All demand mastery of certain basic sciences—basic, that is, to the practice of that profession and/or to the continued education of the practitioner in that profession. Moreover, each demands education and training to prepare its students to perform certain tasks and to play certain roles in the practice of that profession. And, each professional school demands a comprehensive educational plan that includes reference to prerequisites, selection and admission, curriculum (both content and learning experiences), objectives, certification, and continuing education. Finally, all of them share the dubious distinction of facing problems like the following:

1. Conflict between professional education and professional licensure.
2. Conflict between "town" and "gown."
3. Explosion of knowledge.
4. Separation of basic sciences from clinical studies.
5. Changing patterns of delivery of services.
6. Inadequate statement of "objectives"—i.e., inadequate definition of the "product."
7. Inefficient educational practices.
8. Separation of professional education from general education.
9. Perceived lack of emphasis on interpersonal skills and societal concerns.

Education for health professions may best be described by illustration. The next pages are devoted to a study of the standard practices, the trends, and the problems that characterize medical education today.

MEDICAL EDUCATION

Conventional medical education originated in the wave of reform that followed the famous Flexner Report. While modest evolutionary changes managed to take place, basically the structure of present-day medical education has persisted from about 1920 until today. Some notable exceptions began to appear starting in 1952, but essentially American medical education has been as follows.

1. **Prerequisites.** For the most part, students are expected to have completed a baccalaureate degree prior to entrance into medical school. Many medical schools will permit some few students to enter after only three years, but these students are still exceptional. (Under "Trends," below, there is reference to the few programs that accept high school graduates and provide a five- or six-year program leading to the M.D. degree.) Most medical schools require such courses as physics, calculus, organic chemistry, and/or embryology.

2. **Selection and admission.** Typically, American medical schools select their students on the basis of their prior achievement in college or in a university setting; scholastic achievement and aptitude reflected in scores on the Medical College Admissions Test; personal attributes inferred from a) the premedical college advisor's "ratings" and/or comments, b) an essay written by the applicant, and c) an interview of the applicant. One out of three applicants is admitted to some American medical school each year.

3. **Curriculum.** Again, the typical (conventional) medical school includes four years of attendance by its students. The first two years deal with basic medical sciences almost exclusively while the third and fourth years provide clinical learning experiences. In outline form, the program is as follows:

Year One

Anatomy (including gross anatomy, neuroanatomy, histology)
Biochemistry
Physiology
Introduction to Clinical Medicine (in many schools)
Biostatics (in many schools)

Year Two

Microbiology (including immunology, genetics)
Pharmacology (including nutrition)
Pathology
Physical Diagnosis
Community Medicine (in some schools)

Years Three and Four

Medicine (and selected specialties)
Pediatrics
Psychiatry
Surgery (and selected specialties)
Obstetrics and Gynecology
Other clinical electives

In the first two years, the learning experiences include lectures, laboratories, some small group discussions, and occasional self-instructional units. There is a heavy emphasis on lecturing, and basic science laboratories have tended to occupy less and less student time. In the third and fourth years, the experiences are, for the most part, "clinical clerkships," in which students learn the role of physicians by performing familiar patient-care tasks under supervision usually in the hospital setting: taking history, performing physical examination, formulating a "problem list," keeping written records, making case presentations, and the like.

4. **Objectives.** Over the past several years, many medical schools have begun to define their specific educational objectives. For many this task has still not been accomplished. While it is probably generally acknowledged that the *primary goal* of undergraduate medical education is the preparation of students for the practice of medicine, there are some medical school faculty who contend that the primary goal is the preparation of "medical scientists" or of faculty members for tomorrow's medical education. This kind of divided view on the goals of medical education makes it more difficult for medical education to make its adjustments to changing times, changing demands, and changing conditions. Indeed, in the absence of consensus on the general goal, it is virtually impossible even to *discuss*, let alone agree upon, specific learning objectives such as requisite information, essential understanding, basic skills, desirable habits, and sound attitudes for the practice of medicine.

5. **Certification.** More than 80 of the 120-odd American medical schools require that their students take examinations prepared and administered by the National Board of Medical Examiners, a voluntary agency that has prepared high quality examinations to determine "competence to practice medicine" since its establishment in 1915. Indeed, licensure (a state function) is granted by every state in the United States to students who pass Parts I, II, and III of the National Boards'. But within the schools, there are internal examination procedures to assess students' knowledge, and observation and rating scales to assess students' clinical performance. External examinations (like the NBMEs) generally serve as a form of confirmation to the individual medical schools that their respective programs and educational efforts are "producing" the results that are nationally "approved."

6. **Continuing education.** With the growing practice of requiring evidence of continuing education for recertification and/or for relicensure, more

and more effort is now being put into provision of educational experiences for practicing physicians—designed to "bring them up to date" or introduce newer information or practices to their attention. These efforts take the familiar form of "courses" for the most part, although there are notable other activities like "Audio-Digest" (audio tapes for physicians to listen to), Medical Television Network (video tapes circulated to medical schools and teaching hospitals), and "Self-Assessment Examinations" (examinations with accompanying educational materials), to mention a few.

Turning from "typical" medical education to a consideration of trends, one must not begin to examine today's apparent directions without some review of the modification of the Flexner model that began in 1952 and took place until 1972.

The first major change in American medical education occurred at what was then Western Reserve University (now Case-Western Reserve University) School of Medicine in 1952, following a period of intensive self-study and planning. The "Western Reserve Plan" was best known for its shift in approach to the teaching of the basic medical sciences. The faculty believed that there was much unnecessary duplication of instruction because of the way in which the sciences were organized. They said, in effect, that it was possibly inefficient to teach the structure of the cardiovascular system in anatomy and then the function of that system in physiology and then the deviations from normal in that system in pathology. They proposed that teaching should be organized around organ systems and that teaching should become the responsibility of teaching committees of an interdisciplinary nature. That organization has been adopted by almost 40 American medical schools at this time.

But the contributions of the Western Reserve curriculum change included many more innovations of that time, in addition to the subject-teaching committee approach to teaching basic medical sciences.

1. **Multidiscipline laboratories.** Whereas basic science teaching laboratories had been purely disciplinary in organization prior to that time, it occurred to the curriculum planners that there were a number of advantages to making laboratories multidisciplinary. First of all, the only students to use the physiology labs, the histology labs, the neuroanatomy labs, and the biochemistry labs were first-year students. Since medical students, like other human beings, are capable of being in only one place at a time, they reasoned, would it not be logical to have laboratory space for first-year students? In that way, whatever lab exercise was scheduled, the students could always use that lab. Indeed, the lab space then became the student's own academic home for study, for research, for reading, and the like. These multidisciplinary labs (commonly known as "MDLs") have been copied in many other American medical schools by this time.[5]

2. **Family clinic.** In this part of the revised educational program, provision was made for students to have much earlier encounters with patients than had been the case in the Flexner curriculum model. In fact, a first-year medical student was assigned his or her own patient in the first week of school: a pregnant woman in the newly established "family clinic." This patient (and her family) became the patient of the student who was expected to be present at all of the visits made

by the patient and, indeed, to follow the patient through her normal pregnancy and delivery and then follow the family through postnatal care and other care for members of the family. At the time of adoption of the "new" curriculum, students were expected to follow the patient and the family through all four years of medical education. While that has been modified (the last two years certainly might not be expected to make as significant a contribution to the education of the student as the first two) it is still part of the program and has been emulated in many other medical schools in one form or another.

3. **Basic clerkship concept.** In medical schools prior to this time, students rotated through clerkships in the various clinical areas, some starting in medicine, some in surgery, and others in any one of the many specialty areas. This "new" idea was that students should start in a clerkship in which the basic principles and practices were taught prior to their rotating through different, more specialized clinical areas.

4. **Grades and examinations.** Peter V. Lee's description of this change probably sums it up best:

> In an attempt to treat the student as a maturing individual, the faculty has devised a mature system of examinations and grades. . . . Class rankings and numerical or letter grades are not used. An examination is given at the end of each major subject-committee topic . . . and at the end of each phase . . . No grade is recorded unless a student is doing failing or borderline work. In this case, the examination results are used for counseling the weak student. Class standings are not recorded; instead there is an attempt to have each instructor who has had contact with a student describe his strengths and weaknesses. These comments are used for counseling, not for ranking.[6]

5. **Free time.** During the first two and one-half years of the curriculum, one and one-half days were designated as "free time" for students to use in elective study and/or truly free time. Indeed, the concept was so new at the time that the term, "free time," had to appear on the formal schedule in order for it to be honored in the program.

So many of the major contributions of the Western-Reserve plan have since become commonplace in other medical schools. Indeed, the period from the time of the Western-Reserve curriculum change until 1972 was one of considerable unrest and ferment in medical education. It became a matter of humor that almost every medical school in the country was engaged in self-study leading to possible curriculum change. The early changes are described in Lee's work. Later changes appear in the medical education literature. Not one of them, however, represents a significant deviation in *concept*, with a couple of notable exceptions. That is, the changes seem to be "adjustments" in scheduled hours and shifts in "blocks" of time. Medical education *still* consists of two years of basic medical sciences followed by two years of clinical clerkships with an early introduction to patient care, some elective time increasing each year, and *formal* scheduling of "free time" necessary to guarantee students some time for themselves. The "adjustments" involve possible organ-system organization of basic sciences, introduction of pathology in the first year, emphasis on molecular biology, introduction of behavioral sciences, and the like. All of these kinds of curriculum characteristics can be found in the AAMC's *Curriculum Directory*, published annually.

Lee's description of the nine "experiments" in medical education that took place between 1950 and 1960 includes three programs that accepted high school graduates into a six-year combined college and medical school program, four that introduced special programs in the teaching of comprehensive medicine, a special chapter on the Western-Reserve curriculum reorganization, and a chapter devoted to a new medical school: the University of Florida. These changes and the others of that extended era tend to be more mechanical than philosophic. That is, attention is paid to the timing of learning experiences and the arrangement of courses rather than to the objectives of medical education, how students learn, and the needs of society.

And that situation persisted into the expansionist period of medical education in which so many new medical schools were founded in an effort to increase the number of new physicians graduated each year in the United States. Edwin F. Rosinski reviewed the curriculum status of the 11 new schools that had appeared and taken their first students by 1969 and reported at the Annual Meeting of the Association of American Medical Colleges in November 1969 that all but one of the new schools had ended up as "traditional" as the established schools despite the promises at the outset by the founding deans that their respective programs would be innovative in response to the needs of society in general and of medical education in particular. In an editorial, Rosinski said that by July 1970 in each of the 11 new schools there was a ". . . rather standard curriculum with parts of it innovative but, by and large, stereotyped."

It is important to note that during that era in medical education when there was both money and encouragement for schools to be innovative with regard to the curriculum and also with regard to the teaching program, very few schools were *truly* innovative. Today, the most notable innovation in undergraduate medical education is *not* in an American medical school; it can be found in Canada (McMaster University School of Medicine) and in Australia (The University of Newcastle Faculty of Medicine). The core of their programs is both curricular and pedigogic. The curriculum consists of a series of problem-solving exercises for students to study in small groups. There are no lectures or other formal, all-class, learning exercises during that period of time given to the basic sciences in the first two years of American medical education. The program involves much more than that, of course, but it is enough to say here that the student's experiences are significantly different from those in conventional medical schools. It is also interesting to note that the one American medical school cited by Rosinski as being innovative among the new schools he reviewed (i.e., Michigan State University) has some of these characteristics. It is probably also important to note that the University of New Mexico has introduced this format as an *option* for students who are interested in pursuing it while most of the students remain in the conventional program.

One other program of note, perhaps, is that which began as the "Pilot Medical School" at Ohio State University College of Medicine about 1970. That school prepared a number of self-instructional units in the basic sciences, essentially including the content of the first two years. These units were administered to students through the aid of a computer so that each student was able to learn at his or her own rate and progress was measured not by the all-too-familiar passage of time (and tests) but rather by achievement on examination without regard to passage of time. And the faculty was able to assume a role of educational counselor much more than that of lecturer.

What has been presented is a very personal view of a 20-year period of sincere concern for medical education and honest effort at meeting changing times. It is, in this writer's view, sad that much of the ferment and excitement of that era seems to have resulted in little real change in undergraduate medical education. There is no need to explore the reasons for that situation; the important factor here is that understanding that little change has taken place helps us to examine "trends" and to offer some predictions about the future.

It is difficult to find "trends" in medical education that are distinct and unequivocal. On the one hand, there is still a rapidly increasing body of knowledge in molecular biology areas and it is clear that medical schools continue to try to include these new developments. Of course, since little is ever ready to be dropped from inclusion in the curriculum, a continuing problem is the enormous overload for students. Still, one "trend" is the inclusion of the biochemistry and molecular biology still rapidly evolving.

On the other hand, there is still increasing concern for inclusion of learning experiences that will help make the future physicians more humane and more concerned about patients as total human beings. This, coupled with the recent emphasis on some form of return to the "family doctor," has led to an expansion of learning experiences in community and family medicine including 1) early introduction to the patient, 2) more community-based clinical encounters, 3) more ambulatory medicine experiences, and 4) increased emphasis on problems of the aged and indigent, along with emphasis on problems of cost containment and of health maintenance. Thus, one other trend is clear and, unfortunately, in competition with the first.

But the most dramatic trend in medical education is not really in evidence as yet. Indeed, it may not be possible to begin to describe it. It is "in the wings" and will truly be the most traumatic "trend" since the immediate post-Flexner modifications. The high cost of medical education and the inflationary conditions of the times are about to bring changes in medical education that cannot be predicted . . . but the *problem* can be described and some guesses might be offered.

For more than 25 years following World War II, American medical education enjoyed an ever-increasing subsidy provided by the federal government. Through research grants, and the like, the "Feds" (as they are often called) provided money in support of faculty positions, office equipment, student fees and stipends, laboratory equipment, and much more. Indeed, when it was proposed in 1966 that funds available for the National Institutes of Health might be held at a *constant level* rather than continue to increase at the rate at which they had been, the outcry among medical school personnel was as one voice: this will destroy medical education! And when the "training grants" for basic sciences were discontinued, the same cry was heard.

Today, the movement is clear: there will be *at least* a leveling-off of and at worst a reduction in federal subsidy for medical education. That action, along with the continued inflation that has driven both the institutional costs of operation and student tuition and fees to a once unbelievable level, surely will have an impact on medical education. What that impact will ultimately be is not clear. It could bring a reduction in the number of faculty resulting in more large group instruction and less small group instruction. It could bring an increase in participation by "voluntary faculty" leading to greater control by the practicing community with possible de-emphasis of what is perceived as less relevant basic sciences. It could bring a significant decrease in biomedical research activities resulting in fewer basic science faculty and a significant slowing of the development of knowledge. It could mean less money available for curriculum development, and consequently, fewer attempts at educational innovation and a solid retrenchment in conventional educational practices.

Twenty years ago there were problems and trends that were evident as they were evolving. Today—as then—there are some problems, but it is not clear how these problems will affect medical education. In a strange "long view," it is possible to say that little (except some content of science and practice) has changed in 30 years; thus, probably little will change now. This time, however, the problems will force significant change—just as they would have in the 1950s except for the federal response of large sums of money to be used to solve those problems of that time. Now, there will not be that financial intervention—and the problems are not inconsiderable.

If it is not possible to discuss trends in American medical education, it is still feasible to list some problems and speculate on the potential impact of such problems on medical education. It is quite apparent that the most pressing problem facing American medical education in 1980 is that of providing an adequate financial support base. With the federal government indicating clearly and strongly that it will no longer provide the extent of support it has in the past and with costs of everything continuing to rise, the problem is vast and still growing. Tuition in private medical schools is already prohibitive and yet does not begin to cover the true cost of education for the student. State schools are trying to collect from out-of-state students the *real* costs—well in excess of $20,000 per year. Needless to say, the net result of that action is restriction of student population in such schools to residents of those states, respectively.

One must also examine the internal structure of the medical school to consider possible outcomes of this financial crisis. Basic science teachers have been able to devote most of their time to "scholarly" activities, often limiting their "contact hours" with students to as little as two hours per week (on the average for a department). In a tight-money situation, this practice will be examined closely—but with what results, it is difficult to say.

On the other side of medical education, clinical faculty will probably be asked to participate more in institutional practice plans designed to generate funds for the medical school. This has been a practice in many schools, it is true, but now it will become essential for the other schools to do so—and it will become a new institutional value, just as "grantsmanship" among basic scientists has been for all these years. That is, administrative decisions about salary levels and space may now be influenced much more by these considerations.

But there are other problems. There is still the problem presented by the continuing growth of knowledge bases in the sciences. It is quite evident that the rate of generation of new information is still exceeding the rate at which faculty members are willing to drop dated material from the curriculum and study their own teaching programs with an eye toward streamlining them.

This problem is exacerbated by the lack of skill in educational planning evident in so many of the schools. There is often no "standard operating procedure" for 1) making decisions about curriculum, 2) obtaining participation from faculty members in curriculum planning, and 3) implementing educational policy. Rosinski's view of 1970 is still operant: the education of medical students is, unfortunately, not the first priority of medical school administrators. Worse, it is probably not even a high priority when compared to such matters as finding financial support, creating and distributing sufficient working space, and maintaining cordial relationships among the school's many constituencies—the faculty, the students, the alumni, the practicing community, the board of trustees, the hospitals, and the sources of support. Finally, it is sad to add that the education of the students is probably not a high priority item among most of the faculty who are faced with an almost absurd application of the "publish-or-perish" doctrine that governs promotion, a need to obtain grants to support either themselves or the personnel needed to carry out their research, and an "academic community" of their respective disciplines that tends to place a high value on "scholarship" (all too often measured by publication) and a low value on teaching.

But the health care community adds a number of problems for medical education. The runaway costs of health care pose a serious problem for society. In turn, medical education is being asked to "teach" students practices which will result in "cost containment." Thus, the medical educators must first investigate the whole area of medical economics (and are generally not well prepared to do so), then develop practices that might be less costly (and try these experimentally in controlled settings), and finally find some way to introduce those ideas into an already crowded curriculum (with the strict academicians resisting these inroads into their "territory").

Furthermore, third-party payers are having an increasingly significant impact on how health care is delivered. It is quite clear that this will continue—particularly if a national health insurance plan is adopted.

The emergence of a "new" specialty, family medicine, has already introduced new problems for medical education. The first problem deals with "time" in the curriculum: if students are to have learning experiences in family medicine, what disciplines will lose time? Another deals with the "logistics" of the learning experiences: since much—if not most—of family medicine practice occurs *not* in the hospital (inpatient) setting, how are such experiences to be designed? For much of this, there is no good, sound precedent. Thus, there exists a wide latitude for innovation in addition to an enormous challenge demanding intensive study and collaborative effort.

Finally, putting medicine back into the context of total health care, patterns of delivery of health care are changing. While predictions about the ultimate pattern to evolve from the present changing patterns are probably not clear enough to explore, one can predict comfortably that health care practices in the year 2000 will be quite different from those today. (And keep in mind that our present health professions students will be at the peak time of their respective practices in that year.) While the future is unclear, it is quite clear that more and more of health care delivery will be done by health care personnel other than the physician. The newer mid-level health practitioners will clearly play a more important role. The physician's role is the least clear in many ways.

Medical education's problem, then, is at least doubled: 1) How can we best prepare medical students to assume their appropriate roles in today's health care arena—with all its problems of spiraling costs, exploding knowledge bases, and changing delivery patterns? 2) How can we best prepare medical students to assume their appropriate roles in *tomorrow's* health care arena—with all its problems as yet undefined but surely including the resolution of complex interrelationships with other health professions, each with its own undefined problems?

NOTES

1.   Morris L. Cogan, "The Problems of Defining a Profession," *The Annals of the American Academy of Political and Social Science*, 297 (January 1955).

2.   Morris L. Cogan, "Toward a Definition of Profession," *Harvard Educational Review*, 23 (Winter 1953).

3.   Lloyd E. Blauch, *Education for the Professions* (Washington, DC: U.S. Department of Health, Education and Welfare, 1955).

4.   Myron Lieberman, *Education as a Profession* (Englewood Cliffs, NJ: Prentice-Hall, 1956).

5.   P. V. Lee and J. Bamberger, "Multidiscipline Student Laboratories: University of Southern California School of Medicine," *Journal of Medical Education*, vol. 39, no. 9 (September 1964).

6.   Peter V. Lee, *Medical Schools and the Changing Times* (Washington, DC: Association of American Medical Colleges, 1962).

7.   Edwin F. Rosinski, "The New Medical Schools and Curriculum Innovation," *Journal of the American Medical Association*, vol. 216, no. 2 (April 12, 1971).

BIBLIOGRAPHY

Blauch, Lloyd E. *Education for the Professions*. Washington, DC: U.S. Department of Health, Education and Welfare, 1955.

Cogan, Morris L. "The Problems of Defining a Profession." *The Annals of the American Academy of Political and Social Science*, 297 (January 1955).

Cogan, Morris L. "Toward a Definition of Profession." *Harvard Educational Review*, 23 (Winter 1953).

Lee, P. V., and Bamburger, J. "Multidiscipline Student Laboratories: University of Southern California School of Medicine." *Journal of Medical Education*, vol. 39, no. 9 (September 1964).

Lee, Peter V. *Medical Schools and the Changing Times*. Washington, DC: Association of American Medical Colleges, 1962.

Lieberman, Myron. *Education as a Profession*. Englewood Cliffs, NJ: Prentice-Hall, 1956.

Rosinski, Edwin F. "The New Medical Schools and Curriculum Innovation." *Journal of the American Medical Association*, vol. 216, no. 2 (April 12, 1971).

PHARMACEUTICAL EDUCATION

by
John A. Biles

Dean, School of Pharmacy
University of Southern California

In the twentieth century several surveys have been reported concerning pharmaceutical education and the practice of pharmacy. In 1948 *Findings and Recommendations of a Pharmaceutical Survey*[1] was published as well as *The General Report of the Pharmaceutical Survey*,[2] 1946-1949, with Edward C. Elliott as survey director and author. The pharmaceutical survey was a broad scale study of American pharmacy including pharmaceutical education and originated via the united efforts of the American Pharmaceutical Association, the National Association of Boards of Pharmacy, and the American Association of Colleges of Pharmacy. The survey was conducted under the auspices of the American Council on Education and was supported by funds provided by the American Foundation for Pharmaceutical Education.

The stated risk of the pharmaceutical survey was to assemble, as far as the available resources and means would permit, the important facts relating to pharmaceutical education, practices, services, and trade. The members of the survey committee were asked to interpret these facts and to develop proposals for the improvement of pharmacy as a profession and as a public service. The membership of the pharmaceutical survey recommended a conclusion of great significance, stating that for pharmacy to gain respect as a health profession, pharmacists should spend a minimum of two years in prepharmacy education and four years in a School of Pharmacy and that a Doctor of Pharmacy degree (Pharm.D. degree) should be granted to each graduate.

The University of Southern California was the first to adopt the Doctor of Pharmacy degree program, graduating its first Pharm.D. class in 1954. The second School of Pharmacy to adopt the Doctor of Pharmacy degree was the University of California, School of Pharmacy. However, debating this issue, the American Association of Colleges of Pharmacy adopted a five-year educational plan for graduates, thus leading to a baccalaureate degree in pharmacy. By 1960 all but the two above schools of pharmacy had adopted the five-year plan.

In the summer of 1978 the American Association of Colleges of Pharmacy again discussed whether or not to adopt the five-year degree (B.S.–Pharmacy) or the six-year degree (Pharm.D.) plan as the sole degree, concluding to endorse the six-year program. At the present time, in spite of budgetary constraints, schools of pharmacy are adopting the Doctor of Pharmacy degree as a sole degree program. By 1985 it is possible that 50% of the schools of pharmacy in the United States will have adopted the Doctor of Pharmacy program.

In 1952 the report *The Pharmaceutical Curriculum*[3] was published as an outgrowth of the pharmaceutical survey. The authors devoted considerable time to objectives of pharmaceutical education, a statement on the need for general education at the college level and the need for courses of study in the physical sciences, in mathematics, and in the biological sciences. The authors were specific, recommending the number of units or hours that should be spent in each of the courses that make up those sciences.

In 1975 the Study Commission on Pharmacy was appointed by the American Association of Colleges of Pharmacy. John S. Millis, president emeritus of Case Western Reserve, was invited to act as chairman. Members from various educational and professional backgrounds were selected to meet over a two-year period of time. The commission did not examine the content of the educational program in detail as the members believed it was not their responsibility to determine how many units or hours of a given course in the sciences should be provided to students. Nevertheless, after reading the commission's report, the reader can conclude that the commission membership suggested that the schools of pharmacy identify the competency characteristics that a pharmacist should possess and from that determine what courses of study should be provided to students.

In 1971 in an address before the American Association of Colleges of Pharmacy, its president, Dr. Arthur Schwarting, recommended that a careful and external examination of the practice of pharmacy occur. During his presidency he reported that little or no innovation in pharmaceutical education had occurred in those colleges offering the five-year program, but that innovation had occurred in those colleges that had offered the six-year Doctor of Pharmacy program as its sole degree.[4]

The Study Commission on Pharmacy published its report in 1975 entitled *Pharmacists for the Future*[5] and reported that:

- One of the inadequacies of the health care system was the unavailability of adequate information for those who consume, prescribe, dispense, and administer drugs, and that this deficiency has resulted in inappropriate drug use and a frequently unacceptable coincidence of drug-induced disease;

- It advanced the concept that pharmacy should be conceived basically as a knowledge system that renders a health service by concerning itself with understanding drugs and their effects upon people and animals;

- It concluded that a pharmacist must be defined as an individual who is engaged in one of the steps of a system called pharmacy;

- It recommended that major attention be given to the problems of drug information, to define who needs to know, what he or she needs to know, and how these needs can best be met with speed and economy;

- It recommended that every school of pharmacy promptly find ways and means to provide appropriate practice opportunities for its faculty members having clinical teaching responsibilities so that they may serve as effective role models for their students;

- It emphasized that the pharmacist must have knowledge about drug products and must understand the needs and behavior of people with which the pharmacy should interact;

- It recommended that quality of pharmaceutical education would be enhanced by the services of a national board of pharmacy examiners.

The commission's report provided guidelines by which pharmaceutical education could reexamine curricula and provide the necessary education to pharmacists so that these graduates could, in turn, provide an appropriate health service to the consumer. The commission's report will continue to provide direction for pharmaceutical educators in the 1980s.

During the 1980s health science educators are faced with a significant degree of uncertainty. This constitutes an imposing challenge and calls for commitment on the part of faculty to the planning process. Dr. Donald C. Brodie, adjunct professor of medicine and pharmacy at the University of Southern California School of Pharmacy, has written a cogent statement regarding the need for planning by pharmaceutical educators.[6] He stated that university administrations periodically require future plans from their constituents, and periodically ask for review and/or revision of existing plans. He further stated that many of these requests are for projections of manpower, facilities, and budget. He identified external and internal factors as follows:

EXTERNAL FACTORS

1. government regulation of the economy, higher education, health care education, health care delivery and cost containment
2. changes in societal expectations and demands for health services and public acceptance of expanded roles for pharmacists
3. changes within the health care delivery system; changes in medical practice; growth of preventive, self-care and home-care programs; changes in the management and use of health care institutions (acute care, long-term care, outpatient and inpatient care); growth of the regionalization of health services
4. scientific and technological breakthroughs; for example, gene splitting, immunosuppressive agents, anticancer therapies, population control, cardiovascular therapies, automation applied to pharmacy practice
5. the number of students attending universities. The Chronicle of Higher Education (2) projects that, nation-wide, there will be a rejection of 18-19 percent in the numbers in high school graduating classes from 1980 to 1995.

INTERNAL FACTORS

1. changes in university policies that ultimately influence the resources allocated for pharmacy education. (Note: These changes may reflect governmental intervention in the economy and higher education)
2. actions taken by the AACP and the ACPE, particularly as they relate to curriculum, academic standards, special programs, and management of pharmaceutical systems
3. the continued development of the clinical pharmacy concept; the balance between the basic and clinical sciences; the effectiveness of clerkship programs; the level of clinical performance of students and faculty; improvements in competency-based curricula, and innovation in providing clinical experiences for students, particularly in ambulant patient care settings

4. the integration of the social and behavioral modernization of departments of "pharmacy administration" with strong research programs in such areas as social pharmacy, health promotion, management of pharmaceutical systems, health behavior, and health care economics

5. changes in the patterns of health care delivery, to include the services of pharmacists, physicians and hospitals

6. changing patterns of use of pharmacy manpower; supply and demand for practitioners, clinical specialists, pharmacy managers, clinical scientists, technicians and those with graduate and post-graduate training in the pharmaceutical sciences; improvement in the productivity of pharmacy manpower

7. changes in the patterns of financing and containing the cost of health care including those necessitated by a national health insurance program

8. the degree to which pharmacists are able to cope with the changing world and integrate their services with those of physicians, nurses, dentists and other providers

9. the success pharmacists have in achieving reimbursement from third parties for their services, in addition to those for the products they dispense.

All the factors listed will have a significant impact upon pharmaceutical education during the next 10 to 20 years. Four are worthy of further comments: cost containment, patient behavior, government regulations, and manpower.

Cost Containment. The cost containment factor is of utmost concern. In 1980 the Health Care Financing Administration (HCFA) projected that the cost for medical care in 1990 will be $760 billion, up from the actual cost of $162 billion in 1977. Costs per capita in 1977 for medical care totaled $800 as compared to a projected cost of $3,100 in 1990. During this same period of time the cost of drugs will increase from $64 per capita to $158 on an annual basis. In 1977 it was estimated that as much as 60% of the medical care costs was allocated to those individuals who would die within a year. It is evident that our medical care system is concentrated on the care of the acutely ill patients.

The Surgeon General of the United States has stated that six of seven major causes of illness are those of life-style. Examples of illnesses related to such causes include cardiovascular disease, lung cancer, alcoholism, and obesity. The greatest percentage of deaths is caused by cardiovascular disease followed by oncology. All other causes of death represent 30% of the total.

The continued escalation rates for costs of medical care and the diseases of life-style suggest that a new emphasis should be placed within the medical care system. The emphasis, which is a national priority, should be placed on the promotion of health and the prevention of disease. This provides a difficult task for curricula planners, since changes in curricula emphasis require patience, persistence, and time.

Patient Behavior. Not only will it be difficult to modify the emphasis in health science education, it will be difficult to bring about a change in the behavior of those patients receiving the service of health care providers. The consumers' responses to change in behavior and life-style may be paradoxical. The consumer is complaining about the costs of medical care delivery and the access to providers. At the same time the consumer has not fully demonstrated a desire to alter behavior. This is exemplified by the continued consumption of alcohol and use of tobacco despite the well-known statistical evidence linking cirrhosis of the liver to alcohol use and lung cancer to smoking. There is ample evidence that the consumer does not comply with physicians' orders regarding the treatment of disease; individuals are guilty of multi-drug abuse. Yet it is recognized that some of the consumers are vitally interested in exercise and diet restriction.

Government Regulations. An external factor affecting the pharmacist and pharmacy is government control and restriction. Pharmacy is regulated and controlled, more so than medicine, dentistry, or nursing. The pharmacist is perhaps the most regulated of all health care professionals. Pharmaceutical manufacturing is among the most controlled and regulated of all industries. This regulation has resulted because consumers believe that a substantial amount of control is necessary in order to protect the public interest relating to drug efficiency and safety. Pharmacists and pharmacy will be further regulated by continued control over the cost of drugs. The Social Security Administration (SSA) has imposed maximum allowable costs on multi-source drugs (drugs available through many companies/manufacturers). This agency has provided estimated acquisition costs on single-source drugs (drugs available through one company/manufacturer).

Manpower. The health science educators and practitioners face a dilemma regarding the number of individuals being educated. It is a general belief that too many physicians, dentists, and pharmacists are being educated and that surpluses will exist in the latter part of the 1980s. At the same time there will be a reduction of 19% in the number of high school graduating classes in 1990; this suggests increased competition among the professions for a reduced application pool. Several hundred different kinds of professional training and education programs exist. At the present time a satisfactory three-dimensional matrix consisting of health care decision makers, supportive staff, and patients does not exist. This contributes to an ineffective and inefficient system for delivery of care. It also contributes to patient confusion and frustration and to increased costs.

In summary, it is suggested that:

1. Pharmaceutical educators modify the emphasis on the pharmacists' role in acute care to include their activities in health promotion and disease prevention.
2. There will be an increased emphasis on care management and cost effectiveness.
3. The curricula will be expanded to include behavioral sciences in order to increase the practitioners' ability to understand and communicate effectively with other health care providers and patients.

It should also be noted that at the same time that the educators are providing an expanded curriculum, school administrators will be faced with increased university budgetary constraints. The 1980s will be a decade of uncertainties, opportunities, and challenges.

NOTES

1. E. C. Elliott, *Findings and Recommendations of the Pharmaceutical Survey* (Washington, DC: American Council on Education, 1948).

2. E. C. Elliott, *The General Report of the Pharmaceutical Survey* (Washington, DC: American Council on Education, 1950).

3.   L. E. Blauch and G. L. Webster, *The Pharmaceutical Curriculum* (Washington, DC: American Council on Education, 1952).

4.   A. E. Schwarting, "Foresight," *American Journal of Pharmaceutical Education*, 35 (1971), p. 495.

5.   J. S. Millis, *Pharmacists for the Future* (Ann Arbor, MI: Health Administration Press, 1975).

6.   D. C. Brodie, "A Time To Plan," *American Journal of Pharmaceutical Education*, 44 (1980), p. 203.

BIBLIOGRAPHY

Blauch, L. E., and Webster, G. L. *The Pharmaceutical Curriculum*. Washington, DC: American Council on Education, 1952.

Brodie, D. C. "A Time To Plan." *American Journal of Pharmaceutical Education* (April 1980), pp. 203-204.

Elliott, E. C. *Findings and Recommendations of the Pharmaceutical Survey*. Washington, DC: American Council on Education, 1948.

Elliott, E. C. *The General Report of the Pharmaceutical Survey*. Washington, DC: American Council on Education, 1950.

Millis, J. S. *Pharmacists for the Future*. Ann Arbor, MI: Health Administration Press, 1975.

Schwarting, A. E. "Foresight." *American Journal of Pharmaceutical Education*, 35 (August 1971), pp. 495-96.

SOME THOUGHTS ON THE PAST, PRESENT, AND FUTURE OF ARCHITECTURAL EDUCATION[1]

by
David Stea

Professor of Architecture and Urban Planning
University of California at Los Angeles

This paper addresses, in reasonable order, some questions of architectural practice, education, and research, from the perspective of one who has spent most of the past 15 years as an educator and sometime practitioner in the fields of architecture, urban design, and planning.

It is better to avoid such platitudes as "architecture is at a crossroads," because they are always at least partly untrue. In fact, many of those who currently practice architecture in a "traditional" way will probably be able to continue doing so for some time to come: there are people of means who want and can afford residences that are tastefully designed as well as spacious and expensive; large corporations will continue to want high-rise office blocks; cities will commission civic structures and monuments, etc. Architecture may well have been the hardest hit of all professions in America's 1974-1975 recession (and there are, no doubt, lessons in that), but the largest offices, at least, seem to have managed to "bounce back" without having to undergo any major changes in their modes of operation.

Thus, if forced to look "toward the year 2000," an astute observer might predict that existing emphases in architectural practices will continue for those already in practice, but that the market for these emphases will not expand. Some new graduates, therefore, will be able to fill spaces vacated by death or retirement in very traditional practices, but the majority may have to break new ground. Will this mean redefining architecture? It is probably safest to say that *whatever* definition seems currently popular may have to be expanded. For, if the winds of change have given way to the doldrums, there are still a few breezes around.

First, the broad trends: young architects, on whom this discussion is primarily focused, seem dissatisfied with a choice between the "slave market" drafting room of the large office, and the insecurity of individual practice (in spite of the fact that many are glad to get *any* job right now). Most are neither effective specialists nor well-trained generalists at the B.Arch. level, and do require some period of internship, which usually constitutes an economic hardship. It appears, even further, that the positions (or thrones) of the great form-givers are not being filled as they die; there are fewer generally-acknowledged great "styles" to follow. But there is a "movement."

This recent movement, or trend, or direction in architecture gained considerable popularity in certain schools (and aroused considerable controversy in others) at the end of the 1970s. Labeled "Post-Modernism" (Jencks, 1977), it combined a form of historical eclecticism with an interpretation of architecture in the vocabulary of linguistics ("semiotics" is a frequently-heard word), combining well-known phrases with neologisms created by Frampton (1975) and others. It is based on a reaction to the so-called "modern movement" that flowered in the 1950s and 1960s, whose death is traced by Jencks to the demolition by dynamite of the notorious Pruitt-Igoe housing project in 1972. According to its critics, Post-Modernism has replaced the platitudes of its predecessor with an obscure new language of visual aesthetics, and the banality of modern architecture with the elitism of self-consciously executed forms. Some find these forms excitingly new, while others see a reduction of architecture to a formalist exercise:

> The strongest criticism against the new design is that its aesthetic investigations "glorify subjectiveness and purely personal expression," as Robert P. Burns put it, "at the expense of the more serious architectural needs of society."[2]

In the extreme, the new movement involves an active rejection of the interdisciplinary activity that characterized architectural education in the 1960s, an abandonment of behavioral research (e.g., Bennett, 1977) and social relevance. The irony of this is that many exponents of Post-Modernism trace its roots to the architect Louis Kahn, whose ideas were rather different:

> In Kahnian theory, Form comes from a careful consideration of the human activities that will go on in the building . . . he talked about a building in terms of what its effect on the human being is.[3]

The prognosis for Post-Modernism is unclear. It may indeed be the wave of the future—or merely a "flash in the pan," a transition to another position commanding greater consensus within the next five years.

ARCHITECTURAL PRACTICE, POST-1984

The first trend we may see in the post-Post Modernist period is an *in*crease in specialization and a *de*crease in narrow specialization. This apparent paradox is resolved if we consider the function of architecture not just as synthesis alone but as a *blend* of synthesis and analysis. The "old" specialist was one who had often been trained not to see the forest for the trees; the generalist, of course, has the opposite problem. The "new" specialist, hopefully, will be a person who can see both, who has a great deal of "expertise" in one or several areas but the trained capacity to see how these areas relate to a synthetic or synthesized whole, an intuitive grasp of "fit" from a certain well-considered perspective. Avoiding catch phrases, the broad specialist appreciates the point at which "less is more" begins to imply that least is most, or even that nothing is everything.

Young "broad specialists," of course, face the same problems when entering the work market as other beginners. The solution may be the formation of loosely-knit "architectural cooperatives" that dilute the liabilities of private practice (as well as the possibilities of considerable wealth; who, however, enters architecture purely for the money?), enabling the organization to take on slightly more "risky" (but also more interesting and more innovative) projects. In such projects, a subgroup of the cooperative, consisting of broad specialists who can work constructively together and whose specialties are appropriate to the task, combine forces to achieve a richer and better outcome (words such as "solution," "form," and "product" seem inappropriate).

The formation of such cooperatives was suggested to young architects in Southern California in 1977. Rather than being met with hostility, as a potential threat to their individual artistic creativity, this suggestion was greeted with almost universal enthusiasm.

Possible areas of broad specialization include the following:

1. New and expanded approaches to building rehabilitation.
2. Low-cost industrialized building.
3. Low-cost housing alternatives to the mobile home; an emphasis upon the design of "housing" rather than upon residences.
4. Energy-conserving design. The sensitive architect will be interested in pursuing this not because of a so-called "energy crisis" but because decreasing dependence upon corporate suppliers of energy gives clients and users more control over their lives, and because designing with energy considerations is an aesthetic as well as an economic challenge. The question of energy is, to at least some extent, therefore, a question of values.
5. More efficient use of public space in public buildings (including such educational facilities as universities), which inevitably involves *genuinely* flexible design.
6. Architectural responses to changes in concepts of public services, such as emphases upon paramedical practice, preventative rather than strictly curative health services, community schools operating on a 16-hour day, halfway houses in place of expanded prisons, alcohol and drug rehabilitation centers, etc.
7. "New" vernacularly-based housing for the third world. Educationally, this may mean that some architecture students coming from third world countries will not accept training in Western forms as adequate for the problems they encounter at home.
8. Creative uses for recycled materials in design.
9. Community architectural practice.
10. Projects funded by the "public sector."
11. Regional emphases in the use of construction materials and techniques, giving official sanction to "funky Oregonian" and "New Mexican new adobe."
12. Architecture for specific user groups (child/adult/"senior citizen"/ male/female, etc.).

ARCHITECTURAL EDUCATION

In its role of training professionals, architectural education tracks, to some extent, the requirements of professional practice. To the extent that practice incorporates the projected specializations mentioned above, educational areas associated with these specializations will require strengthening. Professional education will need to display greater flexibility, encouraging a broad outlook on the part of design instructors. Since many schools already find themselves somewhat overextended, this may also mean that schools themselves will have to become "broadly specialized," in terms both of what is taught and of the particular groups of students served.

To meet these requirements even within a broadly specialized framework, schools will have to analyze two trends of the past few years, regarded by some as disturbing and even counterproductive: 1) a conservative reaction to the partial failure of attempts at interdisciplinary collaboration during the 1960s (throwing the baby out and keeping the bathwater), and 2) an increasing schism between "design" and "non-design" faculty. Both trends have been markedly accelerated in the years following the ascendancy of Post-Modernism.

Some views on the general nature of the educational process in architecture are: that the often accepted division between research and design is artificial; that research is interlaced with design insofar as each design is regarded as an *hypothesis* testing the architects' program within the context of the building's actual use—analysis and synthesis are thus seen as proceeding together in an iterative fashion; that problem-formulation is at least as important as solution-generation, avoiding the production of solutions to which there correspond no problems; that the architectural studio is properly an *integrator* of everything the student is learning and that both the content *and* the faculty of both studios *and* lecture and seminar classes must therefore be better integrated; and that courses in or related to professional practice ought to put more emphasis than at present upon societal concerns, and especially upon dealing with the public sector and with architects working in the public sector.

As any but the very largest schools cannot hope to deal effectively with *all* possible content areas, so any one school cannot serve all students. Students wanting an architectural education (other than architectural history) appear to fall into seven categories:

1. Students with no university education and no experience (B.Arch. candidates).
2. Students with a university degree but no professional architecture degree.
3. Students already possessing a B.Arch. degree.
4. Students with architectural experience but no architecture degree, who can attend school full-time.
5. Potential students in category "4" who cannot attend school full-time (candidates for an "extended university" program).
6. Students with a nonprofessional background and serious nonprofessional objectives, such as research (e.g., UCLA's M.A. in Architecture Program).
7. Students with a professional architecture background, and research objectives in graduate study (candidates for a Ph.D. or D.Arch. Program).

In American architectural education, on the whole, it seems that the first four categories are somewhat better than served than the last three. As it is unlikely that any one school can serve *all* of these effectively, the task of those who shape the nature of architectural education on a national level is to generate national educational plans and policies that will help to serve those groups in proportion to their relative demands.

ARCHITECTURAL RESEARCH IN ARCHITECTURAL EDUCATION

The role of research in architectural education and practice requires separate comment. It is a sticky subject, partly because "research" is taken as meaning anything from reading magazine articles to field work in exotic locales. Part of the problem of incorporating research into architecture is that, quite sadly, because architecture is seen as "creative," research is seen as the opposite. A physicist called "uncreative" would react with justifiable dismay; why then is architectural research so demeaned?

In point of fact, few students will become researchers; in the professional roles to which most aspire, they will, however, become "consumers" of the *results* of research. As part of their education, they must learn to become sophisticated con-sumers; at very least, to sift applicable from inapplicable information. Since much of the research architects need and eventually use is written by academics to be read by academics, this is no mean task. They will need to understand work done by social and behavioral scientists, political scientists, economists, and others (e.g., experts in land economics), in addition to the more traditional areas of research in materials and structures, the engineering aspects of building. Beyond even that, some students will need to familiarize themselves with design research, directed at an understanding of the architectural process and the nature of decision making in environmental design; and with the more global forces and value systems shaping architecture today. This is especially true of students planning to work in foreign areas or in cultural contexts outside the USA.

In an ideal university, some of these requirements could be met by taking courses in other departments. Unfortunately, however, these courses are almost always structured by and for their mother disciplines (research methods courses are usually taught primarily to graduates, as well); the typical architecture student rarely finds more than 10% of such a course relevant to his or her concerns. A bright student seriously interested in person-environment relations would be ill-advised to try distilling what he or she needs from an Introductory Psychology course, much less a seminar on Perception!

All of the above implies greater emphasis upon the nature and nurture of research— of a certain kind—in architectural education. This further implies a greater commit-ment to research itself on the part of faculty. Instead, quite a number of schools have *reduced* their commitment to research. Fortunately, however, such architecture departments as those at the University of Wisconsin—Milwaukee and The Massachusetts Institute of Technology are expanding their research components to meet anticipated needs of the profession.

The above suggests that one research emphasis ought to be upon the development of those techniques most applicable to the problems and time scales of architectural practice: those using "mid-range" research techniques (necessarily somewhat less precise than traditional scientific approaches) and "fast research," accomplished over periods considerably shorter than those usually available to the traditional sciences. In the late 1960s, for example, as a partial bending to the winds of social change, the American Institute of Architects initiated a program entitled "Regional Urban Design Assistance Teams" (R/UDAT). The objective was to blend on-site research with envi-ronmental design and planning to provide alternatives for communities lacking financial means to accomplish things on "normal" time scales. R/UDAT members assembled for the first time on a Thursday afternoon and published their final reports the follow-ing Monday morning (!). Team members (who served without pay) and local archi-tecture students combined forces on a 4-day "charette," often working 20-22 hours per day. (Some teams put in as much as one person-*year* of effort in a single 80-hour period.) Both students and professionals (usually interdisciplinary teams of architects, planners, urban designers, lawyers, economists, land-use and transportation experts, etc.) generally agreed that the educational value of the experience was unsurpassable.

Any research, however, requires the commitment of individuals and, usually, of money to individuals. The formation, in schools of architecture, of committees on *research* and *extramural funding* has been advocated a number of times. The era when one could write a "blind" (not specifically solicited) grant proposal in response to an RFP, with any reasonable expectation of funding, is over. When a school must do its own research, and when such research must be externally funded, it is important that economy of means be exercised; the (often enormous) expenditures of time required to assemble a formal proposal can turn out to be only so much wasted effort. The energy expended, then, must relate to known risks and likely returns. As a "rule-of-thumb," the following formula has been found to serve quite well:

$$\text{minimum amount to be requested (from funding agency)} = \frac{\text{estimated value of time expended in proposal preparation}}{\text{a priori probability of funding}}$$

One function of a committee on extramural funding would be to determine the values of the variables in the above equation. Its importance extends beyond issues of mere research to questions of morale: expending enormous amounts of time and energy to achieve an "approved but not funded" decision on one's proposal is demoralizing and debilitating.

ARCHITECTURAL PRACTICE IN ARCHITECTURAL EDUCATION

Few architectural students—especially those pursuing their professional degrees in graduate school—can afford to attend school without working for money at the same time. For many, this involves employment in an architectural office. Some obtain additional educational experience thereby, but others find themselves assigned only to repetitive jobs on drafting boards; nearly all are forced to commute, often considerable distances, from school to work, and then back home again. Faculty who wish to practice are faced with similar commuting problems, and all the expenses associated with opening and maintaining an office.

Several schools, such as SUNY Buffalo, UCLA, and the University of Oregon, have responded to this dual problem by setting up quasi-independent professional practice "arms." The specific intent of these offices is to provide practice opportunities for professionally-oriented faculty and internship for students. The "work/study" offices generally seek architectural design contracts on the same competitive basis as offices unaffiliated with academic institutions, but the educational role of the former is more explicit. Some subsidy from associated academic institutions is occasionally involved.

SUMMARY

Architectural education, like almost every other branch of education, is in the process of at least some change. Whether the current direction of this change is progressive or reactionary remains to be determined. During the late 1970s the "Post-Modernist" movement emerged as a reaction to the banal aesthetics of "modern" architecture, and to the interdisciplinary trends of architectural research and education that characterized the preceding decade.

What will happen in architectural education depends in some part upon the success of this movement, and upon its influence on the schools. It also depends upon the response of the architectural profession to the needs of the nation (and the rest of the world) for real innovations, rather than mere novelty, in production of the built environment. This paper has examined the relationship of architectural education to professional practice and to environmental design research. The importance of the *interaction* among these three, especially the influence of the interesting and significant issues now facing the profession upon the directions of both architectural education and architectural research, has been stressed. The success of architectural education in producing professionals capable of solving built environment problems in the 1980s and 1990s will depend, in large part, upon how it deals with this necessary interaction.

NOTES

1.   Few books have been written about architectural education, *per se*, and the exceptions, which include Rittel's (1966) work and publications of the A.I.A. Educational Research Project, on this side of the Atlantic, and RIBA (1970) publications in Britain, are by now rather dated.

2.   C. Ray Smith, *Supermannerism: New Attitudes in Post-Modern Architecture* (New York: E. P. Dutton, 1977), p. 325.

3.   Ibid., pp. 83-84.

4.   David Stea, "Cultural Change and the Values of Environmental Designers," in *American Values and Habitat: A Research Agenda*, ed. by Mayra Buvinic (Washington, DC: American Association for the Advancement of Science, 1977).

BIBLIOGRAPHY

Bennett, Corwin. *Spaces for People: Human Factors in Design*. Englewood Cliffs, NJ: Prentice-Hall, 1977.

Blake, Peter. *Form Follows Fiasco: Why Modern Architecture Hasn't Worked*. Boston: Little, Brown and Company, 1977.

Brolin, Brent C. *The Failure of Modern Architecture*. New York: Van Nostrand Reinhold, 1976.

Education for Architectural Technology. Proceedings of conference sponsored by Washington University, St. Louis, and the American Institute of Architects Educational Research Project, April 1966.

Frampton, Kenneth. "Frontality and Rotation," in *Five Architects*. New York: Oxford University Press, 1975.

Jencks, Charles. *The Language of Post-Modern Architecture*. London: Academy Editions, 1977.

Rittel, Horst. *Some Principles for the Design of an Educational System for Design*. Berkeley: University of California Institute of Urban and Regional Development, 1966.

Smith, C. Ray. *Supermannerism: New Attitudes in Post-Modern Architecture*. New York: E. P. Dutton, 1977.

Stea, David. "Cultural Change and the Values of Environmental Designers," in *American Values and Habitat: A Research Agenda*. Ed. by Mayra Buvinic. Washington, DC: American Association for the Advancement of Science, 1977.

The following publications, available at many libraries, contain articles of interest:

Journal of Architectural Research (formerly entitled *Journal of Architectural Education*). A publication of the Association of Collegiate Schools of Architecture.

Proceedings of the Annual Meetings of the Environmental Design Research Association.

Research and Design. A quarterly of the American Institute of Architects Research Corporation.

Student Publications of the School of Design. North Carolina State University, Raleigh, North Carolina.

ENGINEERING AND ENGINEERING EDUCATION
IN THE 1980s

by
Melvin Gerstein

Associate Dean, School of Engineering
Professor of Mechanical Engineering
University of Southern California

INTRODUCTION

The goals and problems of technology and of education in engineering will respond more than ever in the next decade to the demands of society. These problems, arising from an increasing world population, will impose conflicting demands on technology, and the solution will often create new problems or aggravate the problems that were to be solved. Technical advances to house, to clothe, to feed, and to otherwise support the needs of larger numbers of people will further strain the limited energy resources of the earth, and advances in technical sophistication to accomplish some of these goals may well require less human labor while the pool of people in the work force continues to grow. The developed nations providing the means for improving the quality of life in underdeveloped areas may find that these advances come at the expense of their own standard of living.

Engineering education will continue to have an important but ambivalent role in technological advance, leading applied technology in some areas and following it in others, and, at times leading the way to technological change in areas not accepted by society. The peaceful uses of nuclear energy are probably the most apparent example of a technology that was rapidly incorporated into science and engineering curricula in the late 1940s and early 1950s, only to be left waiting 30 years later while society still debated whether fission represented a boon or a curse.

The demands on the education of engineers will require a reexamination of the objectives and curriculum of engineering education. On the one hand, the complexities of modern technology demand increased technical knowledge, while on the other hand, society demands that the engineer be educated in terms of the societal impacts of technology and in the liberal arts. Merely lengthening the term for the baccalaureate degree in engineering has not accomplished these goals and is not likely to be proposed in the 1980s.

SOME ENGINEERING PROBLEM AREAS

Some of the technological areas that will influence engineering education will be reviewed first, followed by a discussion of some of the goals and problems of engineering education directed toward solutions of the technological problems facing society in the 1980s.

Energy

As one looks into the future of technology, energy certainly stands out as the single most important resource that must be developed. Presumably, if enough energy were available, one would use even the most inaccessible resources and could process the wastes produced by an industrial society.

The long-term solutions to our energy problems seem more evident than do the short-term solutions. It seems clear that nuclear fusion, using the vast oceans as the source of hydrogen fuel, and solar energy, the only important resource that comes to the earth from outside its boundaries, will provide the energy of the future. If one attempts to look ahead only 10 or 20 years, however, the area of progress in technology is much less certain, if indeed there is any progress at all.

It appears that the next decade will represent a period in which conservation of nonrenewable energy resources will be emphasized, while the growth in the other available energy resources will continue slowly.

In the United States, the greater use of coal will be emphasized with three major problem areas receiving most of the attention: 1) extraction of coal from the ground, 2) transportation of coal, and 3) control of pollution related to coal usage.

Although technological advances in coal mining may still be expected, the major problems are social, ecological, and economic. These pressures will accelerate attempts to recover the energy from coal by so-called in-situ processes—the production of gaseous and liquid fuels within the coal bed without removing the coal from the earth. Various techniques for partial burning of coal underground and for reaction with steam are under investigation. The production of gaseous and liquid fuels from coal, whether in-situ or in processing plants at the source, also simplifies the problem of transportation of the energy resources and of reducing pollutants during combustion. The economic pressures and the nature of the technology being developed both tend to reduce the amount of human labor involved in the extraction, the transportation, and the use of this energy resource compared with the traditional coal industry of 50 years ago and even today—an example of a reduced dependence on human labor in a world producing an ever-increasing labor supply.

The discussion of the problems associated with the extraction of oil from shale, another important energy resource in the United States, would almost duplicate that for coal with the major emphasis being given to in-situ recovery processes and a reduced dependence on labor.

Solar energy has become the favorite of the public, but its emergence as a major supplier of energy for the needs of society is still probably 25 years away. The economic problems associated with the use of solar energy have been discussed, but the ecological problems associated with its use and the production of facilities for its use have received much less attention. The sun provides a large quantity of energy, but the intensity of the energy is low. The immediate impact of this fact is that major solar facilities are large and have an effect on the local environment. The construction of solar power plants requires large quantities of material whose production uses energy and may introduce pollution problems.

While there was an initial surge in engineering education to provide "energy degrees," this trend has subsided, and in the near future we can expect an emphasis on the traditional areas of engineering relevant to the technological problems associated with changes in energy production along with selected specialized courses highlighting some of the new areas of energy technology.

Food

The need for increased food production, like the need for more energy, is also driven by the population growth. The technological changes necessary to supply more food in less space are also energy-intensive. The continued growth of automated farms and a growing dependence on the use of synthetic chemicals for farming will dominate the technological scene. Again, the reduction in the use of labor for both economic and productivity reasons comes in the face of a growing pool of labor, particularly in the less developed areas of the world. It is ironic that the very advances in food production necessary to feed these regions may, for economic reasons, aggravate the problems of hunger.

The increased use of synthetic chemicals to increase the productivity of farms (to increase the yield per acre as agricultural land gives way to urban and industrial expansion) brings with it a growing energy dependence and increased concerns with the effect of chemical agents on the food itself, on the earth in which it is grown, and on the water resources. Increased research on the processing and packaging of food to protect its quality and extend its shelf life will grow in importance. Even today, the packaging of food represents a major part of the cost of food and consumes large quantities of disposable materials. New areas of technology and of engineering education are being developed to cope with this problem; degrees in packaging are now being offered, and an institute devoted to packaging education has been formed.[1]

Materials

This isolated sphere that we call Earth contains all of the material resources available to support the population of the earth. We depend for our mineral resources on concentrated pockets of various materials, pockets that are economically accessible and from which we can efficiently remove and process raw materials for our needs. As we use these raw materials, two factors tend to degrade them as future sources of the same elements. First, the final product combines materials in a manner that often makes it more difficult to recapture the mineral from a product than from the crude ore from which it was derived. A simple, but not trivial, example was the steel tab on aluminum beverage cans. The separation of the aluminum from this product was uneconomical and led eventually to the design of all aluminum, economically recyclable cans. Second, we spread the materials almost randomly across the earth. Instead of concentrated deposits, the materials are thinly distributed, making reclamation difficult and costly. Technology has already begun to respond to this problem. Modern design techniques consider the need to reclaim and reuse materials. Conservation and recovery will continue to be recognized as a major aspect of engineering design in the years to come.

Although many plastics depend upon petroleum as a raw material, technology is available to produce organic materials from waste and from the basic elements. As we consider renewable energy sources, we may consider plastics in the category of renewable materials.

Transportation

The problems of energy resources and increased population will accelerate the trend toward mass transportation in the 1980s. Little technological change is expected in this period, however. The major changes will occur with respect to the automobile, continuing the trend toward smaller size and more efficiency. An electric or a hybrid engine will assume more importance toward the end of this decade. Educational emphasis will be focused on new design techniques using lighter materials, greater automation, and sophisticated control systems.

Computers and Communication

Solid-state devices, which have revolutionized modern electronics—particularly in the area of the computer and in communications—will continue to lead major advances in these fields in the 1980s. The most needed advances are in the area of input and output devices. Automated readers and voice inputs will decrease the drudgery of manual input operations and will further reduce the personnel required for computer operations and computer controlled systems. The continued effect of the computer on every aspect of daily life (including the home) will have a large effect on the education of engineers and non-engineers, with a growing trend toward teaching technology to non-engineers.

Global communications through wider use of satellites and the continued expansion of video-telephones into offices and homes, three-dimensional television, and interactive television will not only require advanced education for both engineers and non-engineers, but these advances will also be used to extend and improve engineering education. Interactive television, now in use at the University of Southern California (USC) and at several other universities, not only expands the concept of the extended university but also permits experiments with new teaching methods. The decade of the 1980s should see innovations in engineering education using modern techniques of communication to improve the quality of learning and to reduce the cost of education.

Weapons

While it would be desirable to exclude weapon development as a focus of technology in the 1980s (and its impact on education), in reality the same developments expected in other fields will influence the technology of weaponry. The emphasis on automation will continue with reduced demands on personnel in warfare, and improvements in the accuracy and effectiveness of weapons can be expected. Weapon production and weapon-testing, detection, deterrents, and defense will also require engineering activity.

Environment

All areas of technology—indeed all areas of human activity—affect the environment. Distracted by energy problems, the problems of the environment will receive major emphasis in the 1980s. Programs in environmentally related education will grow, many of which had stagnated or decreased in the late 1970s. The preservation of the earth, its waters, and its atmosphere will have an impact on all phases of technology and of education.

PROBLEMS IN ENGINEERING EDUCATION

Technology, engineering education, and society represent an interactive system with each segment influencing the other. The peaceful applications of nuclear energy, principally fission power plants, are an example wherein college programs preceded the industrial development and the needs of society. In other cases, an industry can develop and grow before the college curriculum changes in a dramatic way. The area of computers and solid-state electronics is one in which an industry advanced faster, at first, than the engineering curriculum. This is not to say that courses did not exist dealing with these topics, but the bulk of the curriculum changed slowly at first and then dramatically.

The diversity of technical problems outlined in the previous section, representing only a fraction of the technical challenges that face the engineer today, poses an almost overwhelming burden on engineering education. Coping with these problems within the constraints of time and cost will be a major challenge in the 1980s. Because of the relatively slow evolution of educational processes and curriculum, this will not be accomplished easily.

There is a basic structure to an engineering curriculum—much of it dictated by accreditation requirements—that has been relatively fixed in the past and is not likely to change dramatically in the decade of the 1980s. A typical curriculum consists of these elements: 1) Mathematics, 2) Physical Sciences, 3) Social Science and Humanities, and 4) Engineering. While the number of courses associated with each category varies somewhat with the particular engineering discipline, this variation is not large. The primary accreditation body for engineering is the Accreditation Board for Engineering and Technology, Inc. (ABET), formerly Engineers' Council for Professional Development, Inc. The curricular criteria established for accreditation at the BS level (basic level) are:

1) The equivalent of approximately two and one-half years of study in the area of mathematics, science, and engineering. The course work should include at least one-half year of mathematics beyond trigonometry, plus one-half year of engineering sciences, and one-half year of engineering design.

2) The equivalent of one-half year as the minimum content in the area of the humanities and social sciences.[2]

In a four-year program, these requirements would leave a maximum of one year for highly specialized courses in a technical area. In fact, there is less than this in most engineering curricula. Such courses as English composition, speech, foreign language, accounting, finance, and others are not recommended as a part of the humanities and social sciences requirement. In a typical engineering curriculum approximately one semester remains for highly specialized courses or for courses in an emerging field of technology.

There are three principal ways to maintain a relevant curriculum while retaining the traditional elements of the fundamentals of the field. These are: 1) extend the degree period, 2) require an advanced degree, or 3) replace portions of the existing program. None of these can be accomplished without problems.

The five-year baccalaureate degree in engineering was tried by many schools and still exists in a few. It was non popular for several reasons, but primarily because it discouraged many students from choosing engineering and, from the point of view of many employers, delayed the time when students would become available for employment. The same arguments would apply to the requirement for an advanced degree. The third approach brings with it the obvious question of what shall be dropped if new courses are added.

At the level of the first degree, all of the above approaches are doomed to fail because of the diversity of opportunities open to engineering students in each discipline. The objectives of an engineering education vary with the point of view of the individual or group defining these objectives. These range from ". . . development of a capability to delineate and solve in a practical way the problems of society that are susceptible to engineering treatment . . ."[3] to ". . . sound general education for individuals who may later enter upon different career paths."[4]

The concept of engineering as a form of general education at the baccalaureate level comes closest to the objectives that will be emphasized in the decade of the 1980s. Engineering education dances to a tune played by many pipers, from the most applied interests of industry to the broadest demands of society. At best we can hope to educate the young engineer to learn; to provide enough of a fundamental background in mathematics, science, liberal arts, and engineering from which a more specialized knowledge can be developed based on the career objectives of the engineer, objectives likely to be defined after the student leaves school. The emphasis on developing skills to further the acquisition of knowledge reduces the problem of justifying courses in terms of specific career objectives and, coupled with the concept of lifelong learning, could eliminate the problem of obsolescence. Industry must be prepared to provide the specialized knowledge needed by the students they employ. These students have been "programmed" to learn and can only apply a thorough knowledge of the fundamentals of science and engineering to a wide range of problems.

Humanities and Social Science

The demand of society to "humanize" the engineer or to make the engineer more aware of social impacts will probably not change engineering education in the 1980s. In part, neither the society asking for social involvement knows clearly what it wants nor, in addition, do educators know how to accomplish these ill-defined goals. Similarly, the request of both industry and society to provide engineers with better communication skills may not be easily realized and at best would have to be done at the expense of technical courses or a lengthening of the curriculum. Let us examine both of these in more detail.

In a limited sense, one may define engineering as the application of natural science to the solution of practical problems. Some of these problems were discussed earlier. None of them has a single solution, and it may not even be possible to define an optimum or best solution from an engineering point of view, let alone from the viewpoint of society. Presumably, the engineer's education should include the necessary skills to solve the technical problem and an awareness of other technical and nontechnical implications such as the environment, economics, human factors including technologically induced unemployment, aesthetics, and many others. One semester of humanities and social science or, in fact, a degree in the liberal arts would not provide enough education for this purpose; nor do we know the solutions to these social problems with sufficient confidence to teach the engineering student how to influence his technical work with these concerns.

It is necessary to examine carefully the goals of the humanities and social science requirements in an engineering curriculum and, after suitable definition, select or create courses to meet the needs defined.

If we accept that the primary role of engineering education at the baccalaureate level is to teach a student how to learn, then any humanities and social science courses that can provide the background and stimulation for future learning serves the same purpose, provided that it includes these basic ingredients: fundamental knowledge and stimulation. Many of the liberal arts courses taken by engineering students do not provide both of these elements, and some fail to provide either. Some of these liberal arts courses are as narrow and as specialized as engineering and science courses are accused of being narrow and specialized. I believe that the 1980s will be a period in which the liberal arts will take more seriously their responsibility to serve society and the learning needs of the nonspecialist. The pressure of engineering students demanding the liberal education promised them may well produce the momentum for these changes.

It is not wrong, however, to provide engineers with a working knowledge of the behavior of individuals and the behavior of groups of individuals. A course in human behavior designed especially for professionals of all sorts who must deal with other individuals, and a course dealing with the behavior of groups—a social science course dealing with society—would serve useful purposes. Such courses would be service courses for engineers and other professionals. At least these courses would provide a broad exposure to the problems and behavior of individuals and of groups; it is also hoped that these courses might also provide a meaningful experience for the engineering student interacting with students with a variety of academic experiences.

It has often been expressed that one goal of the liberal arts portion of the engineering curriculum is to bring the engineering student into contact with students in other academic areas. While it is true that many of the humanities and social science courses taken by engineering students include students from a variety of disciplines, little contact actually occurs. Groups of engineering students leave the engineering quadrangle, sit together in a lecture, and leave together. Only planned group effort would expand the interaction of students. Certainly the courses designed to teach individual and group behavior could include direct experience in the classroom through group projects, guided discussion, and the "encounter" concepts that the social scientists reserve for their own students. This writer would expect to see more humanities and social science courses with a "laboratory" component in the 1980s.

Engineers should be taught to write and to speak effectively. No one would argue with this statement, if applied to all students, but it seems frequently directed only toward engineering students. In spite of the general agreement for a need to improve the communication skills of engineering students, it is not likely that much will be done in the 1980s to change the nature of the curriculum dealing with communication. The accreditation guidelines do not accept composition and speech as suitable courses to satisfy the humanities and social sciences requirements. To augment the present curriculum would mean to reduce the engineering content or extend the unit requirements, neither of which is likely to be done.

It would be desirable to improve the quality of the communication courses without increasing their number, and some progress is being made. It is necessary first to define the objectives of such courses. Industrial representatives who visit the campus to hire engineering students generally refer to the ability of engineers to communicate with each other, while teachers of composition often refer to communication in a more literary sense. It is unlikely, at least in the next decade, that we are going to change the literary talents of engineering students in a major way. It is both necessary and possible that we will improve the ability of engineers to communicate with each other and with others. The stress will be on simple declarative writing with an emphasis on precision and clarity and not on literary style, complexity, and the qualities that, added to precision and clarity, make for great writing. At USC, composition courses created especially for engineering students are making headway in this direction, and with a better perception of what composition courses are intended to accomplish, student interest has grown. Speech courses remain a student option, usually replacing a free elective. However, most engineering students do not opt for a speech course, although oral communication is a necessity in all technical work.

THE FUTURE

What can be done with engineering education to improve its effectiveness and prepare for the challenges that continue to grow?

Let us assume that we will continue to have a four-year baccalaureate degree in the 1980s and that a majority of the graduates will seek engineering employment following graduation. The prognosis is that jobs will exist. At the same time the growth of automated processes will reduce the need for routine engineering services while increasing the need for sophisticated engineering services. Many will return to the university for advanced education, while others, unable to make the sacrifices associated with a return to school, will suffer problems in their jobs or will leave the field of engineering. Yet the process of getting some practical experience following the baccalaureate may still be a sound concept.

It is the area of continued education that will be highlighted in the 1980s, particularly using the modern communication and teaching systems becoming available. We may see, in fact, the growth of a four-day work week in the 1980s. What better use of that "extra day" than to provide or, in fact, require increased education in its broadest sense—technical, cultural, economic, social, etc.

At a time when the number of people required for many tasks is decreasing, and the available work force and the cost of education is increasing, what more appropriate action can be taken than to provide advanced education for employees working a reduced work week? Technical obsolescence could be reduced and the nature of the education could be programmed to meet the requirements of employment as these change with technical advance and with the age and experience of the employee.

While we will see a dramatic change in the engineering curriculum in the 1980s, we will see major changes in the efficiency of education and, most importantly, in the concept of lifelong learning with an emphasis on the needs of the individual rather than on specific degree programs following the traditional degrees. Only in this way can the engineer dance to all of the tunes played by the pipers of industry and society.

NOTES

1.   The Packaging Education Foundation, Reston International Center, Reston, VA 22091.

2.   *46th Annual Report 1977-78* (Engineers' Council for Professional Development, 345 East 47th Street, New York, New York 10017), p. 45.

3.   Ibid.

4.   *Issues in Engineering Education. A Framework for Analysis* (Washington, DC: National Academy of Engineering, April 1980), p. 11.

THE PROFESSIONAL SCHOOL OF BUSINESS ADMINISTRATION FOR THE 1980s: A CRISIS OF MANAGEMENT

by

V. Thomas Dock

Associate Dean, Administration and Budgets
School of Business Administration
University of Southern California

INTRODUCTION

The political, social, and economic environment of the world, and in particular the United States, has undergone great change since World War II. However, the evidence indicates that many organizations are not making internal operational changes accordingly, and many of the changes that have occurred were more by default than by design. Also since World War II, organizations in general have become large-scale, complex, diversified systems. These facts have brought into focus the major institutional problems of organization and management.

Unfortunately, the developments in science and in the knowledge of social phenomena have been greater than our ability to manage them. The management of many organizations—profit and not-for-profit alike—either is inefficient and ineffective or is thought to be so by individuals inside and outside the organizations. Unfortunately, a primary need of society that is not being satisfied is a systematic perspective of the management of the organization, as contrasted with the need for professional expertise in the functional areas of business—finance, production, marketing, etc.

BUSINESS EDUCATION AFTER WORLD WAR II

Prior to World War II, not much attention, relatively speaking, had been given by university educators to a special curriculum or educational program for students aspiring to careers in business. Agreed, some of the country's great university business schools predate World War II—some to a considerable extent—but it is safe to say that the present university-level programs of business education on a national scale have developed since the war. This development was primarily due to the increased educational funding provided by the GI Bill of Rights enacted by Congress after World War II, combined with the postwar growth in business activity. Schools of business administration have evolved since World War II from either departments of economics and accounting or from pressure exerted by industry and business for specialized courses such as retailing, insurance, or banking. Prior to 1960, this was not only acceptable, but in all probability may have been best for society.

Since the publication of "Higher Education for Business," by R. A. Gordon and
J. E. Howell, and "The Education of American Businessmen," by Frank Pierson in
1959, schools of business administration faculty have closed the academic credibility
gap on most university campuses. The faculties have been a source of research in such
basic disciplines as mathematics, statistics, economics, and the behavioral sciences.
Courses have been introduced into the curricula that are based upon theories and
concepts from these disciplines. The productive research and teaching effort of the
faculties during the past decade has begun to earn the academic respect of faculties
from other academic units. As such, schools of business administration faculty have
academic status on university campuses that they never before enjoyed. They have
come far from the Ford Foundation report's statement of: "They—schools of business
administration faculty—search for academic respectability, while more of them continue to engage in unrespectable vocational training."

As indicated in the Gordon and Howell reports, prior to 1960 schools of business
administration had a well-defined and widely-accepted societal identity and purpose.
The curriculum was made up of courses labeled Accounting, Marketing, Finance,
Production, etc. The focus in these courses was on the practice and the techniques
of these various areas. Although it was not always explicitly stated, students were
generally trained for their first job in an organization that had profit as its ultimate
objective. The emphasis in most courses was on the "how to do" rather than upon
"why we do it." The central thrust of research emanating from the faculty during
this time was descriptive rather than explanatory in nature.

In summary, the mission of a school of business administration during the late
1940s and the 1950s was basically to educate students for entry-level jobs in profit-
oriented organizations. The classroom content and the faculty research effort reinforced this mission, resulting in stability for most schools of business administration.
This stability was gained—in most cases—at a cost of being isolated from other academic units and of being considered vocational by university colleagues. However, the
acceptance of graduates and the rapport of schools of business administration faculties
with business organizations was excellent.

THE SIXTIES

In the 1960s, some of the greatest economic and social changes in the history of
the United States occurred. Society developed an egalitarian perspective toward higher
education. This evolvement was institutionalized by the introduction of various
"legalistic" federal and state education-oriented programs.

One of the premises upon which higher education functioned was that it was
"apolitical." In the middle 1960s, this premise began to be shattered. The basis for
this occurrence was four-fold: 1) the tremendous increase in students demanding
a higher education; 2) the exponential increase in governmental funding; 3) the
development of faculty unions; and 4) the involvement of faculty and students in
the political process. The result was that by the end of the 1960s, higher education's
self-perception, and, more importantly, society's perception of it, was no longer that
of an apolitical institution.

During this period, business, governmental, and not-for-profit organizations experienced tremendous growth in size and complexity. In the business sector, the growth
of service industries was greater than that for product industries. An increasing number
of career opportunities in government and not-for-profit organizations became available. Opportunities abounded for positions as well as for research in such fields as
health care services and pollution. It thus was difficult to reconcile the fact that, on

the one hand, the United States offered to students more opportunities for positions in organizations that could give growth, satisfaction, and contribution than ever before yet, on the other hand, many young people suffered an identity crisis.

THE SEVENTIES

The revolutionary changes in the organizational structure and in the modus operandi of higher education during the latter 1960s have been greatly impacted by, and to some extent dominated by, the bearish economic realities of the 1970s. The results have been 1) student and faculty frustration; 2) an exponential increase in faculty unions; 3) greater faculty/student involvement in the governance of higher education; and 4) greater involvement by faculty and student organizations in the political process. A by-product of this economic reality has been society's realization and acceptance that post-high school education, via vocational-technical and community college institutions, is not only acceptable but most appropriate for many high school graduates. (This is in contrast to the widely held belief in the 1960s that every post-high school student should be expected to graduate from a four-year college or university.)

A CRISIS OF MANAGEMENT

The Professional Business School

The problem facing society in the 1980s is the understanding and application of knowledge, rather than the acquisition of expertise per se. One of the business school's objectives therefore should be to give students an academically rigorous and relevant educational experience instead of mere exposure to knowledge and acquisition of data. (In the latter situation, the faculty are teaching the students, not educating them.) Thus, it is imperative that faculty recognize the salient distinctions between cognitive and affective learning, and their appropriate application inside and outside the classroom. Unfortunately, the lack of this recognition often results in students being involved in learning activity that might be charitably described as "mental masterbation" at best.

The above objective can be accomplished within a school's departmental structure. The difference would lie in the objectives behind offering the courses within that structure. Presently, the primary objective in most required and elective courses is to impart knowledge about a functional field of study. The model that instructors have tended to follow is one which assumes that their students are a homogenous population, and that they are going to a homogenous marketplace. Therefore, they have identical needs and should receive essentially the same knowledge exposure. Yet the evidence is fairly obvious that our entering students are heterogeneous in terms of their motivations, abilities, and backgrounds. Their educational needs are, therefore, different. We also know that the jobs they accept will vary tremendously. In addition, most longitudinal studies indicate that students will probably change jobs and functional areas approximately six times in their careers.

Unfortunately, many "professional" schools of business administration are still oriented toward the study of the narrow functions of the field. The problem with this approach is that emphasis is placed upon the tools and techniques of subsystems of the organization rather than upon a systemic perspective of overall organizational operations. The departmental structure, which encourages the continued specialization, makes the description of business administration primarily dependent upon the faculty members' departmental affiliation. The problem of managing organizations in the 1980s is so important that a business school can no longer afford the luxury of traditional departmentalization. (Traditional departmentalization tends to focus internally rather than upon the total educational experience of the student.) The faculty's emphasis must be on each student's educational program within the school rather than just his or her specific functional area. Otherwise, there is a tendency for the student to perceive that he or she is taking just a sequence of courses. The faculty must appreciate the interdisciplinary implications of being a member of a school of business administration who has a primary interest in accounting, finance, business economics, marketing, etc., rather than being just a member of a department within a business school.

Issues and Problems Confronting the Administration and the Faculty

Management is one of the functional areas within the professional school of business administration. Unfortunately, the administration and faculty of most business schools are guilty of "not practicing what they preach." The political-economic impact of the 1960s, combined with the economic-political realities of the 1970s, has created a crisis in the management (planning, organizing, staffing, directing, and controlling) of most business schools; a crisis that must be systematically addressed by the administration *and* by the faculty. The issues and problems are not only complex in and of themselves, but the dynamics of the external environment have a compounding effect on addressing and resolving them.

While the administration and the faculty of each professional school of business administration must identify and resolve its unique situation, one or more of the following salient issues and problems permeate most schools, and either are or probably will be the basis for a management crisis:

1.   The environment established within the school is critical to the effective and efficient accomplishment of its mission and, in turn, its objectives. One of the salient questions that should be addressed in the process of establishing the desired environment is: "What is the appropriate mix of 1) structure and certainty and 2) planned ambiguity?" The desired mix should have a major impact on the development and implementation of the school's policies and procedures.

If the structure and certainty is proportionally increased, it is more appropriate to have a school administration and faculty whose orientation is that of "maintaining and fine tuning the status quo." For example, the administration and faculty of Harvard's Business School made the long-term commitment to support the development of an environment that has allowed the faculty to establish a national academic reputation for using primarily the "case method" approach to teaching. Similarly, the administration and faculty of the University of Chicago's Business School made the long-term commitment to support the development of an environment that has allowed the faculty to establish a national academic reputation for conducting and publishing theoretical research. The "maintaining and fine tuning the status quo" has been the framework within which each of these schools has developed and implemented its policies and procedures. This has resulted in an environment which, for new and existing faculty, has a high degree of structure and certainty with respect to earning annual merit salary increases and being granted promotion and tenure.

Conversely, if the planned ambiguity is proportionally increased, it is more appropriate to have a school administration and faculty whose orientation is that of "change agent." Unlike the administration and faculty that makes a long-term commitment to support a particular type of academic environment such as the above mentioned ones, a commitment is made to establish a school mission and the appropriate policies and procedures within the framework of uncertainty. It is recognized that the political, social, and economic environment of the world, and in particular the United States, is changing at an increasing rate. This recognition necessitates the establishment of an academic environment that, on the one hand, is "planned" but that, on the other hand, is "ambiguous" and thus flexible enough to continuously proact to this change.

A second salient question that should be addressed is: "Will a productivity ('balanced excellence' with respect to teaching, research, and service) or perish environment, or a research environment (commonly referred to as "publish or perish"), with secondary financial and promotion and tenure recognition given to teaching and service excellence be more appropriate?" The basis for awarding faculty merit salary increases and promotion and tenure will be quite different depending upon the environment established.

2.   For many schools, the establishment of a school mission involves consideration of the impact of its attainment on the school's regional, and possibly national, ranking by other business school deans and faculty. It is important that the administration and the faculty recognize the distinction between the statements "one of the benefits of accomplishing the school's mission will be that the school will be ranked ahead of say, Harvard and/or Stanford," and "one of the benefits of the accomplishing of the school's mission will be that the school will be considered a 'school of the first rank.'" The former statement implies a "me too-ism" with respect to faculty, research, and teaching. This is due to the fact that most business school rankings, such as the one conducted by *MBA* magazine, are subjectively based. Thus, when a school administration and faculty make the decision to develop an environment that will be conducive to establishing a "better" academic reputation than another particular school or group of schools, there is a tendency to attempt to emulate the subjectively determined outstanding scholarly and educational characteristics of those schools. The latter statement implies an identification and evaluation of the internal and environmental strengths and weaknesses of the school's faculty, research, and teaching. In addition, there is a formal assessment to determine the faculty and supportive resources necessary to accomplish the desired mission and the comparison of the results of this assessment to the school's present and realistic future faculty capabilities and support resources prior to making a final decision. Depending upon the statement accepted, the allocation of the school's resources for the type of faculty recruited and for the structure of the faculty reward system should be quite different.

As progress is made toward attaining the school's mission, the kinds of problems that must be addressed by the administration and the faculty will be of a different origin. The problems encountered while working towards success will not only change but must be addressed from a different perspective. This shift in perspective should be reflected in discussions concerning the necessary increase in scarce resources like travel and research funds, and in the recognition that the policies that determine the allocation of these funds must change as the "problems of *working toward* success" shift to the "problems of *achieving* success." The perspective must permeate all facets of the school's policies, especially in regard to faculty recruiting. Recruiting efforts should be initially oriented toward the rank of assistant professor and secondarily toward the rank of associate professor. As success begins to occur in the attainment of the school's mission, the recruiting efforts should be broadened to include appropriate "targets of opportunity" at the rank of full professor. The purpose of this faculty recruiting modification is to provide the necessary senior leadership to the assistant and associate professors for professional development in the various areas of expertise. Like travel and research, the budgetary implications of this faculty recruiting modification must be addressed by the faculty and by the business school administration in consultation with the appropriate central administration.

3.   The economic-political realities of the 1970s necessitates the determination of which departments, and which areas of concentration within each department, will reflect the overt attempt to establish faculty expertise and faculty competence. The process of determination should be affected by such factors as:

  a.   The economic-political realities of the 1970s

  b.   The demographic fact that during the 1980s the 18-22 age group will decline by approximately 18%

  c.   The growing demand for "continuing education" and "retreading" courses and professional programs

  d.   The fact that a business school is a subset of an organization (the university) that has a product (students) that must be marketed (attracted and sold to business, government, and/or not-for-profit organizations) in a competitive environment (other business schools)

  e.   Established academic programs and research centers

  f.   The professional qualifications of the present faculty

  g.   Student functional area (accounting, finance, etc.) demand

  h.   The perceived opportunity to recruit additional faculty for specific expertise and competence areas of research and teaching.

4.   Most business schools are attempting to recruit net additional faculty to "catch up" to the greater-than-normal student increase of the past several years, which is expected to continue at least into the early 1980s. At what professional ranks should faculty expertise and competence be reflected within each department or area? What percentage of the overall school faculty, and/or each departmental or area faculty should be tenured? These questions should be answered prior to the design of a

faculty recruiting program, since that is when there is the greatest flexibility to respond to them.

5.   Traditionally, the majority of faculty research has been "microfunctionally" oriented. However, the exponentially increasing dynamics of managing organizations requires a systematic perspective. Thus, the faculty must undertake more joint intradisciplinary and interdisciplinary research and the school administration must recognize and support this kind of research via the appropriate resources.

6.   The political-economic impact of the 1960s, combined with the economic-political realities of the 1970s, has resulted in a great amount of discussion between the administration and faculty concerning their respective *rights*. It is imperative that these discussions also include an understanding of and appreciation for the *responsibilities* that accompany those rights.

Inherent in these discussions should be the distinction between commitment and loyalty. Commitment is reflected in an understanding and acceptance of the mission of the school and in a desire to actively and constructively participate in its accomplishment. Loyalty, on the other hand, is reflected in the almost "blind faith" acceptance of the perspectives of an individual or individuals concerning the organization. It is imperative that the administration and faculty recognize this distinction and its implications.

7.   A school administration and faculty cannot expect to function within the framework of external—outside the university—non-interference, if they overtly become involved in the affairs of the external environment. Thus, it is important that the administration and faculty address the issue of whether or not the mission of the school involves just the education of students to analyze and solve future professional and personal problems, or also to become involved in economic and/or political attempts to influence moral issues and problems in the world, such as the investment by the university in companies who conduct business with South Africa.

Mission in the Eighties

Although no one can predict the future, it is fairly well accepted that change at an ever accelerating rate will be the norm. Thus, schools of business administration should use the following statement as a conceptual framework for future change.

We are trying to focus on a world of tomorrow where knowledge will be temporal and fleeting, where unlearning is potentially more important than learning, where proaction is more crucial than reaction, and where any undying principle can make an intellectual pauper.

The process of education must be coordinated with its goal. To 'produce' a person of action, different methods may have to be employed than to 'produce' a person of thought. Developing aptitudes involves different techniques than disseminating knowledge. (C. J. Grayson)

The mission of a *professional* school of business administration is to close the gap between the abstract theory that has been developed about business administration and the application and implementation of that theory as practiced by management in our postindustrial society. In contrast, the primary mission of the *academic* college (Letters, Arts, and Sciences) is to prepare its students for society and possibly graduate school with its curricula being oriented within functional areas. The challenge and opportunity that business school faculty should address is to develop a curriculum that will find a middle way between vocationalism and esoteric theory, which will result in a student being capable of making a contribution to profit-oriented, governmental, and/or not-for-profit organizations. In addition, the curriculum should be a learning experience that develops a student's attitude so that he or she views learning as a life-long endeavor and not something that is crammed into two, three, or four years. The result, hopefully, will be: 1) to provide students with the capacity for analyzing and solving problems that confront them in their occupations, in society, and within themselves; and 2) to improve the students' management ability.

With respect to research, a majority of the faculty should concentrate on management-oriented problems of application and implementation. While a voluminous amount of esoteric theory has been generated during the past 15 years, some of it, unfortunately, has been concerned with answering questions to problems that managers are not and probably will not be asking. There are two reasons for this. First, the world of esoterica is a "safe place" because a faculty member can say to the practitioner: "Here is something I find interesting; I hope you will find it useful." (In contrast, a faculty member desiring to concentrate on management-oriented problems of application and implementation says to the practitioner: "I have the expertise to assist you in solving your problem; let me work with you.") Secondly, universities have rewarded theoretical research, but not applied research. Both types of research must be performed by the faculty of a school of business administration. Hopefully, the university will recognize the distinction between these types and will support both activities. The second thrust of research should be in the area of implementation. If an application proves to be successful, the problems associated with implementing it must be addressed if the application is to be of value to management.

The research scope can and should be all pervasive, providing a foundation for a link between the many activities and responsibilities of the business school. This means that teaching faculty who have both developed and employed the concepts of their disciplines should be better able to communicate them to their students, to learn in an atmosphere of intellectual inquisitiveness, and to gain an appreciation for the orderly seeking of knowledge. To this end, the business community oftentimes provides the laboratory for the academic researcher and, in return, learns new approaches for the solution to its own problems. In addition, a school is primarily known by the productivity of its faculty. This external awareness is largely created by the contributions of its faculty to their respective disciplines. Thus, the role of research is not to provide an objective in and of itself, but rather to provide a means by which several objectives can be reached.

Lastly, the faculty of a professional school of business administration should support an "advocacy role" with respect to the competitive market system. They should be concerned when polls show that a small minority of the population has confidence in business. They should be concerned with the dearth of capital formation and with declining employee productivity. The framework in which these concerns exist is a society in which approximately 65% of our GNP is service-based and in which only approximately 3% of our labor force reside in rural areas. A professional school, in concert with management, should proact and not react to these and the many other problems facing the private and public sectors of our economy.

CONCLUSION

The issues and problems that must be addressed by the administrations and the faculties of most schools of business administration are potent, emotional, and inter-dependent. It is imperative that the administrations and the faculties of the schools assume the appropriate responsibility to avoid a management crisis or at least minimize and effectively and efficiently resolve one through a proactive and not a reactive decision-making process. A fundamental requirement for this to occur is the demo-cratic establishment of formal communications between the administration and faculty. The result of these communications should be the development of the: 1) mission of the school, 2) organizational structure most appropriate to facilitate the accomplishment of the mission, and 3) policies and procedures to guide the administration and the faculty in effectively and efficiently performing the appropri-ate activities.

The issues and problems that should be addressed by the administrations and the faculties of most business schools are identifiable and solvable. They have the option of either adopting a proactive philosophy and a professional orientation or reacting to crises and probably not being satisfied with the results. The crisis of management is a reality. The salient question is whether or not the administrations and the faculties of these schools will respond to and resolve the crisis.

BIBLIOGRAPHY

Collier, Peter. "Stanford Means Business." *New West* (October 6, 1980), pp. 49-53.

Steele, Jack D. "Executive Education." *The Executive* (November 1980), pp. 81-98.

Toffler, Alvin. *The Third Wave*. New York: William Morrow and Co., Inc., 1980.

ISSUES IN HIGHER EDUCATION FOR THE PROFESSION OF PUBLIC ADMINISTRATION IN THE 1980s

by
David Mars

Professor of Public Administration
University of Southern California

At this writing, the federal government of the United States has approved a $613.6 billion budget for the next fiscal year (FY 1981). This staggering amount, which some forecasters have already said will be $50 billion short before the fiscal year is over, represents over one-quarter of the gross national product. Add to this amount the hundreds of billions of dollars that will be spent in the next fiscal year by state governments, county governments, municipal governments, school districts, and other special districts, and it becomes quite clear that government—or public administration—in the United States has developed into very big business.

It was not always thus. President Washington's first annual budget, late in the eighteenth century, was less than what is spent today on any single small federal program. But clearly the country has changed since 1789, and so too has its government. Increased population, industrialization, mobility, urbanization, economic uncertainties, foreign policy problems, and global interdependencies have drastically changed the nature of life in the United States (and in many other parts of the world) in recent decades; with these changes, have come drastic changes also both in the ways in which government is viewed and in the ways in which government operates.

Public administration as a separate profession in the United States has about a 100-year-old history. The two events generally regarded as the launching pads for such a separate profession are the Pendleton Act and the early work of Woodrow Wilson.

The Pendleton Act, passed in 1883, in direct response to the public outcry resulting from the assassination of President James Garfield by a disappointed spoils-seeker, led to the installation of the merit principle in federal public administration.[1] The act also created the Civil Service Commission to watch over the operation of the merit principle within the federal government.[2] The Civil Service Commission was the first "independent regulatory agency" created by the federal government, to be followed in later years by many others, including the Interstate Commerce Commission, the Federal Trade Commission, the Federal Communications Commission, the Federal Power Commission, the Securities and Exchange Commission, the Federal Reserve Board, and others.

Woodrow Wilson, destined for later greatness as a university president, state governor, and president of the United States, wrote an essay entitled "The Study of Administration" in 1887. In contrast to earlier American writings on political philosophy, public affairs, political economy, and public law (e.g., the Federalist papers, de Tocqueville's *Democracy in America*), which had been largely descriptive, Wilson's

25-page journal article[3] was—in the words of two authors—"epochal in delineating the conduct of government as a field for analytical study and generalization."[4] Thus, Wilson's early effort is generally regarded as making possible the study of public administration as a field or discipline in its own right.

During the century since the creation of the Civil Service Commission and the publication of "The Study of Administration," public administration has grown apace in the United States, to the point where a large fraction of our gross national product now is spent by government and where one person in every seven in the labor force derives his or her salary from a public agency.

How has this come about? What factors have been responsible for the astonishing growth in public administration in the United States during the last century? The following items, not intended to be exhaustive, do provide some answers to the questions posed.

Population Growth. In 1790, at the time of the first census, the population of the United States was 3,900,000; in 1979, the estimated population was 217 million, more than a 50-fold increase.

Increased Urbanization (and density). In 1790, about 5% of the population of the United States was characterized as urban (and there were only 24 "urban places" of 2,500 or more). The 1920 census was the first in which more than half the population of the country was classified as urban rather than rural. And in the 1970 census, the urban percentage figure had risen to 73.5%. Dense, urbanized populations always require more public (governmental) regulation and intervention.

Technology. Advances and improvements in technology, including most particularly those in communications and electronics, have simplified our lives in some ways, but in many other ways have complicated them, again bringing about more government regulation and intervention.

Business/Labor. The last century has seen first the growth of big business (involving giant corporations, massive mergers, and the like) followed by the growth of big labor (with nationally-organized unions counting their members in the millions). Inevitably, the third factor, government, has had to respond appropriately, and this has brought about an accretion of activity and power in the public sector.

Economy. The great depression of the 1930s, and the periodic recessions that have punctuated the economic news of the past several decades, have made it clear that the government increasingly has a vigorous role to play in the economy. Though such a role continues to be resisted by some economists and even by some public officials, most persons now accept the notion that the government has a responsibility to take measures to help maintain a stable and productive economy. However, debate continues to rage over the level, intensity, and timing of these measures.

Civil Rights. Beginning with the adoption of the Fourteenth Admendment in 1868, but more particularly in the twentieth century, we have witnessed a number of movements designed to secure for previously-disadvantaged "minorities" the same rights accorded to the majority population. Extending these rights to racial minorities and to women has occupied us for a long period of time; in more recent years, we have become concerned with the rights of older persons, children, gays, handicapped, and others. Much of the progress in this area has come about through legislation, both federal and state, setting forth these rights. This legislation has also required and resulted in the creation of administrative machinery to monitor and to guarantee the enforcement of the legislated provisions.

Energy. Recent changes in the pricing and availability of fossil fuels have made it clear that we need to consider developing alternative sources of energy. It is also clear that government programs of various sorts, including research and development efforts, tax incentives, and so forth, will be required, in addition to massive efforts in the private sector, to end our historic dependence on nonrenewable energy resources, especially imported ones (e.g., oil from OPEC countries).

Global Interdependence. Our heavy reliance on imported petroleum is but one example of a phenomenon becoming ever more evident. With the advances in transportation and communication we have witnessed in the past century, the world has been symbolically shrinking, and various countries and regions have been growing increasingly dependent on one another. Though much of this development has impacted heavily on the private sector (as in the growth in number and power of multinational corporations), it also has focused considerable attention on public administration: much of the activity that takes place across national boundaries and within/across regions is governmental in character and operation.

War/Foreign Policy. While the United States was a small and unimportant nation, and while there was not much international governmental intercourse, the foreign policy dimensions of our government were not very significant. This picture has changed completely, and now the United States plays a major role in world politics. This has become true especially in the decades since World War I. Our activity in that war, reinforced more strongly by our activity in World War II, Korea, and Vietnam, and our role in the creation of the United Nations, has made us unquestionably a world power and world leader. Almost all of this power and leadership is exercised through official governmental machinery.

Space. The last two decades have seen the emergence of a new area of concern for public administration that was likely never dreamed of by our Founding Fathers: exploration of space. This new effort, seen as closely coupled with or as an extension of our foreign policy and military concerns, has been carried forward completely under governmental guidance and control (though obviously the private sector has been closely involved also, as in the construction of space vehicles and equipment).

One final note: the governmental growth that has come about during the past 100 years as a result of the factors cited has also generally been centralizing in character, bringing about greater growth at the national government level than at the state/ local government level. State/local governments have also grown substantially during the same period, but the general thrust of most of the changes cited (e.g., civil rights, energy, foreign policy, space) has been to focus increasing attention on what the national government is doing (or not doing).

Education for public administration, particularly at the university level, seems to have lagged somewhat behind the fast growth in the practice of public administration. The first professional school of public administration in the United States was not on a university campus: it was the Training School for Public Service, created in 1911 by the Bureau of Municipal Research of New York City (the Bureau itself had been incorporated only five years earlier, in 1906).

In the university world, around 1900 Harvard reportedly considered creating a graduate school for civil servants and foreign service officers. This idea was soon abandoned, ostensibly because of a lack of career opportunities in those fields, and the university instead established the Harvard Business School.

In 1924, Syracuse University became the first university offering academic work to prepare persons for public service careers, when it created the Maxwell School of Citizenship and Public Affairs. Much of the work being carried forward by the Training School for Public Service was transferred to the new school. It should be noted that the Maxwell School encompasses graduate work in a number of the social sciences (e.g., economics, sociology), as well as a public administration program.

In 1929, the University of Southern California established the first totally professional school of public administration in the nation, a unit first called the School of

Citizenship and Public Administration, later the School of Government, and since 1941 simply the School of Public Administration. The school offers undergraduate, master's level, and doctoral programs in public administration, as well as a wide variety of mid-career training programs.

New schools of public administration were created at a fairly slow pace during the 1930s and early 1940s, but after World War II the pace quickened. Today, the National Association of Schools of Public Affairs and Administration, which represents the academic dimension of public administration in the United States, consists of close to 200 institutional members, generally called departments or schools of public administration. In a number of colleges and universities, the public administration program functions as part of a department of political science; in a number of other places, the term public affairs or public policy is used in lieu of public administration.

TRENDS IN THE 1980s

In the following section, we will look at certain social trends that seem likely both to continue into the 1980s, and to have a significant impact on the practice of public administration in the United States. In the section that follows thereafter, we look at steps that academic programs in public administration should take, are likely to take, or have taken to help prepare public administrators who will have to live with the impact of those trends. Again, as in the items selected to explain the growth of public administration in the United States, neither of these lists is intended to be all-inclusive.

Continued Rapid Rate of Change

The ancient Greek philosopher Heraclitus (c. 540-480 B.C.) once wrote, "Nothing endures but change." This suggests that change is a phenomenon that has been thought about (and worried about) for a very long time.

More plausible seems to be the position that though the world has always been in the process of changing, the *rate* of change has accelerated in modern times. Things are changing at a faster pace today than they did years ago, and much faster than they did centuries ago. Certainly this seems to be true for scientific and technological change. In these areas, new discoveries always provide the basis for yet newer ones, and as the bases of knowledge expand, so too does the likelihood of further knowledge being developed. We are told, for example, that 90% of the scientists who have ever lived are alive today. This is a significant measure of the potential of new scientific and technological discovery we can expect in the immediate and near-term future.

Gerald Feinberg has pointed to the contracted time scale over which changes take place in the modern world. In 1969, he wrote:

> While the Agricultural Revolution took several millenia and the Industrial Revolution several centuries to develop . . . . because of the interdependence of different parts of the modern world and the greater magnitude of the forces controlled by modern technology . . . . we should expect that the time scale for major changes in human civilization will soon be about one generation.[5]

Other authors also have pointed to the increase in the rate of change in modern times. Alvin Toffler, for example, has written of "the roaring current of change, a current so powerful today that it overturns institutions, shifts our values, and shrivels our roots," and that "the acceleration of change in our time is, itself, an elemental force. This accelerative thrust has personal and psychological, as well as sociological, consequences."[6] Toffler, of course, is the author who invented the term *future shock*. First, in an article in 1965 (in *Horizon*), and later in a 1970 book bearing that title, Toffler defines future shock simply as "the shattering stress and disorientation that we induce in individuals by subjecting them to too much change in too short a time."[7]

There is little evidence to suggest that the rate of change is decelerating[8] (though clearly it cannot continue to accelerate indefinitely). Accordingly, the public administrators of the 1980s and those responsible for educating and training them can look forward to a world substantially different from the one they have known.

Loss of Confidence in Public Institutions

Another trend that seems to be increasing in intensity is the loss of confidence in our social and political institutions. The political crisis surrounding the Watergate revelations, culminating in the first-ever resignation of a sitting president of the United States, is seen by some as the beginning of this trend. On the other hand, there is considerable evidence that the failure of confidence in our institutions, and particularly public institutions, may have begun considerably earlier. Some observers of the American social and political scene point to the growing disenchantment with America's role in the Vietnam conflict, beginning in the late 1960s, as the root source for much popular discontent, eventuating in weakened confidence in public institutions. This loss of confidence coincided historically with such developments as the emergence of the "counter-culture," of "hippies," "flower children," and alternative living arrangements (e.g., communes), and so forth.

That the current loss of confidence in public institutions is fairly widespread and pervasive is seen in the following data, reflecting a poll taken early in 1978 under the sponsorship of *U.S. News & World Report*. The poll surveyed a national sample of 5,873 men and women, including business people, professional people, laborers, and government workers, and discovered the following: 1) widespread distrust of government in practically all its forms, with a feeling that elected officials are not up to coping with many national problems; 2) reluctance of people themselves to make financial and other sacrifices required to solve national problems; and 3) shrinking support for organized labor by a public fed up with strikes and unrelenting demands for more money for less work.[9]

When asked to rate 25 social/political institutions on ability to get things done, and on honesty, dependability, and integrity, the results were as follows:

HOW AMERICANS JUDGE BASIC INSTITUTIONS[10]

Using a scale of 1 (poor) to 7 (excellent), here is the way those surveyed rated national institutions, including business and professional groups and their leaders:

Ability to Get Things Done		Honesty, Dependability, and Integrity	
Relatively Good	Average Rating	Relatively Good	Average Rating
1. Science, technology	5.07	1. Science, technology	5.09
2. TV and radio news	4.85	2. Small business	4.64
3. Papers, news magazines	4.66	3. Consumer groups	4.47

4. Medical profession	4.65	4. Organized religion	4.44
5. Large business	4.47	5. Medical profession	4.39
6. Business executives	4.43	6. Supreme Court	4.35
		7. TV and radio news	4.32
		8. Environmentalist groups	4.27
		9. Educators	4.25

Medium		Medium	
7. Small business	4.25	10. Papers, news magazines	4.18
8. U.S. military	4.21	11. U.S. military	4.03
9. Consumer groups	4.18	12. Postal Service	3.87
10. Supreme Court	4.15	13. The White House	3.81
11. Organized religion	4.05	14. Business executives	3.65
12. Environmentalist groups	4.02	15. Legal business (tie)	3.49
13. Legal profession	3.99	16. Legal profession (tie)	3.49
14. Educators	3.84	17. House of Representatives	3.45
15. Labor union leaders	3.80	18. State, local government	3.41

Relatively Poor		Relatively Poor	
16. Postal Service	3.43	19. Regulatory agencies	3.29
17. State, local government	3.38	20. Democratic Party	3.27
18. The White House	3.37	21. Republican Party	3.13
19. Senate	3.33	22. Federal bureaucracy	2.74
20. Democratic Party	3.29	23. Labor union leaders	2.59
21. House of Representatives	3.26	24. Politicians	2.42
22. Regulatory agencies	3.20		
23. Republican Party	3.10		
24. Politicians	2.69		
25. Federal bureaucracy	2.68		

The above data are revealing as to current social/political trends and institutions. They show that even the most highly rated institutions on a relative scale do not come off too well on an absolute basis (barely scraping above 5 on a 7-point scale). Second, the public administration sector, narrowly defined, comes off extremely poorly: on ability to get things done, the White House, regulatory agencies, and federal bureaucracy rank 18th, 22nd, and 25th, respectively, out of the 25 institutions surveyed; and on honesty, dependability, and integrity, they rate only slightly better— 13th, 20th, and 23rd, respectively. Finally, public institutions, broadly defined, fare only a little better: the military and the Supreme Court get respectable marks, but the rest of the public sector does not. Note that the 10 institutions doing the poorest on getting things done are all public institutions, and of the 11 rated lowest in honesty, dependability, and integrity, all but 2 are public institutions.

The loss of confidence in public institutions is dramatically reflected in—and probably reinforced by—the same trend in nonpublic institutions. Perhaps most revealing in this regard is what has been happening in recent decades to the family and marriage. We have witnessed drastic increases in divorces, separations, one-parent family units, living-together arrangements by couples, and a variety of other alternative living arrangements. These trends have all had significant, if sometimes indirect, impacts on public administration. And if they continue into the 1980s, as they seem likely to do, they will likewise continue to have at least as much impact as they have had until now.

Citizen Tax Revolt

Related to the loss of confidence in institutions, particularly public-sector institutions, is the growing reluctance of American citizens to support many governmental programs with their tax dollars. The bellwether for this movement is generally regarded as having been California's Proposition 13. In that initiative-generated proposition, the citizens of California in June 1978 overwhelmingly voted to roll back property taxes to a maximum of one percent of the market value of real property in an earlier base year. The effect was to reduce the revenue available to local governments in California (counties, cities, school districts, and other special districts) by about $7 billion a year.[11]

Though there were special circumstances present in the 1978 California vote, including the rapidly escalating real property values in the state (particularly in the populous southern portion) and the accumulation in the state treasury of an unusually large surplus, the size of the plurality signalled a high level of taxpayer discontent. In a number of other states, the same or similar measures were proposed, and in some of them enacted. A number of different kinds of limitations on state/local taxing and spending powers became popular, and at the national level, a movement calling for a constitutional amendment to require a balanced budget for the federal government quickly gathered momentum.

For a short time, something close to panic seemed to prevail in some governmental circles. The backers of Proposition 13 had urged voters to "send a message" to their government. Some public administrators interpreted this message to be to pare down government programs, to "cut out the fat" in government spending, and so forth.

But as some public programs were reduced or phased out, and as it started to become clear that lower taxes generally means fewer or lesser services, citizen reaction changed somewhat. The longer-range message emerging from the "citizen tax revolt" seemed to have become reduce or phase out unnecessary or ineffective government programs, but keep essential services (e.g., schools, fire, police, health). Another part of the message, dealt with below, was to take steps to increase productivity in the public sector.

The view that the public wants better public services for its tax dollars rather than simply lower taxes was reinforced by the experience with another California proposition. Buoyed by the success of Proposition 13, many of its backers also supported Proposition 9, which was on the ballot in June 1980. This proposition would have generally cut the state income tax collections in half, making it extremely difficult for the state government to continue the so-called "bail-out" money, i.e., state-raised revenue pumped to cities and counties to help them out of their post-Proposition 13 financial doldrums. Citizens of the state, apparently worried about the effects of such government revenue reduction on public services, especially on local school systems, decisively defeated the proposal.

Though the virulence of the citizen tax revolt seems to have abated somewhat, with many taxpayers apparently willing to take a longer look at the complex issues involved, American public administrators have clearly been put on notice that the message for the 1980s is: deliver or else.

Concern for Productivity

American public administration has seen many slogans and catch-phases come and go. Two terms that have persisted are *economy* and *efficiency*. These terms were used in citizen commissions almost 100 years ago, and are still in use in many governmental quarters today. Economy, in the public administration setting, means simply spending the fewest tax dollars possible; efficiency means extracting the greatest product possible from tax dollars spent, at whatever level of expenditure. A more recent term is *effectiveness*, or the relationship between goods and services produced and appropriately-adopted goals and standards. Effectiveness is concerned not only with how much is produced (economy) or how well it is produced (efficiency) but also with the *quality* of what is produced.

All of this relates directly to productivity, which focuses on outputs or outcomes, or what is actually produced. The American economy as a whole has been able until recent years to give us a constantly improving standard of living because of increases in productivity. Our more recent economic problems, including most particularly those associated with our recent high levels of inflation, stem from the fact that American productivity generally is lower today than it has been in the past, with significant increases only in limited industry groups, relative stability in many others, and declines in still others. Increases in the costs of certain factors in the production of goods and services, (labor, for example) without corresponding increases in productivity result in inflationary pressures. The higher relative costs of labor, in the example, if they do not lead to more production, can be recaptured only by charging higher prices.

Given that the public sector is such a large part of our economy/polity, and not really separable from it, we could expect to find the same concerns for productivity. The concern is there. During the past few years, productivity has become a featured topic at professional conferences and symposia, in government reports, in journal articles and books, and in all the places consulted by public administration practitioners and students. Governments at all levels are seeking ways to improve productivity, to provide more and better goods and services with the same level of tax expenditures, or to provide the same level and quality of goods/services with a lower level of taxes, or—in the idiom popularized by the military—"to provide a bigger and better bang for the buck."[12]

This concern for productivity in the public sector is obviously reinforced by citizen concern over taxes. A large part of the taxpayer resistance that has developed in recent years has resulted from a perception that many public agencies have not always spent their revenues wisely or efficiently. To the extent that public officials convey a concern for the effective expenditure of tax monies, and to the extent to which they try to improve the productivity of their agencies and programs, citizen support for government will grow.

Two authors of a recent textbook in public administration have summed up this situation very well, as follows:

> Productivity improvement, then, is both an old and a new concern for public administration. Efficiency in agency operations has traditionally been a concern for public administration studies. In recent years, however, the costs of government and the increasing demands placed upon the public sector have exacerbated the situation. Likewise, the growing concern with government effectiveness has added a new dimension to the sole question of efficiency. Public administrators today find themselves on the horns of dilemma—one that promises to be one of the most vexatious problems that today's administrators must face—how to provide a continuing upward spiral of public services, yet at a cost that is acceptable to American taxpayers. This is perhaps one of the major issues that will face public administrators in the years ahead. Like so many other contemporary issues in public administration, it promises to thoroughly tax the resources, ingenuity, and skills of public managers in the years ahead.[13]

Equality, Equity

To the three E's discussed thus far (economy, efficiency, effectiveness), another pair must now be added: *equality* and *equity*. Though these two seem to be related concepts, they are distinguishable.

Generally speaking, we assume that governmental services will be distributed equally among all social racial, and ethnic groups. This assumption is given philosophical, legal, and juridical reinforcement by such things as the language in the Declaration of Independence ("all men are created equal"), and the legal protection of the laws clause of the Fourteenth Amendment.

There may be circumstances or conditions, however, in which equity considerations override those of equality. For example, if police services within a given municipality were distributed exactly equally (by ward, district, neighborhood, or some other grouping), we would probably find that some areas are overserved, while others are underserved. This comes about because the circumstances requiring the governmental services vary widely by area. In the example, criminal activity is likely to be more rampant in certain areas than in others, logically requiring differential levels of police service.

Lucy, Gilbert, and Birkhead have proposed three tests for equity, "intended to be practical, concrete applications of an otherwise elusive concept," as follows:

1. Equal treatment should be the norm.
2. Deviations from that norm should have specific justification.
3. There should, in any case, be a minimum level or floor for each service below which quality and quantity delivered should not dip.[14]

Closely tied with the civil rights movements of the past few decades have been assertions that American governmental units and agencies have not always acted in an egalitarian or equitable fashion in distributing tax-supported services. Pressures from civil rights groups have brought about some changes in the practices and procedures of many governmental bodies. But these pressures have continued, frequently fueled by the changes made and by a rising level of expectations. We can expect that these pressures will continue into the 1980s.

HIGHER EDUCATION RESPONSES

In this section, we turn to suggestions for steps that educational programs in public administration can take to meet the impact likely to result from the trends discussed in the previous section. Most of these suggested steps have already been taken in one form or another at some institutions; they need to be strengthened and extended.

Flexible Curricula

To keep up with the rapid rate of change, academic programs in public administration need to stay flexible and responsive. As economic, political, and social conditions change, corresponding changes must be considered—and, as appropriate, implemented—by institutions educating and training the public managers of today and tomorrow. This means constant attention to the curriculum, to weed out outmoded or irrelevant materials and requirements, and to incorporate fresh (and interesting) material as it becomes available and salient.

Academic readers will recognize very quickly that this prescription is easier to make than it is to adopt. College and university rules and regulations, tradition, financial exigencies, faculty/student/administrator resistance to change, jurisdictional issues, and many other factors may stand in the way of effective implementation of this recommendation. To the point here is the old saw that the only place harder to reorganize than a university is a cemetery.

But if public administration programs are going to keep pace with the rapid rate of change in modern society and to act responsively (and responsibly) in the face of that change, they must recognize the need for flexible curricula.

Innovations in Learning

Related to flexible curricula is the notion of incorporating into them new or non-traditional ways of learning. Many new approaches in learning have been discovered and developed, and these should be closely examined for their relevance to a public administration curriculum.

Among the new approaches that would seem to have some merit in learning public administration are: 1) cases (both the study of previously-prepared cases, as well as having students write their own cases, based generally upon direct experience they have had); 2) simulations (again, both pre-packaged ones as well as others that students themselves might develop); 3) audiovisual materials (films, filmstrips, slides, drawings, audio tapes, video tapes); 4) individually-paced instruction and programmed learning (both manual and machine-interactive); 5) observation tours (where students observe practitioners in their own work settings and get an opportunity to question them about their work); and 6) debates, both among students and among invited practitioners. (*See also* the "Sponsored Experiential Learning" section below.)

Interaction with Professionals

Public administration curriculum should be developed in close interaction with representatives of the professional practitioner community. Many public administration programs include faculty with limited direct experience in the public service or whose experience in the public service is dated. Such faculty may, with all the best intentions, construct curricula that do not fully or effectively meet the current needs (or future needs) of public managers. To avoid such a contingency, public administration faculties should be in constant touch with practitioners, in order to keep abreast of the latest changes (and anticipated changes) in the public service.

To say this is not to suggest that the public administration curriculum should be turned over to practitioners. There is ample opportunity for curriculum development and educational leadership by public administration faculties. But that development and leadership should be appropriate, timely, and informed.

Direct interaction with practitioners in the course of curriculum development can have much additional favorable fallout. Practitioners who have participated in the design of an educational program in public administration can normally be expected to assist the program in a number of other significant ways: making internships available, helping to recruit students, providing job prospects, opening agencies for research opportunities, providing community liaison opportunities for students and faculty, making guest appearances and serving as lecturers in classes, etc.

Sponsored Experiential Learning

This area includes a large and growing variety of experiences that are built into a student's academic program while he or she still has student status. Beginning with the first cooperative education program for engineers, sponsored by the University of Cincinnati shortly after the turn of the century, this approach has become quite diversified in recent years. It now includes various kinds of work-study programs, "Antioch-type" programs, cooperative education agreements, internships, residencies, "semester" programs, "year-abroad" programs, directed research, individual study, field work, observation tours, and others. The basic purpose of all these approaches is to build some practical elements into academic programs.

Advantages seen as accruing to these appraoches are many, including most prominently: 1) giving students a chance to test the academic/theoretical knowledge that they are acquiring in classrooms and libraries; 2) making classes more interesting for everyone, as students bring into their classes insights and knowledge that they have acquired in the world of practice; and 3) giving students a chance to test, in relatively low-risk fashion, whether or not the career path they have chosen is in fact one that they really want to pursue.

These advantages apply with particular force and relevance to "practice" fields such as public administration. Providing opportunities for off-campus experiences while still maintaining student status may not be important if the student is pursuing a degree in the classics, or in literature, history, or philosophy. But in those fields where the student hopes to apply the learning acquired on campus later in practical/ professional settings, getting some practical experience in the field while still a student can be quite important. Clearly, public administration is such a field. For example, a student doing an internship in a municipal budget department while taking a course in budgeting has an infinitely richer experience than does the student taking only the course; similarly, a student sitting in on labor-management negotiations within a city or county department while enrolled in Public Administration 000 (Collective Bargaining in the Public Service). These examples could easily be multiplied a hundredfold.

Nonsponsored Experiential Learning:
Assessment of Prior Learning for Academic Credit

This is a newer area, involving academic recognition of learning from experience not sponsored by an academic institution, but which a student has had prior to enrolling in the institution. Such assessment of prior experiential learning, with a view toward granting academic credits toward a degree for this learning, was rare until relatively recently, but is now going on in a growing number of academic institutions. One survey estimated that while in 1963 fewer than 10 institutions were granting credit for noncollege learning, by 1974 close to 200 institutions were doing so, and the number of colleges/universities doing this has been growing steadily since.

Assessment of prior experiential learning has particular importance to education for public administration, and predictably will have even more importance in the future. The reason for this is found in two trends, one demographic and the other financial.

All demographic forecasters tell us that we are heading into an area of decline in those groups of the population from which college students normally are drawn. The end of the war baby boom, later marriages, later childbearing, fewer children per family, more divorces, more two-earner families, and the pressures of social movements like zero population growth, ecology, and conservation, have all contributed to this decline. Enrollments have already started down at a number of colleges and universities, and are expected to continue to slide. In some cases, declining enrollments have brought about the cancellation of programs, and even the closing of institutions.

Given the decline in traditional college-age populations, colleges and universities will have to turn to other populations, meaning primarily adults and foreign students. This brings us to the second trend, the financial one. From the viewpoint of public administration, dealing with an adult student population means mid-career people already in the public service or adults seeking to enter the public service. As discussed in the preceding section, the last several years have seen some drastic changes in the way citizens in the United States view governments, government services, and government-imposed taxes.

The results of these changes have been twofold: 1) mid-career people are finding it more difficult to secure government sponsorship and financing of their efforts at education and development; and 2) persons who have been considering entering public service as a career are having second thoughts, based on the perceived or actual decline in employment opportunities in that sector. Both these pools of potential enrollees for public administration programs would have a more favorable view of these programs if they could fold in some of their pre-enrollment professional or other experience, and thereby find themselves confronting something less awesome than the 120-130 units generally required for a bachelor's degree, or the 36-50 generally required for a master's degree.

As tuition costs continue to rise, and as public administration programs continue to upgrade themselves (with the number of units required to graduate floating upwards), the need for some way for students to mitigate the effects of these trends will become even more sharply focused. Schools of public administration should be prepared for increasing numbers of applicants seeking to convert experiential learning into academic credit. More proactive schools will probably want to recruit students by anticipating some of this activity and systematically offering credit, as appropriate, for prior experiential learning.

The words *as appropriate* are the key. When is it appropriate to grant academic credit for prior experiential learning? How much credit should be granted, and under what conditions? How can we avoid a situation in which schools go into the business of awarding such credit almost as a commercial enterprise? Are there satisfactory methods for the assessment of prior experiential learning?

Fortunately, the answer to the last question is affirmative, and that makes it possible also to answer all the other questions raised.

During the past several years, an organization known first as Cooperative Assessment of Experiential Learning and now as the Council for the Advancement of Experiential Learning (CAEL) has been deeply concerned about this area, and has published a substantial amount of material on its various dimensions. The 26 reports issued by CAEL during 1975-1977 culminated in a final report, entitled *Principles of Good Practice in Assessing Experiential Learning.*[15] This report "summarizes in succinct form what CAEL has come to view as sound procedures in the assessment of experiential learning," and seems to indicate that the state of the art in assessment has reached a point where a firm basis has been laid for answering the questions raised above.

Concern for Quality

Given that public administration has become such an important enterprise in modern American society, we should be concerned about the quality of the programs dedicated to the education and training of the managers of that enterprise. This concern is even more relevant today, with some public administration programs struggling to maintain enrollments, and possibly tempted into lowering standards as a way to meet the situation.

Fortunately, the professional association of academic programs, the National Association of Schools of Public Affairs and Administration (NASPAA), has taken steps reflecting that concern. Late in 1977, the member institutions approved the establishment of a voluntary peer review process for master's degree programs in public affairs and public administration. The process combines a self-study with peer review, including a site visit. The review is based on standards for professional master's degree programs, as developed by a specially-constituted Standards Committee of NASPAA. NASPAA's stated purpose in establishing the peer review process was "to facilitate the continuing development of the quality of our profession and to encourage peer review and communication of these developments within our field."[16]

After the completion of the review of those programs submitted to the process, NASPAA's Peer Review Committee determines whether the program reviewed is "in substantial conformity" with the standards, and NASPAA publishes a list of those programs.

In preparing their self-studies and going through the peer review process, a number of public administration programs have taken substantial steps to improve their offerings in order to meet the NASPAA standards. Other programs have taken such steps in order to prepare for future reviews. The result has been an upgrading of many such programs.

NASPAA has also published guidelines and standards for undergraduate and doctoral degree programs in public affairs and public administration, and for internship programs in those fields.

NASPAA sees itself as "a professional education association dedicated to the advancement of education, training, and research in public policy and administration . . . a national center for information about programs and development in this field, fosters goals and standards of educational excellence, and represents the concerns and interests of its membership in the formulation and support of national, state and local policies for education and research in public policy and administration."[17]

Continuing Education

Because public administration is such a dynamic field, with the conditions of practice constantly changing, particular attention must be paid to the needs of its mid-career practitioners. The notion that a person can acquire a degree and then use the skills and knowledge thus obtained for a lifetime professional career has become completely obsolete. Conditions and circumstances change, information and knowledge obsolesces, and opportunities must therefore be provided for conscientious professionals to keep up with the most current learning materials in the field.

College and university public administration programs have the responsibility of making opportunities easily and widely available for mid-career persons, including the following populations: 1) trained mid-careerists who are seeking to upgrade themselves in their current specializations, or who are seeking to change to different specializations; 2) other mid-career persons who have not completed formal educational programs and who now seek to do so, 3) other mid-career persons who had had no (or little) prior college-level work who would now like to start; and 4) persons who have had careers, interrupted them, and now seek to get back into the employment mainstream, either in their previous specializations or in different ones.

Dealing with mid-career persons obviously means employing different approaches from those generally used with pre-career audiences, both in process ways and in learning arrangements. First, classes involving experienced persons rely more on class-oriented learning approaches (seminar methods, discussion groups, participant reports, etc.) than on traditional lecturing approaches. Second, given the fact that the members of the class are all employed, accommodations are made in terms of class meeting times (evenings, weekends, concentrated sessions, etc.) and sometimes in class meeting places (e.g., where a number of persons working for the same jurisdiction are involved in the same class, sessions can be held in the workplace: a city hall, a county hall of administration, or in a governmental training facility).

Ethics and Values

Increasing concern over ethics in government has come about because of two developments: 1) the growing role of government and the greater possibility of intrusion into people's lives, and 2) various recent scandals involving public officials, sometimes at the highest levels within government, e.g., Watergate, the General Services Administration revelations, the ABSCAM operation, and others. In consequence, citizens have grown to expect and to demand not only economic, efficient, effective, equitable, and egalitarian behavior by their public servants, but also ethical behavior. Public administrators must therefore pay more attention to the ethical and value dimensions of their work, and in turn academic programs in public administration must include these areas in their offerings.

In fact, they are doing so. Until a few years ago, the subjects of ethics and values were generally foreign to public administration curricula. A search of older introductory texts in the field reveals almost no references at all to these subjects. Today, courses and modules in ethics and values have been added in many public administration programs, and textbooks devote considerable space to discussion of these topics.

People generally agree that ethics and values are not subjects that can be taught successfully. A person's value system and ethical sense are parts of that person's character, which has likely been molded long before entering a college classroom. What can be taught, however, are such things as respect for values (one's own and others'), ways of making values held explicit and operational, the importance of ethical behavior, and related matters. Academic programs can help persons going through as students develop their value and ethical systems, and thereby make these persons potentially more conscientious public servants. Most important is the conveyance of the significance of ethical behavior in today's public administration milieu: the notion that the most efficient/economical/effective public manager somehow has failed if he or she behaves in an unethical way in discharging assigned responsibilities.

Futures Orientation

Concern for the future has swiftly come to the fore in recent years. Fueled by much uncertainty both at home and abroad, and by the rapid rate of change being experienced, many persons are anxious and worried about tomorrow.

At the same time, there has been an explosion of interest and concern in the future in academic and professional circles. Under labels such as futuristics, futurology, futures research, alternative futures, and others, scholars in many disciplines and in a variety of academic and think-tank settings have been working at perfecting their skills in futures forecasting, technological assessment, scenario construction, and related matters. A considerable body of literature and techniques has been developed in the last two decades.

Some citizen groups and government agencies have also been engaging in these and similar activities. A few states and a number of cities have undertaken goals programs, under which citizens in large numbers are encouraged to make their views known on the kinds of communities they would like to live in and on the directions in which these communities should move in the future.

Academic programs in public administration seem to be moving rather slowly in incorporating the newly developed material on the future. Given the obvious and simple fact that the future is where all of us are going to live, and the notion that our public leaders should be forward looking, public administration programs need to pay closer attention to this area.

What do public administrators themselves think of the future of their profession? A revealing report was issued in 1979 by the Committee on Future Horizons of the International City Management Association, the professional and educational association of appointed administrators in cities, counties, and councils of government (7,000 members). Speaking specifically for city/county managers, but saying things very relevant for all public administrators, the Committee on Future Horizons made five statements about future ideals, and eight statements about the nature of their profession in the future, as follows:

*More than ever, our idealism must prevail.

*The prime ideal of the profession must be that of excellence in management.

*We must be the strongest believers in democracy.

*The concept of equity is also one of our ideals for the future.

*Our commitment to ethical conduct should remain high.

- - -

*The prime role of the manager will be as a broker or negotiator—but not a compromiser.

*Local governments will require managers who can lead by being led.

*The intergovernmental role of the administrator will grow.

*The power of the administrator will be more widely shared.

*The legal basis for professional management positions will not be as firm.

*The job of manager will be no more secure in 2000, but careers will be less capricious.

*A new profession within the profession—that of internal manager—will emerge.

*An intensification of the profession's quest for its own humanity will develop.[18]

Public administration is important, responsible, fulfilling work. It can also be exciting work. Academic programs in public administration must try to convey some of that importance and excitement to students interested in careers in that field and to mid-career practitioners striving to improve themselves and their work. In concert with public managers, political leaders, and citizen-group leaders, these programs can help substantially in building a better society.

NOTES

1.   Prior to the inauguration of the merit system, jobs in government were generally awarded on the basis of partisan connection, and sometimes on other kinds of connections: family, personal. This type of arrangement, known politely as the patronage system, was also known as the spoils system, from the old catch phrase, "to the victor belongs the spoils," meaning in this context that the political party that had prevailed at the polls exercised the power of filling all governmental positions. Understandably, most of these positions were allocated as rewards to the party faithful.

2.   This agency is now called the Office of Personnel Management.

3.   *Political Science Quarterly*, II (June 1887), pp. 197-222.

4.   Alice B. Stone and Donald C. Stone, "Early Development of Education in Public Administration," in *American Public Administration: Past, Present, Future*, ed. by Frederick C. Mosher (University, AL: University of Alabama Press, 1957), p. 27.

5.   Gerald Feinberg, *The Prometheus Project: Mankind's Search for Long-Range Goals* (Garden City, NY: Doubleday & Co., Inc., 1969), p. 55. Feinberg makes another interesting point about much of the change taking place in the modern world: its irreversibility, i.e., that as a result of some decision, possibility of returning to the previous ways, and that the change may foreclose forever a whole range of options that might otherwise have been possible.

6.   Alvin Toffler, *Future Shock* (New York: Random House, 1970), pp. 3-4.

7.   Ibid., p. 4.

8.   For example, Robert Oliphant, commenting on future problems of the aging, speaks of "the present and near future, when ever more rapid change threatens our very existence." *Los Angeles Times*, II (July 8, 1980), p. 5.

9.   *U.S. News & World Report* (February 13, 1978), p. 39.

10.   Ibid., p. 42.

11.   Though the revenue reduction to local governments amounted to $7 billion, the citizens of California did not realize that much in the form of reduced taxes. About one-third of the tax relief went to corporations doing business in California, and about one-third of the money went to the federal government because of decreased deductions on federal income tax returns.

12.   However, as recently as 1974, a federal survey found that fewer than one percent of the country's 80,000 local governments were involved in significant productivity efforts. U.S. Congress, Joint Economic Subcommittee on Priorities, *Federal Productivity, Hearings*, 93rd Congress, 1st Session (Washington, DC: U.S. Government Printing Office, 1974), p. 83.

13.   Robert D. Pursley and Neil Snortland, *Managing Government Organizations: An Introduction to Public Administration* (North Scituate, MA: Duxbury Press, 1980), pp. 479-80.

14.   William H. Lucy, Dennis Gilbert, and Guthrie S. Birkhead, "Equity in Local Service Distribution," *Public Administration Review* (November-December 1977), p. 688.

15.   Warren W. Willingham, *Principles of Good Practice in Assessing Experiential Learning* (Columbia, MD: Council for the Advancement of Experiential Learning, 1977).

16.   *NASPAA Peer Review Process: Policies and Procedures for the 1980 Initial Roster, Professional Masters Programs* (Washington, DC: NASPAA, 1978), p. 1.

17.   *Guidelines and Standards for Baccalaureate Degree Programs in Public Affairs/ Public Administration* (Washington, DC: NASPAA, 1976).

18.   *New Worlds of Service* (Washington, DC: International City Management Association, 1979), pp. 14-20. In the report, each of the statements is followed by several paragraphs of explanatory text.

SCHOOLS OF EDUCATION: A CURRENT SAMPLE

by
Leslie Wilbur

Professor of Higher Education
University of Southern California

Education has in recent decades been the target of several vigorous assaults. The most dramatic, thanks to television, were directed toward universities during the years of campus unrest. The public became keenly aware of confrontations between militant students and institutions, the destruction of university property, and the violent rejection of traditional curricula. Although the participants were proportionately few in number and were not always students, a lay impression, largely inaccurate, was that colleges and universities were in general disarray.

Other assaults have been directed against public elementary and secondary education. Critical charges have appeared frequently in newspapers, magazines, and various books, pointing out declining student test scores, lack of personal security, and indifferent or fearful or hostile classroom teachers who seem unprepared or unwilling to teach urban students. *Why Johnny Can't Read* and *Death at an Early Age* are examples of popular denunciations of public education. In the pattern of most popular criticism, the achievements current and past are ignored partially because they are not stimulating reading.

Schools of education are perceived by the public as related to the problems of inadequate public schools, even though many are identifying and responding to the need for teachers trained to teach inner city and bilingual students. Institutional responses to complex needs require more planning than do individual responses and attract less attention than do crisis and confrontation, and the time lag often arouses further resentment.

Even an abbreviated discussion of education and its current professional schools requires at least a brief survey of the precedent processes and institutions. In addition to external assaults, most schools of education have not yet achieved on their own university campuses status equivalent to other professional schools. Part of the explanation seems to lie in the humble origins of teacher education and the movement toward professional status.

PROFESSIONAL STATUS OF EDUCATION

Teacher training is the common bond between the early normal schools and present schools of education. An examination of the normal schools exposes the roots of many issues that continue to resist satisfactory or enduring resolution. For example, from the outset of colonial education elementary teaching was identified as a low-status occupation, one typically carried out by women who had few alternative occupational choices. Male teachers, although distinguished for being literate, were viewed as men either unfit or incapable of success in more demanding employment.

While the normal schools and academies introduced formal preparation of elementary school teachers, they did little to enhance teaching as a profession. Elementary teachers were needed in increasing numbers during the nineteenth century. As the American dream of education for all citizens was expanded, both the academies, more common in the east, and the normal schools, more prevalent in the west, were responsible for meeting the demand for elementary teachers.

At the outset admission standards in the academies or normal schools were generally modest: an eighth-grade education. The preparation for teaching was usually brief: two years. Thus teacher training was identified as limited in its goals, functioning out of the mainstream of higher education, and applying minimal standards for admission. However, it should be pointed out that during the nineteenth century in the United States, the standards for admission to practice in law and medicine were based more on apprenticeship than on academic competence.

In addition to its early identity as preparation for semiprofessional status, teacher training in nineteenth century America developed in a relatively disorganized manner. The uneven evolution reflects the constitutional relation of the federal government toward education, which was clearly left to the states. Consequently each state could establish whatever educational system its legislature, resources, institutions, and constituencies would allow. Thus both private and publicly supported institutions established teacher training programs, largely independent from the federal government until the mid-twentieth century.

The effects of the absence of centralized authority at the federal level are reflected in another manner in the development of teacher preparation programs at public and private universities, largely from the beginning of the twentieth century. Colleges and schools of education, orienting teacher training to state credentials, began to exert an increasing influence on the methods and content of teacher training.

The increasing role of universities was accompanied by an expansion of state influence on teacher training, due to the demands of the public for uniform state requirements. The authority of the states to require licensure and credentialing was clearly established and exercised more vigorously in the twentieth century. However, the standards and methods of licensing the professions were generally conceded to require the participation of representatives of the practitioners. A typical result of this mixture of legislative and academic needs and interests was the establishment of a teaching credential that reflected the recommendations of the various institutions of higher education.

Before the beginning of World War II, in many states the state department of public instruction or its counterpart virtually delegated to teacher training bodies the authority to credential. Credentials could be obtained only through programs approved by the state; moreover, in many states the applicant was required to be recommended by the institution. Elementary and secondary teaching required a state credential; the credential required an institutional recommendation; eligibility for a recommendation required admission to and completion of a program established by the institution.

As the universities began to play a more aggressive role in teacher training and research related to learning, the body of knowledge related to education expanded rapidly after World War I and dramatically after World War II. Prior to World War I, normal school elementary teacher training had been largely an apprentice process, including supervised teaching if possible. New teachers continued to train while teaching independently and immediately after completion of the program.

Research-based teaching and learning were limited for both secondary and elementary levels, but they were beginning to reflect research findings related to the discoveries of psychologists. In the early twentieth century, research and debates related to the findings of researchers in psychology were affecting, albeit slowly and unevenly, teacher preparation programs. During the same period, growing attention was being given to educational matters other than teaching. Counseling and administration started to emerge as subjects worth systematic attention. Accompanying these changes and reflecting the status of influence of expanding knowledge, professors of education began to work toward recognition.

World War II can be seen as a watershed in the development of American higher education. The rapid expansion of college and university enrollments, accompanied by an unprecedented baby boom, expanded the demands for teachers at all levels. Research and specialization in education also expanded. Such specialties as educational sociology, student personnel, school finance, instructional technology, and higher education blossomed and established departments, usually apart from teacher education.

The bachelor degree in education, which had been well-established prior to World War II, continued to be the basic degree for elementary and secondary teaching credential programs. Moreover, a fifth year was often added to teacher preparation requirements. However, an expansion in graduate degree programs, particularly the master's degree, accompanied the establishment of a variety of specializations in education departments. Although the education doctorate was established at Harvard in 1920, there were numerous institutions that offered Ed.D.s prior to World War II. The postwar demand for education doctorates, both Ed.D. and Ph.D., increased the need for graduate program faculty until the mid-70s.

Increasing public recognition of the roles and pervasiveness of education brought with it an increasing amount of controversy about the effectiveness of public elementary and secondary education. The crest of the postwar baby boom was accompanied in the 1960s by a rising wave of criticism directed toward the performance and preparation of public school elementary and secondary teachers. One most visible and articulate critic was Dr. James B. Conant, president of Harvard University. His book, *The Education of Teachers*, aroused vigorous support and opposition from within and without education.

His was one of a series of critical books and articles that took aim at the shortcomings of public education, personified in its teachers. Teachers were often perceived as the products of programs that emphasized teaching methods to the detriment of subject matter. Professors of education, especially those responsible for teacher training programs, were criticized typically as being divorced from the realities of life outside the university, particularly the public school classroom, and especially in an urban setting, and devoid of competence in any established subject matter field.

In the early 1970s it became clear that the wave of elementary student enrollments was passing and that it would be followed by an enrollment trough. The declining demand for elementary teachers and the subsequent decline in secondary teaching placements resulted generally in a surplus of teacher applicants in the precollege level of education. On the other hand, changing demands created a shortage of teachers who were effective in urban school classrooms, who were bilingual, or who had special skills in a technical or scientific field. Although some schools had discontinued or sharply reduced programs for the preparation of elementary teachers, many changed the design and content, responding to new demands.

By the end of the 1970s, a substantial number of outstanding schools of education had been established at major universities. Furthermore, most normal schools have for several decades been transformed into state colleges and universities, with a wide variety of programs other than teacher training. In many states the state universities have become graduate level institutions with faculty and research facilities comparable to those of the state senior universities. Their normal school origins and functions have been historical rather than actual. The granting of the doctorate has generally been withheld from the state universities, reflecting the resistance of the legislature to do more than allow a change in nomenclature.

SCHOOLS OF EDUCATION: SOME EXAMPLES

There are many institutions maintaining teacher training programs, including small independent colleges, state colleges, and universities, both independent and public. These examples are restricted to doctorate-granting institutions, all selected from the schools listed in the Cartter Report in *Change* of 1977. The schools were chosen as illustrative of the mission statements and organizations of some leading schools of education.

The illustrations of missions and examples of organizations were drawn from the following schools of education, generally conceded to be among the outstanding professional schools. They have been listed alphabetically rather than according to Cartter's rankings:

Private	Public
1. Cornell University	1. Michigan State University
2. Duke University	2. Ohio State University
3. Harvard University	3. University of California, Berkeley
4. New York University	4. University of California, Los Angeles
5. Northwestern University	5. University of Illinois
6. Stanford University	6. University of Indiana, Bloomington
7. Syracuse University	7. University of Michigan
8. Teacher's College, Columbia	8. University of Minnesota
9. University of Chicago	9. University of Texas, Austin
10. University of Southern California	10. University of Wisconsin

Bulletins of these institutions are a rich source of information related to the current status of schools of education.

An examination of their recent bulletins reveals basic similarities among the missions, even though their statements vary. One common mission is that of educating and training teachers, administrators, researchers, and specialists in various areas of education. The prevalence of international graduate students confirms that this mission is no longer restricted to American educators.

Another generally accepted mission of the schools of education is that of conducting research. This mission reflects the general commitment of the school to faculty performance. It seems evident that faculty must demonstrate competence in their research as well as their teaching.

The subjects of research extend well beyond the traditional teaching and learning processes although the emphases differ at different institutions. The impact of the study of higher education as one increasingly important focus is reflected in numerous subdivisions of the established divisions as well as being a specialist; for example, college counseling and the administration of higher education seem to be generally accepted as specialties in most institutions.

Typical comparative responsibilities to research are conceded to be the discovery, synthesis, dissemination, explication, and application of knowledge. The search for knowledge through disciplined inquiry is perceived as a scholarly bond between the student and the professor.

For the majority of schools of education degree programs have survived in similar patterns. The master's degree is the most common goal. Master of arts, master of science, and master of education are common to most professional schools. Such degrees as the educational specialist and the advanced master's represent degree programs for persons who have previously completed a master's degree are options in several institutions. They seem to be responses to students who seek advanced graduate study but who do not seek a doctoral degree program.

Two doctoral degree programs are offered by the professional schools: the Doctor of Education (Ed.D.) and the Doctor of Philosophy (Ph.D.). The Ed.D. is usually described as a professional degree, designed around the competencies needed by the educational practitioner rather than the researcher. The professional degree is largely controlled by the school of education rather than the graduate school.

Doctor of philosophy degrees, including those in education, remain chiefly under the aegis of the graduate schools. Bulletin descriptions stress that the degree program emphasizes the development of research skills oriented toward basic rather than applied research. Whereas school administrators are generally Ed.D. degree recipients, that degree is relatively uncommon for specialists in educational psychology.

Most of the schools maintain credentialing programs, reflecting the role of each state in setting its standards for credentialing a variety of public education specializations. Teaching at elementary or secondary level requires preparation to be eligible for the credential; nevertheless in most states competition is vigorous among colleges and universities for students whose opportunities for job placement have been declining for several years.

Counseling, supervision, and administration are examples of other state credential programs that colleges and universities offer. State colleges, usually with lower tuition costs than professional schools, have been able to compete with success in credential programs and master's degree programs. In contrast, most state legislatures have been unwilling to allow the establishment of doctoral degree programs at the state colleges, even though many have frequently acquiesced to the pressure for changing the titles from "college" to "university."

Most of the schools have a variety of programs other than those for credentials and degrees. There are centers, institutes, and clinics, to name only a few. These represent group efforts, often cutting across the organizational units of the school of education and often in cooperation with public elementary or secondary schools. Nevertheless, every school of education seems to be organized with a structure typically established with departments, divisions, areas, or faculties.

The department pattern seems to be the more traditional, representing the gradual expansion, separation, and addition of areas of research and specialization over the decades since World War I. Administration, history, philosophy, psychology, elementary and secondary departments have been joined by special education, higher education, counseling, and sociology, to name a few examples. Newer departments have expanded and separated, reflecting the effects of specializations in such fields as the administration of higher education or college counseling.

The number and the nature of departments is under general scrutiny. Numerous departmental units may be considered an impediment to cooperative effort among faculty. In schools of education as in other professional schools, the department chair is often perceived as an ambiguous position, neither completely faculty nor clearly administrators. Moreover, the role may be accepted reluctantly and may be viewed as a distraction from more academic activities. On the other hand, the occupant may be viewed as an impediment to positive change rather than a leader.

Departments are occasionally recast into larger, fewer units. One school organizes its degree programs into three broad areas: 1) Social and Philosophical Studies in Education, 2) Educational Psychology, and 3) Organizational and Administrative Studies in Education. Each of the three includes several specializations; for example, comparative and international education, philosophy and history of education, and sociology and anthropology of education are specializations within the first area.

Another school uses a different pattern in reducing its areas of study to three broad categories: 1) Division for the Study of Teaching, 2) Division of Special Education and Rehabilitation, and 3) Division of Educational Development and Administrative Studies. The second division includes the administration of special education, communicative disorders, education of the emotionally disturbed, special education, education of the mentally retarded, and rehabilitation counseling.

The decline in school of education enrollments has been accompanied by a decline in the market for school of education faculty. The decline has been uneven; states with expanding populations have had less severe declines. The declines have also varied among the various specializations. For example, among the early casualties were many faculty whose specialty was training elementary teachers.

Another surplus of candidates for professorial positions has been in social and philosophical foundations. In contrast, there has been a rising demand for faculty members whose expertise relates to allied health professions education and for those who are bilingual education specialists. Moreover, specialties related to faculty development and older students seem to be in greater demand.

ISSUES IN THE 80s

The forecasts for higher education have several common themes: one is that enrollments will decline with an expected increase again following demographic data; another forecast is that operating expenses will increase; another is that decisions related to higher education will be increasingly centralized. State and federal requirements are viewed as increasing in number and aggressiveness. Such issues as these affect schools of education as part of their universities.

In the past most schools of education served largely middle class American students. The past ten years have seen the federal government increasing its support and urging professional schools to assist in the achievement of federal goals by admitting and retaining more women and more minority students. At the same time, the training of teachers for urban students and bilingual students has been vigorously supported as a federal priority to be achieved through schools of education.

The number and proportion of international students has been increasing as the conventional enrollments have declined. Can these new students be served effectively with curricula heavily oriented toward the American public school system? If the traditional curriculum has limited relevance to international students, should the content be substantially revised?

Faculty roles are now under more scrutiny than ever before. Under the pressure of declining enrollments, should faculty be required to give more time to advisement in order to reduce attrition? As "marketing" gains consideration, do faculty have a responsibility to assist in student recruitments? If faculty positions are jeopardized by declining enrollments, can faculty maintain the quality of teaching and academic standards?

Tenure and promotion were relatively casual in the 1950s and 1960s during a period of college and university teacher shortages. One result is an uncomfortably high proportion of tenured faculty. When student enrollments seem likely to decline further, it is not surprising that universities would insist that all units establish high standards for promotion, especially when the step includes tenure.

A pervasive university issue is the conflict between demands for faculty productivity in teaching and research. The standards for both performances seem to be rising. The academic reputation of a school of education is usually the reflection of the quality of its scholarship as measured by the esteem of the academic peer group. The achievement of tenure seems to be a more adversarial process in recent years. At the same time, more emphasis is placed on teaching competence as an institutional requirement.

Financial support for students of schools of education has become increasingly difficult, especially for the private institutions that are tuition-dependent. Although federal loans have broadened eligibility requirements for graduate students, students who must pay their own tuition and whose means are relatively modest seem to be taking fewer units at a time. On the other hand, in programs related to federal priorities, funds are available to assist and encourage students.

An issue that has extended beyond a decade is that of accreditation. Should a school of education apply for specialized accreditation, specifically NCATE? There are strong differences of opinion, even among some of the 20 schools listed in the Cartter Report. The accrediting agency seems to be defining and applying its standards more effectively. Nevertheless, there is an unresolved disagreement among schools of education on the issue of the value of specialized accreditation.

FUTURE DIRECTIONS

Schools of education have been and continue to be sensitive toward their relative status within their universities. There seems to remain some defensiveness, reflecting the early, low status of education. In addition, there is still evidence that in the pecking order of the university and its professional schools, law and medicine and dentistry are considered of higher professional status.

There is a massive amount of research related to the various specializations within education, but the major university departments rarely turn to schools of education for assistance in the improvement of instruction in their own areas such as chemistry or history. Although there is some recognition of the need for better mastery of subject matter, assuring teaching competence still survives substantial contradictory evidence. Until university administrators demand more effective instruction, teaching will remain generally a lecture approach.

Declining enrollments, changing student populations, and a continuing struggle to improve the quality and increase the acceptance of educational research should combine to impose change on schools of education. Some of the earlier patterns have changed: fewer hire their own graduates until their graduates have achieved status elsewhere.

Schools of education are identifying new clientele and forming new university liaisons. Such specialties as continuing education and instructional technology are gaining respectability. Gerontology and health professions education are forming liaisons with schools of education to the benefit of faculty, graduate students, and the general public.

It seems clear that schools of education will face all of the typical problems of higher education in the 1980s. Added to those will be a few special difficulties reflecting, for example, the attitudes of several constituencies that education will somehow resolve social issues as well as educational issues.

BIBLIOGRAPHY

Books

Amitai, Etzioni, ed. *The Semi-Professions and Their Organization*. New York: Free Press, 1969.

Brubacher, Johns S., and Rudy, Willis. *Higher Education in Transition*, 3rd ed. New York: Harper and Row, 1976.

Clark, David, and Guba, Egon. *Studies of Knowledge Production and Utilization Activities in Schools, Colleges, and Departments of Education*. Syracuse, NY: Eric Clearinghouse on Adult Education. ED 139 805.

Conant, James B. *The Education of American Teachers*. New York: McGraw-Hill, 1936.

Frankena, William K., ed. *The Philosophy and Future of Graduate Education*. Ann Arbor, MI: University of Michigan Press, 1980.

Goodlad, John. *The Dynamics of Educational Change*. New York: McGraw-Hill, 1975.

Howsam, Etal. *Educating a Profession*. American Association of Colleges for Teacher Education, 1976.

Kerr, Clark. *The Uses of the University*. Cambridge, MA: Harvard University Press, 1963.

Powell, Arthur G. *The Uncertain Profession*. Cambridge, MA: Harvard University Press, 1980.

Schein, Edgar H. *Professional Education: Some New Directions*. New York: McGraw-Hill, 1972.

Smith, B. Othanel, et al. *A Design for a School of Pedagogy*. Washington, DC: Superintendent of Documents, U.S. Government Printing Office. S/N 017-080-02098-0.

Storr, Richard. *The Beginnings of Graduate Education in America*. Chicago, IL: University of Chicago Press, 1965.

Periodicals

American Association for Higher Education. *Journal of Higher Education* [published bimonthly].

American Association of University Professors. *Bulletin* [issued quarterly] ; *Academe* [issued monthly].

American Council on Education. *Educational Record* [issued quarterly].

Change [published bimonthly].

Chronicle of Higher Education [issued weekly].

Phi Delta Kappa [published monthly]. (October 1980 special issue on teacher education reform.)

ISSUES IN EDUCATION FOR LIBRARIANSHIP

by
Russell E. Bidlack

Dean, School of Library Science
University of Michigan

A typical way to begin a discussion of the present state of an academic discipline
is to note that it is in a period of transition. It has been reported that Adam observed
to Eve as they were departing from the Garden, "We must think of this as a period
of transition." Whether or not that was the first application of this evasive means
of facing reality, we have all used it to disguise our own inability to determine exactly
where we are and where we are going. How much easier is the task of describing where
we have been.

It may be well to note early in this discussion that library education in the United
States has not yet celebrated its one hundredth birthday. It was during the annual
conference of the American Library Association of 1883 that Melvil Dewey, the new
Columbia College librarian, introduced a resolution that the association endorse his
proposal for the creation of a library school. In the ensuing discussion, William F.
Poole, one of the half-dozen most respected librarians of the time, asked whether
there was even a need for a school to educate librarians—was not on-the-job training
a sufficient means to prepare library workers? Furthermore, Poole questioned whether
librarianship could be taught in the classroom—he had little regard for the theoretical
approach to professional training. It was four years after this discussion, on January 5,
1887, that Dewey opened his School of Library Economy at Columbia. Two years
later, amidst controversy regarding the admission of women to the program, Dewey
and his school moved to the State Library in Albany, thus establishing a precedent
for the training of librarians within a major library.

In any backward glance at library education, one must include mention of a publication that appeared nearly 60 years ago entitled *Training for Library Science* by
Charles Clarence Williamson.[1] Now called simply "The Williamson Report," this
slender volume published by the Carnegie Corporation in 1923 had an influence on
library education very similar to that of the "Flexner Report" on medical education
a decade earlier. It was Abraham Flexner's conclusion in 1910 that the value of a
profession to society, as well as the standing of its members in society, is dependent
to a high degree upon the standards of the training required of individuals wishing to
enter that profession. C. C. Williamson applied the Flexner conclusion in his study
of library education, and the picture that he painted of that education, and, therefore,
society's view of librarianship, was a dismal one.

A principal result of Williamson's investigation was the removal of a number of
library schools from libraries to colleges and universities. Also resulting from the
"Williamson Report" was the introduction to library education of what was then

still a relatively new concept, that of programmatic accreditation. In 1924 the American Library Association created a Board of Education for Librarianship (BEL), renamed the Committee on Accreditation in 1956, as a means to improve the quality of the training of librarians and to establish a minimum level of quality that programs would be required to meet. There are presently (in 1980) 69 library education programs leading to the first professional degree (the master's) that are accredited by the American Library Association. Seven of these are located in Canada while the remaining 62 are in the United States. It is not easy to estimate the number of programs not presently on the ALA accredited list for whom accreditation is a goal, but it is worthy of note that 34 programs presently hold associate membership in the Association of American Library Schools, a category of membership available to library schools that have not yet gained accreditation for their master's degree program.

Accreditation by a professional association, regardless of the field of study, implies the need for written standards for measuring quality. The present *Standards for Accreditation* for application to programs leading to the first professional degree in librarianship were adopted by the Council of the American Library Association in 1972. They constitute the fourth such document to appear in what is bound to be an evolutionary process. Earlier editions of the standards were issued by the ALA in 1925, 1933, and 1951.

The Standards for Accreditation of 1972 were written to address the primary issues facing library schools in the 1970s and 1980s and are organized under the headings: 1) Goals and objectives; 2) Curriculum; 3) Faculty; 4) Students; 5) Governance, administration and financial support; and 6) Physical resources and facilities. These six areas of concern provide an appropriate outline for the remainder of this commentary.

It was noted in the introduction to the 1972 standards that the terms "librarianship," "libraries," and "library service" can be interpreted differently by different people. One of the confusing aspects of library management has always been that, to the typical library user, anyone employed in the library is a "librarian." That same library user would not, on the other hand, assume that everyone employed in a law firm is a lawyer nor that everyone who works in a hospital is a physician or surgeon. This confusion regarding the work actually done by librarians, i.e., the lack of distinction between clerical and professional responsibilities, has not only confused the library user, but librarians themselves. Much of the essential work in libraries, such as returning books to the shelves and charging out materials to library borrowers, is routine and nonprofessional, as opposed to such responsibilities as collection building, reference service, and bibliographic instruction. Because, however, there are hundreds of libraries, whether public, academic, school, or special, that are operated entirely by one individual, that individual's responsibilities can scarcely be limited to purely professional tasks. Likewise, in larger libraries, perhaps because of the essentiality of many routine library tasks and the traditionally low salaries received by librarians, there have been all too many examples of professionals being assigned, or even seeking, duties of a strictly clerical nature. An effort better to recognize library personnel who have been professionally trained has resulted in the use of the awkard term "professional librarian." Today there is not only a determined effort in libraries to draw a clear distinction between professional and nonprofessional responsibilities, and to hire personnel accordingly, but also to limit the title librarian to those who have been professionally trained. For the past 30 years, "professionally trained" has meant holding the master's degree, or its equivalent.

There has also been confusion about whether the terms "information science" and "documentation" pertain to aspects of librarianship or whether they represent separate disciplines. The answer to this question has, of course, close relevance to library education. A statement of policy adopted by the Council of the American Library Association on June 30, 1970, entitled *Library Education and Personnel Utilization*, contains a clarification of this issue in a statement that was subsequently incorporated in the 1972 standards:

> Throughout this statement, wherever the term "librarianship" is used, it is meant to be read in its broadest sense as encompassing the relevant concepts of information science and documentation; wherever the term "libraries" is used, the current models of media centers, learning centers, educational resources centers, information, documentation, and referral centers are also assumed.[2]

Of the 69 schools appearing on the ALA-accredited list dated October 1980, 45 have names that emphasize "library" (7), "librarianship" (5), "library science" (27), "library service" (4), "library studies" (1), or "bibliothéconomie" (1). On the other hand, 14 schools now have names that incorporate also the term "information science," such as UCLA's Graduate School of Library and Information Science, while 4 have chosen to add "information studies." One school has added "information services," while another prefers "information management." Reflecting still another point of view, one school has added "instructional technology," another has added "media," while another has added "media and information studies." One school has even abandoned the word "library" altogether—Syracuse University has a School of Information Studies through which the degree Master of Library Science is awarded. Regardless of what a library school may call itself today, one can be sure that its curriculum includes courses that give attention to the application of computer science to library problems and that attention is also given to all forms of media. The degree to which these are emphasized, however, varies and may have slight relationship to the school's name.

Regardless of what it may call itself, a library school must have clearly defined goals and specific objectives for its master's degree program in order to comply with the 1972 *Standards for Accreditation*. This requirement, representing a relatively new emphasis in the accreditation process, has forced library schools during the past decade to visualize and describe their mission with a greater degree of clarity than they have sometimes done in the past.

In the words of ALA's policy statement on "Library Education and Personnel Utilization," library service "is concerned with knowledge and information in their several forms—their identification, selection, acquisition, preservation, organization, communication and interpretation, and with assistance in their use."[3] While choice of terminology differs from one library school to another, and emphases vary, presently stated library school goals generally reflect this definition of library service.

A primary issue in library education today, however, pertains to the fact that the skills required for providing excellent library service, including those based on the application of computer science in the storage and retrieval of information, have equal application to many agencies other than libraries in what has come to be known as the information industry. The extent to which library school curricula should be altered, with the implications for faculty and student recruitment that such a change in emphasis suggests, is a matter of keen interest.

It has been demonstrated frequently in the past that library skills have practical applications outside libraries, to which many former librarians now in related professions can attest, but not until recently have library schools questioned whether they should educate students directly for a profession other than librarianship. This questioning has been prompted in part by the tightening of the job market for librarians in the 1970s and the generally low salaries that graduates of library schools can expect within the traditional library setting. Declining enrollment in many schools is also a strong factor in this debate.

Libraries experienced dramatic growth during the 1960s and librarians were suddenly in great demand. President Johnson's "Great Society" legislation not only contributed indirectly to the growth of library education through federal aid to libraries, but directly through Title II-B of the Higher Education Act of 1965. Fellowships at both the master's and the doctoral level, along with funding for research and continuing education, became available in number and amount never known before in library education. The institutional support accompanying the fellowships not only spurred existing library schools to expand, but encouraged the creation of new library schools as well. Whereas today there are 62 U.S. schools on the accredited list, in 1965 there were but 33 accredited schools.

It is generally agreed that these 62 library schools are distributed across the country in a less than ideal fashion. While California, the most populous state, has four schools, New York has no fewer than nine. Seventeen states (Alaska, Arkansas, Delaware, Idaho, Maine, Montana, Nebraska, Nevada, New Hampshire, New Mexico, North Dakota, Oregon, South Dakota, Vermont, Virginia, West Virginia, and Wyoming) are not represented at all on the ALA list. Of the three accredited programs in Texas, two are located in the same town, Denton.

It is also apparent to many that in relationship to the employment picture during the latter half of the 1970s and the probable job situation in the 1980s, there are more library schools today than are actually needed. That all will survive in the decade ahead is doubtful. Enrollment has declined during the past 4 years in 80% of the schools (an overall decrease of 20%). The master's degree was conferred upon fewer than 30 students in 1978-1979 in each of 6 schools. The number of library school faculty has likewise decreased, especially those employed on a part-time basis. Over half of the schools on the ALA-accredited list have total full-time faculties of fewer than 10, including the school's head; only a dozen have 15 or more regular faculty members.[4] Herbert S. White, dean of Indiana University's School of Library and Information Sciences, has asked: "Is there a point in terms of faculty size, student enrollment, and institutional support below which the offering of the necessary diversity in library education becomes impossible?"[5] The answer must surely be affirmative, but what those minimum figures should be has yet to be agreed upon.

The proper length and level of an educational program for the first professional degree in librarianship has been a matter of debate since Melvil Dewey founded the first library school in 1887. As library schools were established in colleges and universities following the issuance of the Williamson Report, the pattern that gradually emerged comprised two years of study beyond the bachelor's degree. The first year led to a second bachelor's degree (e.g., Bachelor of Arts in Library Science) while the second led to the master's degree. The evolutionary development of library education at the University of Michigan epitomizes its development throughout the United States and Canada and may be used here as an illustration.

Beginning in 1909, a summer course in library methods had been offered by the Michigan librarian and his staff to high school graduates. In 1918, however, the admission requirement had been raised to 30 hours of college credit, or its equivalent. It was not until 1926 that a degree program in library science was established with the creation of the Department of Library Science. Two degrees were authorized, the A.B.L.S. and the A.M.L.S. Senior standing was required for admission to the first-year program while a year of library training, or its equivalent, was required for entry into the master's program. In 1930, entrance requirements for the A.B.L.S. were tightened to include a bachelor's degree; the A.B.L.S. thus came to be called "the first professional degree." (It was also, incidentally, in 1930 that the University of Chicago, where the Graduate Library School had been founded four years earlier, conferred the first Ph.D. in library science—Eleanor S. Upton's dissertation was entitled "A Guide to Sources of Seventeenth-Century History in Selected Reports of the Historical Manuscripts Commission of Great Britain.")

For over two decades, until 1949, the University of Michigan, like most other library schools, thus had what might be called a two-year program in library education. It was assumed that the A.B.L.S. degree equipped one to enter the library profession at the beginning level; i.e., to work as an assistant in a large library or to take charge of a small library. In the words of Michigan's bulletin of the time, "the aim of the second-year or graduate courses is to supply the need of college, university, public, and reference libraries for trained people to fill more advanced positions." Entry into the master's degree program, whether at Michigan or any other library school offering the second year of library education, represented a genuine commitment by the individual to the library profession. (Approximately 40% of those completing the first year subsequently, usually after two or more years of experience, went on for the master's degree.)

Effective in 1948-1949, Michigan, along with such peer schools as Columbia, Illinois, and Western Reserve, adopted the so-called "Denver Plan." The Michigan curriculum was revised to upgrade all courses to the graduate level; the A.B.L.S. degree was dropped, with the A.M.L.S. henceforth to be conferred as the fifth-year, or first professional degree. This quickly became the standard pattern of library education across the country, with a summer session usually added to give the program greater substance. At Michigan, as well as at Illinois and Columbia, and a little later at Berkeley and Western Reserve, a doctoral program was introduced. Of the 62 library schools in the U.S. holding ALA accreditation for their master's degree, 23 presently have doctoral programs. Students entering such programs usually have career goals involving library education or administration.

Today there is again lively debate regarding the appropriate length of the master's degree program in library science. Six of the seven accredited programs in Canada now require a minimum of two academic years (four semesters) for completion of the master's degree, while three American schools (the University of California at Los Angeles, the University of Washington, and the University of North Carolina at Chapel Hill) have either lengthened their programs to four semesters (or six quarters) or are contemplating doing so. The program at the University of Chicago requires five quarters, while three trimesters are required at Michigan. The generally accepted minimum length of the master's degree program is one academic year plus a summer session.

Where the so-called two-year program has been introduced (or perhaps reintroduced is the proper term), a library internship has been incorporated as an important feature. In most schools, in fact, opportunity is now provided students to enroll in a course involving work in a library, whether called an internship, practicum, or field experience. This is by no means a new concept in library education, but represents a return to an earlier practice that had been generally discarded three or four decades ago. Its earlier disappearance had represented a desire to de-emphasize the "how-to-do-it" approach in library education in favor of a more theoretical approach. As the job market for library school graduates tightened in the 1970s, however, students became increasingly insecure regarding their qualifications for their first job. Many faculties responded to that concern by reintroducing practice work into the curriculum.

To be worthy of graduate academic credit, field experience must be planned and directed in such a manner as to transfer to the supervising librarian responsibility for the instruction for the "course," even though a faculty member is normally responsible, at least in part, for the final evaluation of the student's experience. Few library schools are able to provide even token compensation to librarians providing this service. Reliance must, therefore, be placed upon the willingness of librarians, as part of their commitment to their profession, to make this contribution to library education. Schools differ in their manner of assigning faculty to plan and direct this experience in the field—one individual may fill this role as his or her principal teaching assignment, while in another school all faculty may share this responsibility, often on an overload basis.

With rare exception, library schools attempt to provide a sufficiently broad curriculum to recruit and to educate students to fill positions in all types of libraries, whether academic, public, school, or special. Only one program has yet (as of 1980) been accredited under the 1972 standards that can be described as having a single purpose, i.e., the education of librarians for only one type of library or library service. The standards specifically authorize a program of study with a single specialization so long as it provides for "the study of principles and procedures common to all types of libraries and library services."[6] The assumption has always been that there is a core of knowledge to be taught that is common to all types of librarianship, while that which is peculiar to a type of library can be offered in the form of electives. The typical core courses have been cataloging (including classification), reference, collection building (once called "book selection"), and administration or management.

As in all areas of professional education, the curriculum in library education has changed markedly during the past decade. Its broadening to include courses in systems analysis, on-line retrieval, library automation, and statistics, while giving increased attention to the development of managerial, analytical, and research skills, has resulted in changes so basic as to make present programs of study scarcely recognizable to graduates of the 1950s and 1960s.

One result of this dramatic change in curriculum has been the recognition by a growing number of librarians of their personal need for continuing their education. The role and obligation of the library school in providing continuing education opportunities for its graduates and area librarians have provided further opportunity for debate. Just as a library school's parent institution must charge tuition of degree-seeking students, so also must it charge for offering continuing education opportunities to its graduates and others. The degree of willingness and the ability of librarians to pay the costs of their own continuing education efforts, as well as the degree of priority given this activity by the employing library, are likewise elements in this debate.

In accepting a growing role in continuing education, library schools are having some difficulty in determining how best to incorporate responsibility for workshops and institutes of this nature into the faculty's regular teaching assignments. The decline in enrollment in a number of schools has made the diversion of faculty effort in the direction of continuing education somewhat easier, while in other schools, faculty reductions growing out of declining enrollment, have limited their ability to respond to this need. A few schools have been able to assign responsibility for coordinating continuing education efforts to an individual staff member with at least the hope that his or her salary can be recouped from the fees charged participants.

Related to the matter of continuing education for librarians is the question of the need for and place of a formal program resulting in a degree or certificate beyond the master's degree but short of the doctorate. This post-master's specialist program (often called a "6th-year program") is presently (in 1981) offered in 38 library schools in the United States, although the total number of these certificates awarded each year is small. While some 295 individuals were reported as enrolled in such programs in the fall term 1979 by 35 library schools, these same schools reported having awarded only 45 post-master's degrees and certificates during the year 1977-1978.[7]

A major difficulty in designing a "6th-year program" has been that of creating a meaningful credential to be awarded to the individual at its completion. The certificate customarily awarded has usually been accepted in school systems as a basis for salary improvement and promotion, but rarely has it been considered worthy for this purpose in academic, public, and special libraries. What value will be placed by employers on CEUs (Continuing Education Units), now being awarded by a number of library schools for attendance at institutes and workshops, has yet to be determined.

The evaluation of faculty qualifications appropriate for effective instruction has long been a matter of concern in library education. Quite naturally, the first library educators were practicing librarians, men and women who had, themselves, studied librarianship "on the job." In the first library training classes, there was the assumption that competence in instruction should relate directly to success in library practice. The faculty for the early training programs were, of course, the staff members of those libraries offering such programs.

As library schools moved out of libraries to become academic units in institutions of higher education, faculty qualifications came to be weighed very differently. Earned degrees, research activities, and scholarly publications came to the fore as primary appointment criteria in addition to successful library experience. It was recognized that students working toward graduate degrees ought to be taught by persons holding such degrees themselves, while to be accepted as colleagues by faculty members in other disciplines, library educators needed to possess earned doctorates. It has been this latter expectation more than any other that has encouraged library schools to introduce doctoral programs.

Among the 69 library schools in the United States and Canada holding ALA accreditation in 1980, there were 732 full-time faculty members, including the 69 executive officers. Of this number, 503 (68.7%) held doctorates, of which 175 were in disciplines other than library and information science. Rarely are junior faculty appointments made today in the absence of the doctorate, or at least candidacy status, and each year as retirements take their toll among senior faculty, the percentage of those holding the doctorate increases.

The degree of need for library experience by library educators, and how recent and varied that experience should be, continues as a sensitive matter for debate. The more theoretically oriented the curriculum, and the more it expands to include such areas as computer science and educational technology, for example, the less emphasis tends to be placed on library experience in the recruitment of faculty. Many would contend that continuing research into library problems, along with frequent visitation of exemplary library programs, should enable the educator to keep abreast of issues and developments in librarianship regardless of recent work experience. As an increasing number of library school graduates are placed in agencies other than the traditional library, the essentiality of library experience for each faculty member tends also to be lessened.

Nearly every library school employs a number of adjunct faculty each year. Drawn largely from among library practitioners, these individuals give students the sense of "the real library world" that full-time educators are sometimes accused of failing to provide.

While the library profession has long been dominated by women (one male for every four females), such dominance has not extended to library school faculties and deanships. According to a survey made in 1979 by the present writer, among accredited programs in 1980 nearly 57% of the full-time faculty are males and nearly 83% of the executive officers are men. This ratio seems bound to change in the future, however, as a growing number of women pursue the doctorate in library and information science, and as they more actively seek roles of administrative leadership. Another survey made by the present writer revealed that in 1979 nearly 52% of students enrolled in doctoral programs in library science were women (204 females vs. 191 males). This contrasts with a two-to-one male dominance among doctoral students a decade ago and suggests that during the 1980s there will be more women than men appointed to library school faculties. This trend was already evident in the appointment of new assistant professors in 1979-1980—of the 26 such appointments among the 69 schools then on the accredited list, 17 were women while only 9 were men.

In library schools, as in higher education generally in the United States, the 1970s witnessed a new awareness of the need to recruit a larger proportion of ethnic minorities not only to the library profession but to library education itself. Of the 642 full-time faculty members in 61 of the 62 ALA-accredited programs in the United States on January 1, 1980 (data were not available for the University of Chicago's Graduate Library School), 61 or 9.5% were minority (35 blacks, 16 Asian or Pacific Islanders, 8 Hispanic, and 2 American Indians). If one removes from consideration the 21 faculty members (17 black, 4 white) in the 3 historically black institutions on the accredited list (Alabama A & M, Atlanta, and North Carolina Central), the remaining 58 schools had but 40 minority full-time faculty out of a total of 621, or 6.4%. The present writer's 1979 survey of enrolled doctoral students in library schools revealed that nearly 22% of those individuals were minority. On the basis of these figures, it would appear that minority representation on library school faculties should increase rather dramatically in coming years. The shift to greater representation by women and minorities will have to come gradually, however. Annual surveys made by the present writer for the past 7 years reveal that the annual retirement and resignation rate of library school faculty is only 8%.

Perhaps the area in which library schools are most frequently criticized by practicing librarians is in their recruitment of students. It is claimed, in fact, that almost no real recruitment occurs, that library school students are self-selected, that their undergraduate backgrounds fall largely in the humanities and the social sciences, and that as individuals they tend to be shy and retiring. Few deans and directors of library schools would deny that their students are largely self-selected—that they are primarily people whose interest in librarianship developed from having had a part-time library job while they were in high school or as undergraduates, or whose career goals were influenced by a relative or friend who was a librarian. A few became interested in the profession because they were avid library users while growing up. For some, librarianship represents a second career choice resulting from lack of opportunity in, or dissatisfaction with, an earlier choice.

Examination of undergraduate transcripts of library science students easily confirms the charge that it is the rare science or mathematics major who comes to library school; he, more probably she, does, indeed, tend to have majored in English, history, or education as an undergraduate. It is also probably true that the degree of aggressiveness usually found among students in schools of business, engineering, and law is lower among library school students. Few library educators would deny the wish that their pool of applicants might be larger, but few feel themselves equipped to launch aggressive recruitment campaigns to attract and educate a new breed of librarians.

Because of the declining number of applicants for entry to library education programs, deans and directors of library schools in universities in which there is pressure to meet enrollment quotas find themselves sorely tempted to admit individuals whose limited qualifications would have assured their prompt rejection a few years ago. It is always a bit startling to observe the vulnerability of our academic standards and professional principles when we are faced with economic disaster.

Recruitment to a profession is normally based on the personal rewards that will follow entry into that profession. Such rewards are usually expressed in terms of ease in placement following completion of the training period, an attractive salary structure, speed of advancement, and job satisfaction. When one considers the beginning annual salary received by recent library school graduates, $13,127 in 1979, and the fact that nearly one-fourth of the 1979 graduates had failed to find employment four months after completing their master's degrees, one can guess the reason library schools find the launching of recruitment programs to be difficult. There is a further practical limitation imposed upon recruitment by the severe lack of scholarship and fellowship funds in most library schools. Except for the brief period in the 1960s during which federally supported grants for fellowships were available in large number to library schools under Title II-B of the Higher Education Act of 1965, aid for library science students has been limited largely to local sources. The library profession has provided little assistance of this nature in contrast to such professions as law, medicine, and engineering, while alumni giving to library schools to provide student aid has likewise been very limited. The comparatively low salaries received by librarians across the country accounts for these limitations, of course.

Despite the continued criticism of library schools' admissions policies, Ralph Conant in a recent study of library education reported that "employers generally feel that the quality of people entering the field is improving."[8]

The cost of a professional degree, in the view of the individual contemplating entry into the program leading to that degree, must surely relate to the professional salary that subsequently can be anticipated. While there is considerable variation in the cost of the master's degree in terms of tuition and fees among the 69 accredited library education programs (from less than $1,000 to as much as $7,000), when combined with the living costs for the year or more required to complete the degree, the total in some schools comes very close to the entry level annual salary for the beginning librarian. Small wonder that today's library science student tends to be the individual who has already discovered the satisfactions of library work and is determined to enter the profession despite society's reluctance to pay very much for his or her services.

Because of the mounting costs of library education, a growing number of students are finding it necessary to enroll on a part-time basis while holding full- or part-time jobs in order to finance their education. While the part-time student has always been a common sight in library schools, the ratio has never been quite as extreme as it is today. In 40 of the 58 library schools in the United States that appeared on the ALA-accredited list in 1978, part-time students at the master's level outnumbered their full-time colleagues.

In terms of total enrollment, 62.5% of the student body at the master's level in these 58 schools were registered in the fall term, 1978, on a part-time basis (5,128 out of 8,207).

The male-female ratio among library science students has changed little during the past half-century. Carol Learmont, in her annual survey of placement, has reported that of the 5,139 graduates of 1979 reported by 61 schools with accredited programs, 80% were women while 20% were men.[9] This is the division that has existed for many years in the library profession.

When library education programs moved from libraries to universities, or were created there afresh, their status in the academic hierarchy tended to be closely tied to the university library. The director of the library frequently served as the library school's executive officer, and the school was usually physically located in the library. The title assigned to the head of the school was sometimes that of dean, thus enhancing the librarian's own status in the institution, or, if the library school was established as a department, the title was that of chairman or director. Because from the beginning its program tended to be small in comparison with those of most other academic units, the library school did not tend to occupy a very prominent niche in the institution's organizational chart. Only occasionally did the president or vice-president for academic affairs take a strong personal interest in its program.

An effect of the accreditation process, along with the gradual advancement of the library profession, has been to pressure universities to provide increased autonomy for their library schools by separating them administratively from the library while also giving them a status equal to that of other professional schools. Today, no library school on the accredited list is administered by the director of the library—each has its own executive officer whose primary, if not sole, responsibility is the administration of the school. Of the 69 accredited programs, 54 are officially called schools and 3 have the name college, while 2 of the Canadian schools have the designation "faculty." Only 5 remain as departments, each headed by a chairperson, while 5 others are called divisions and are headed by directors. It is significant to note, however, that of the 59 that are called schools, colleges, or faculties, only 43 are headed by deans; the executive officers of the other 16 have the title director. In most of these 16 schools, the director reports to the dean of a larger school or college of which the library school is a part.

The role of the executive officer of a library school is essentially the same as that for other professional schools in the same institution, and subject to the same changes in authority, responsibility, and period of appointment. Because library schools tend to be small in both faculty and student body size, he or she is often expected, or feels compelled, to do more classroom teaching than would this individual's counterpart in other professional schools. Like all academic administrators, library school deans, directors, and chairs have less direct authority in the decision making process today than was true a decade ago, along with experiencing greater frustration from the growing infringement of government into higher education. There is evidence to suggest that, because of the position's changing role, fewer qualified people are seeking these posts. Most search committees charged with recruiting heads of library schools in recent years have expressed disappointment in the number and quality of applicants, and several have had to open a second or even third search in order to attract a suitable candidate. Whereas at an earlier date such appointments were for an unspecified period, they now tend to be limited to three to five years followed by a careful review to determine possible reappointment. In this review process, the library school's faculty play an important role. The lack of security of such appointment is certainly one of the elements making the position less attractive than at an earlier time. While the head of a library school is still able to exercise leadership in bringing about desired change and improvement in library education, a different style of administration is required from what was effective in the past.

A recent survey by the present writer reveals that on January 1, 1980, 41% of the heads of library schools on the accredited list were aged 55 or older; only 17% were 40 or younger. The average term of office for these individuals was 6.9 years. Twenty-one (or slightly over 30%) had held their administrative posts for a decade or longer.

Of the 69 library school deans, directors, and chairs on January 1, 1980, 57 (nearly 83%) were males. Of the 663 full-time faculty, exclusive of the executive officers, however, the ratio was 57% male (376) and 43% female (287). As these percentages suggest, men appear either to be more attracted to these administrative posts, or are more preferred by search committees, than are women.

In 1975, a first in library education was achieved when the fiscal-year salary of a dean exceeded $40,000. By 1980, nearly 40% of the salaries of the heads of library schools reached this total, while the salaries for three had passed the $50,000 figure. With rare exception, the salaries for library school executive officers compare satisfactorily with those of individuals heading other professional schools within a given institution.

Because of the relatively small size of library education programs, only 34 of the 69 on the accredited list have associate (assistant, etc.) deans, directors, or chairs, although 2 schools have 2 such positions. With but one or two exceptions, these people also have teaching responsibilities, sometimes close to full-time. Responsibilities of an administrative nature assigned to them tend to be associated primarily with admissions, student advisement, general correspondence, and placement. A recent study by Lucile Whalen based on questionnaires completed by 33 associate (assistant, etc.) deans, directors, and chairs of library schools, revealed that the post is not often viewed as a stepping stone to that of the executive officer. Fewer than a quarter of the present incumbents expressed such an interest.[10]

It has been a major objective of the ALA's Committee on Accreditation to assure that the financial support of the library school compare favorably with that provided other academic units within the same university. Since the issuance of the 1972 standards, there has also been a determined effort to assure that compensation for women faculty be equal to that of their male colleagues. The committee is now generally satisfied on both counts. The average beginning salary for assistant professors of library science in 1979-1980 (academic year) was $17,000. By rank the average salary among 65 reporting schools (633 positions) in the United States and Canada for 1979-1980 was as follows: professors, $29,194 (fiscal year $36,308); associate professors, $22,985 (fiscal year $30,531); assistant professors, $19,052 (fiscal year $23,538); instructors, $15,623 (fiscal year $14,925); and lecturers, $21,432 (fiscal year $21,134).

In terms of financial support other than faculty salaries, library schools appear to be receiving an appropriate share of their institution's funding for support staff and services in relationship to their size. As noted earlier, an area in which they frequently do less well, however, is that of funding for scholarships and fellowships. This relates to limited alumni gifts and the lack of professional organizational and federal support.

Because library education had its origin in libraries and because it has long been recognized that the best laboratory for the library science student is the library, library schools have tended to be physically located in the university library. In some instances, the university library has been planned specifically to provide quarters for the library school, but more often library space has been converted for this purpose. Because both library schools and libraries tend to grow, the space provided the school, unless it was specifically designed as a separate wing, will eventually be looked upon with a covetous eye by the library director. Added office and classroom space is usually difficult to provide within the library, and the collegial relationship between library staff and library school faculty becomes strained. Stories of such conflict abound in library education folklore.

A number of schools in recent years have moved from the space they once occupied in the library either to new or to refurbished quarters elsewhere on the campus. Since in virtually every instance the new quarters are more commodious and comfortable than those left behind in the library, most of the faculty and students are happy with the change, despite other inconveniences. There is a great personal advantage, of course, for any faculty member to be housed in the library, whether one's research interests be history, political science, economics, or library science.

As library science has expanded to include information science, with the accompanying need for computer and audiovisual facilities, the space and equipment needs of the library school have been altered considerably. Funding to provide for these facilities is proving difficult to acquire. Most library schools continue to provide, either through their own budget or that of the university library, a special library science collection of materials and study area, with support staff, for their students and faculty. A few, however, have found it impossible to maintain such a facility. So long as appropriate materials are acquired and made easily available to students, the Committee on Accreditation does not demand that a special departmental or divisional library exist for the education of future librarians.

As the foregoing remarks may suggest, library education has its full share of unresolved problems as well as issues for continuing debate. It does not differ in this regard from other programs of professional training. Were Charles C. Williamson to return after 60 years to survey library education in 1981 as he did in 1921, he would doubtless find much to commend and much to criticize. He might even be tempted to observe that it is in a period of transition.

NOTES

1.   Charles C. Williamson, *Training for Library Service, A Report for the Carnegie Corporation of New York* (New York: 1923).

2.   American Library Association, *ALA Policy on Library Education and Manpower* (Chicago: American Library Association, 1970) [reissued as *Library Education and Personnel Utilization* in 1976], p. 1.

3.   Ibid.

4.   These data have been taken from the Association of American Library Schools, *Library Education Statistical Report* (State College, PA: Association of American Library Schools, 1980).

5.   Herbert S. White, "Critical Mass for Library Education," *American Libraries*, 10 (September 1979), p. 468.

6.   American Library Association, *Standards for Accreditation, 1972* (Chicago: American Library Association, 1972), p. 5.

7.   Association of American Library Schools, *Library Education Statistical Report*, pp. S4-S16, S27-S34.

8.   Ralph W. Conant, *The Conant Report, A Study of the Education of Librarians* (Cambridge, MA: MIT Press, 1980), p. 163.

9.   Carol L. Learmont, "Placements & Salaries 1979: Wider Horizons," *Library Journal*, 105 (November 1, 1980), pp. 2271-277.

10.   Lucile Whalen, "The Role of the Assistant Dean in Library Schools," *Journal of Education for Librarianship*, 20 (Summer 1979), pp. 44-54.

THE IMPACT OF AGING ON INSTITUTIONS
OF HIGHER EDUCATION

by

David A. Peterson
Director, The Leonard Davis School of Gerontology
University of Southern California

and

James E. Birren
Executive Director, The Leonard Davis School of Gerontology
University of Southern California

Demographic changes have significant impact on social institutions. Whether it be the massive immigration of the early 1900s, the baby boom of the 1950s, or some future cure for cancer or heart disease, business, politics, families, and the media are all affected. Traditional policies and operations are altered because of the demographic change. Currently, the number of older persons in America is increasing more rapidly than the number of children or young adults. This demographic change is affecting all aspects of American society, but is causing especial concerns for institutions of higher education. Decline in the number of college-age students is resulting in decreasing enrollments, a scarcity of financial resources during a time of high inflation, reduced faculty mobility and increased tenure density, and concerns for the relevance of the curriculum. Although most administrators and faculty are aware of the demographic change, community colleges, four-year schools, or universities have shown limited aggressive, proactive steps to assure institutional viability in light of these developments. The size and composition of the potential student body of the future will be greatly different from the past, and adaptions will be required. The time is at hand to begin the planning, organization, and implementation of procedures by which adaption of educational institutions will occur. However, data are needed on just what demographic changes are occurring and how they can best be accommodated.

The purposes of this paper are to provide some of the data by identifying social and demographic changes, indicating the ways in which they are having an impact on America's institutions of higher education, and suggesting actions that may be of help in the future. No panaceas will be included; the future adjustments appear to be neither easy nor painless. However, there are some insights that, if taken seriously by today's educational planners and administrators, could result in greater social relevance and higher quality of institutional responsiveness.

This paper includes five sections. These are: the implications of demographic changes for institutions of higher education; the aging of colleges and universities and their faculties; the growth of a new student clientele; the development of instruction for middle-aged and older persons; and the expansion of the teaching of gerontology. These sections provide the basis for concluding that the aging of American society is a process that presents higher education institutions with a tremendous challenge but one that, if handled skillfully, may result in the strengthening and broadening of academe.

THE EFFECT OF DEMOGRAPHIC CHANGES
ON INSTITUTIONS OF HIGHER EDUCATION

Institutions of higher education have traditionally served students between the ages of 18 and 24. Beginning in 1980, there will be fewer persons in this age category in each succeeding year. By 1997, it is expected that this nation will have experienced a 23% decline in the total number of traditional aged students.[1] The decline in the number of students aged 18-24 is expected to have a substantial impact on college enrollments though some replacement will occur as older students continue to increase their participation in higher education. The expected result is a reduction of 5% to 15% in total college enrollment over the next 20 years.[2]

The magnitude of the demographic shift is causing great concern in institutions of higher education, but other shifts are compounding the problem. An increasing number of traditional aged students are deciding that they prefer not to attend college at all. In 1968, 63% of the male high school graduates entered college; by 1974 this percentage had fallen to 49% and continues to decline.[3] This may be an indication of a decline in the status of higher education or its perceived usefulness in adult life. The best students no longer necessarily choose teaching or research careers. In fact, some of them appear to be questioning the wisdom of their professors in choosing an academic life. As the economic status of the college educated person declines when compared to others,[4] some elements of the public appear to be questioning the value in relation to the cost of college education. This is reflected in state educational institutions having increased difficulty in obtaining expanded tax support. Although they continue to gain annual appropriations, inflation erodes their financial viability so that they must constantly struggle for program quality and plant maintenance.

Undergraduate education is not the only area to suffer. Since many doctoral graduates enter the professoriate, some persons perceive reduced need for doctoral education since undergraduate teaching positions are scarce. In fact, the size of some doctoral programs has declined, particularly in the humanities and arts, and as jobs become more difficult to obtain at both the undergraduate and doctoral level, we may expect further erosion of the attractiveness of academic careers in higher education.

Those of us in higher education tend to associate institutional and program growth with good times. Increasing public support and educational progress go hand in hand, and we have come to expect that the expansive growth of the 1960s and early 1970s would continue. During that period, higher education substantially increased its share of the gross national product. In 1958, each full-time equivalent student had $237,778 in GNP behind him. By 1971, the expansion of higher education had occurred to such an extent that there was only $111,880 for each student.[5] It is obvious, that in constant purchasing power, enrollment and expenditures in higher education increased much more rapidly than did the gross national product of the United States. Although instructional costs per student increased only minimally, most of the additional resources were used to serve new student bodies, to develop new research facilities and activities, and to meet community responsibilities.[6] Community colleges were especially expansionist during this period, moving into community planning, coordination of educational services, and information dissemination as well as maintaining their traditional roles of transfer education and vocational training.

The immediate future of higher education is unlikely to include much expansion, and some schools, subject matters, and programs will certainly experience contraction. Economically weaker institutions of higher education, especially private ones with little tradition of academic excellence or without unique missions to attract students, are likely to suffer the most. Some will find it financially impossible to survive while others will continue to struggle by reducing academic standards and in effect admitting any paying student, retaining them at all costs, and graduating persons who can make only a pretext at having a college education. Public institutions also face significant challenges. As state legislatures consider the declining enrollments, funds will contract as will the number of faculty and other personnel. Instructional materials may be less readily available, and physical facilities may suffer from deferred maintenance. The major threat to higher education in the next 20 years is that of a decreasing quality. As the Carnegie Council on Policy Studies in Higher Education concludes, "the possible downward drift in quality, balance, integrity, dynamism, diversity, private initiative, and research capability is not only possible—it is quite likely."[7]

The demographic and social changes occurring today are not completely detrimental to higher education. In fact, there are numerous developments that have the potential to strengthen higher education and to provide a solid basis for future activities. Perhaps the most pervasive is the increased desire on the part of Americans for a higher quality of life. Most people appear to want to live a more healthy, happy, successful life. To do this they are demanding greater accessibility to sophisticated services that will help overcome deficiencies and develop their potential. Thus, greater numbers of specialized professionals are needed in such fields as medical specialties, allied health professions, social service, mental health, remedial education, long term care, community service, and information and referral. In these areas and others, additional services and assistance are provided to individuals and families in order that they may more effectively deal with their problems.

The desire for expanding the individual's potential is especially evident in the areas of hobbies, avocations, leisure time pursuits, and continuing education. Individuals are interested in developing their capacities in a variety of areas and are increasingly seeking out skilled or knowledgeable persons in order to achieve this. Educational institutions are in an advantageous position to assist in this progress through the training of specialists and through continuing education of the public. As greater specialization occurs, the need for continuing professional education, skill upgrading of practitioners, and development of new subspecialties occur through educational expansion.

One of the clearest insights to be drawn from educational surveys is that those people who have higher levels for formal education will continue to pursue more education. Thus, as the educational level of various professions increases, we can expect that recurrent education will expand and that specialized skills and knowledge will develop. We are beginning to witness a spiral of increasingly effective services, caused by effective professional education that will lead to an improved quality of life. Higher education is in a position to both assist and benefit from this development.

AGING OF EDUCATIONAL INSTITUTIONS

The processes of aging can be observed in social institutions such as colleges and universities. Although the authors have been able to locate no research on the meaning of aging for institutions of higher education and few sources even mention the topic, it is possible to observe some changes that occur over time and to suggest that they can be attributed to the aging of educational institutions. The measure of age of an institution cannot be years alone, just as chronological age does not suffice to measure the development/senescence of an individual. Obviously, Harvard, being nearly 350 years old, is not the most acutely affected of American institutions. Perhaps, a better way to view the age of institutions is by their adaptive capacity, their ability to recognize social and demographic changes, their willingness to design strategies for coping with them, and their success in mobilizing appropriate responses.

It is possible to see this adaptive process in three stages. First, institutions come to the realization that societal, technological, or demographic changes are occurring that have implications for them. This typically does not occur quickly; many institutions have not yet recognized the contemporary demographic and social changes we have noted. For instance Parker quotes the conclusions drawn by a Carnegie Commission survey of college and university presidents in 1976, "The aggregation of responses of the individual presidents yields a basically optimistic set of views. Fewer see growth in total enrollments in the future (1974-1980) than saw them in the past (1968-1974), but fewer also see declines. Many expect to solve present enrollment difficulties by attracting adult, off-campus, and evening students. Funding problems do not dominate the views of administrators in our survey. Growth remains the expectation—not decline."[8]

In the second stage, a reexamination is initiated in which the institution establishes committees, commissions, and study groups to examine the issues. Often these lead to the conclusion that the institution must be more efficient, more industrious, and more productive in its present activities in order to regain prosperity. This is basically a rejection of the realization that fundamental change has occurred and merely results in a more efficient pursuit of the original mission. Some institutions show this by reemphasizing liberal education, by attempting to recruit more merit scholars, or by deprecating the community colleges or others that respond too vigorously to the community and the society. It is seen in the movement that stresses a return to the basics of the past, to the old virtues, and to a resurgence of former values.

Finally, there occurs the third stage of adaptation, the "new goal" stage, where the institution slowly and (hopefully) perceptively reexamines its goals and purposes in light of the demographic and societal changes and eventually reaches consensus on the modifications it will make to achieve continued development. This may only occur with considerable internal struggle, and often results in personnel changes in the governing board, administrative officers, or faculty senate, but if the organization is to maintain itself or develop rather than decline, it must occur. Today, we can see this happening as some schools seek to address the current needs of the community, become responsive to the challenges of a postindustrial society, seek clearer values for social and behavioral science, examine the needs for new knowledge and complex inquiry, and modify curriculum to fit the changing age mix in a maturing society.

Institutional Adaptation

Institutions of higher education obviously find themselves at different stages of adaptation, and doubtless some will need to adapt less extensively and quickly than others. For instance, urban, state-supported colleges, those located in the west and southwest, and prestigious institutions, are likely to continue to recruit students without difficulty and may not have to modify their current practices or purposes extensively. They may continue to grow and expand with only a modest increase in their efficiency. On the other hand, private schools that are geographically isolated, have a lower status, and have limited endowment may find major adaptations necessary. The newest, smallest, least scholarly, and least vocational schools may suffer the most from the demographic changes.

Community colleges are likely to find adaptation the easiest. They are already extremely responsive to community needs and wants through community service programs, noncredit instruction, and courses offered away from the campus. Their orientation to the local community is likely to generate the support needed for further growth. Other colleges and universities, however, that do not have this orientation or an emphasis on vocationalism, may discover that their goal reorientation forces them to move closer to this model since it is much more attainable than attempting a replication of a Swarthmore, Stanford, or Harvard. The result of this reorientation for some schools may be that a lower quality education will result. Less prepared students may be admitted, and traditional academic standards may be sacrificed to maintain an adequate student body. Although community colleges have maintained an open admissions policy, they have experienced very high dropout rates. Liberal arts colleges attempting to recruit additional students are likely to find that retention is difficult and that supplementary tutoring and auxilliary services are needed. These cost money, which is not likely to be available, so little progress along these lines may be achieved.

Faculty Adaptation

The impact of aging on higher education can also be seen in the faculty and their position in the future. The Carnegie study[9] concluded that faculty members are the group that will suffer the most from the coming changes. This will occur because the total size of higher education faculty will remain static in the future and the median faculty age will continue to rise. By the year 2000, it is expected that there will be far more faculty members over the age of 65 than under 35.[10] The 1978 Amendments to the Age Discrimination in Employment Act will accentuate this trend. When they take effect in 1982, no faculty member may be retired because of age before reaching 70 years of age. In several states, laws already prohibit compulsory retirement, especially if inflation remains high and they see the need to maximize their retirement income by working longer. The result will be increasing tenure density at many colleges and universities. It has been estimated that in 1973, 65% of all faculty were tenured; by 1980, it was expected that 78% would be tenured.[11]

There are several implications of this development. Older professors have additional experience that is valuable in many ways. They are likely to be more visible nationally, to travel more to national societies and association meetings, to speak more widely, and to be able to see their specialization area within the wider context of human knowledge.[12]

On the other hand, there are some clear negative implications of increasing faculty age. Senior professors receive higher salaries than young or inexperienced faculty, often twice as much; costs to institutions of higher education are clearly higher than if there was a balance between young and older professors. As jobs become less prevalent, mobility among institutions is curtailed and faculty members spend most of their careers at one college or university. The implications of this are not clear although job change can be a source of stimulation. Some older faculty are likely to do less research and publish less. Their time is often committed to institutional and scholarly organizational maintenance and may not be available for new scholarship. They are farthest from their own education and so are potentially out of date with the latest developments in their fields. This may prove to be a threatening situation, and older faculty members may attempt to protect their positions by seeking the assistance of academic associations and professional unions. These are likely to become even more in evidence during times of economic difficulty or at particularly vulnerable institutions.[13]

This aging of the faculty has particular implications for younger persons who are preparing for or entering the professoriate. Obviously there will be fewer teaching positions for them, and those that are available will likely be outside the normal tenure stream. This occurs through the creation of lectureships, adjunct appointments, or short-term appointments that are not tenure eligible. It also occurs when departments and schools make it a policy to refuse tenure to virtually all assistant professors. Only the most extraordinary are granted this accolade. Thus, for those younger faculty who do secure positions, promotions become almost impossible and a series of short-term appointments and postdoctoral training experiences replace the normal progress through the ranks.

As in most other areas, it is the last hired who are first fired. Presently this impacts most heavily upon women, minorities, and the handicapped. The affirmative action programs of many institutions are jeopardized, and progress toward equality of opportunity for these new groups of faculty is threatened. Accompanying this loss, is the possibility that a whole generation of young scholars is being lost. With jobs appearing difficult to acquire and hard to hold, many younger persons are opting to use their training in professional service rather than academe. Their careers will help raise the quality of service and ultimately of life for the American people, but it detracts from the development of a group of developing scholars who will be the senior professors after the turn of the century.

Another threat of aging to an educational institution is that both individuals and curricula will become obsolescent. Faculty members may settle into service on committees, repetitively teaching courses and working on community projects rather than maintaining their knowledge within their specialization. Valuable as these activities are, they need supplementation through scholarly research, publication, and creative instruction. Faculty will not remain competitive with other institutions and with the corporate world if they do not regularly receive an infusion of new ideas and approaches. On the other hand, faculty may manage to stay up to date, but if they are in fields that are being supplanted by new scientific or professional specializations, institutional assistance may be needed for major curricular reorientation. Both individual and institutional self-renewal are required. This is where the challenge and the potential of higher education in the future lies.

Attempts to retire faculty early are one means of reducing the median faculty age and making room for young faculty members in new subject areas. It is interesting that a concern of many businesses and industries today is the early retirement of highly skilled professionals that leaves the employer with an insufficient skilled work force. In higher education we are concerned about the opposite trend, that faculty members may choose to remain in their teaching and research roles until they are forced to retire at age 70 or beyond. Perhaps both issues can be addressed through increased flexibility of retirement. By providing more options for part-time teaching, by offering increasingly lengthy sabbaticals, and by creating alternative assignments for the older faculty members, we may be able to develop a setting in which both the older and the younger person can continue to have effective roles and contribute to institutional viability.

If individual faculty members are willing to examine the way by which they can contribute best, if colleges and universities will improve their efficiency and reorient their goals, and if the public will continue its acceptance of education's value at any age, then higher education can emerge from the 1980s and 1990s with increased strength and vitality and the ability to face the additional challenges of the twenty-first century. These results will occur, however, only if means are found to take advantage of the aging of our faculty and institutions. The study of aging itself provides much hope for it has shown that persons can change behavior, can learn, and can develop regardless of their age. Institutions, likewise, can maintain their vitality and can undertake new challenges. What is needed is the will to do so, the supportive environment to facilitate it, and the clarity of vision to direct the new activities toward productive ends.

The following sections indicate some of the possible directions that may be chosen. They are certainly not the only ones, but they are available and offer substantial opportunities for both faculty members and institutions for further growth and progress.

GROWTH OF A NEW STUDENT CLIENTELE FOR HIGHER EDUCATION

One of the developing opportunities for institutions of higher education is the increased interest in education of some new groups of students that may partially offset the expected decline in the 18- to 24-year-olds. These groups are composed of students who are older than age 24; who have had their formal education interrupted and are now ready to return after a period of family or work responsibilities; who wish to increase their skills and knowledge; and who are nontraditional students— minority individuals, handicapped persons, and retirees who have both personal and vocational interests in continuing education.

Education has traditionally been seen as being relevant only for the young. Individuals would receive an inoculation of it during their youth, and this was expected to be sufficient to meet the challenges of adulthood and old age. Unfortunately, the inoculation view of education is no longer applicable (and probably never was) since social, technological, and personal change requires recurrent learning throughout the life span. There are several reasons for education for adults and older people becoming more common. First, the demographic changes noted earlier have massively increased the number of persons in this age group. According to the Census Bureau, the median age of persons in the United States is now over 30 years of age.[14] The 110+ million persons over age 30 provides a population for whom higher education is socially desirable and appropriate.

Second, through extensive research on cognitive and personality change over the life span, researchers have shown that adulthood is not a static period but one that includes developmental changes and a variety of decision points where education could be helpful. Individuals, even though they have completed extensive education, still find the need to understand new developmental tasks and seek insight through both formal study and personal experience. Other research has shown that healthy adults are able to continue learning regardless of their age. Intellectual capacity may show decline with the onset of chronic disease or approaching death, but most individuals maintain their verbal and knowledge abilities well into later life. This research supports the assumption that older people can use instruction to address their problems and continue psychological growth.

Third, more frequent and more pervasive career changes are occurring for adults in American society. Increasingly, people shift careers several times during their adult years and return to the classroom to acquire new knowledge and skill retooling to facilitate this process. Persons with higher levels of formal education generally have developed the learning skills necessary to succeed in many areas; they do not require huge amounts of education for admission to a new field. For instance, the master's degree in some areas requires relatively little in the way of specific undergraduate content. Rather the ability to complete an undergraduate program is sufficient recommendation for enrollment in the master's program.

Retirement may also be considered one of these points at which additional information will assist in adjustment. As greater numbers of persons reach retirement age and as more persons choose partial or flexible retirement, it will be increasingly useful to have organized information on available options and to understand more clearly the experiences that others have had. This can be provided through preparation for retirement education programs that assist people in planning for alternative work or leisure roles.

A fourth cause of increased interest in education results from the past educational accomplishment of today's adults. One of the clearest correlates of participation in education during the mature years is level of formal education. That is, those persons who have completed the most education are those who are most likely to continue their involvement.[15] Since the educational level of younger cohorts is higher than older ones, it is likely that a substantial increase in voluntary enrollment in education will occur in the years ahead. As persons become more familiar with colleges and universities and see them as available sources of aid to meet their needs, participation rises.[16]

The differences in cohort interest in education are shown in a recent national survey of the quality of life of 30-, 50-, and 90-year-olds.[17] Older persons indicated learning to be less important in determining the quality of their lives than did younger persons, but when reviewing the importance of learning to them at ages 30, 50, and 70, the oldest men reported no decline and women indicated an increase with age. This supports the general conclusion that the present older cohort has had less involvement in education and so has less interest in it. Younger cohorts have had more formal education; thus, they see it as more important. Differences between cohorts, then, are not age-related changes but a function of different experiences and historical impact.

In the same study, Flanagan reported that 70-year-olds viewed learning as one of their top three needs currently not being met.[18] This indicates a clear recognition on the part of many older people that instruction can be of assistance to them if it is offered at an appropriate time and place. It is likely to be perceived as a remedial function but one that can be developed in many institutions of higher education. If appropriately done, it can prove to be very popular with older people and to help them solve current problems and continue their personal development.

A fifth spur to educational participation is technological change. Individuals find that increased knowledge and skill are needed to improve their ability to function and to complete successfully. The instruction may be in the form of job retraining, involvement in consumer education, or in citizenship instruction designed to help individuals understand the complex and sensitive issues that confront each of us as voters and participants in the public business. The increased availability of leisure time also results in educational needs. Persons find that they benefit from the stimulation of education and use it to expand their appreciation of art, letters, and the individual. Physical exercise is currently an important topic, but other years have seen involvement of large numbers of persons in other recreation and education activities that benefit the esthetic life of the individual.

Sixth, higher levels of professional service also lead to increased educational participation. As the community realizes the need for services provided at a sophisticated level of competence, social workers, counselors, psychologists, educators, recreators, engineers, inspectors, librarians, nurses, physicians, and many other service providers decide that they can improve their service and their value through education. This is the area where the benefit may fall to graduate education. In the past, the master's degree has been sufficient preparation in several areas. Today, there is a move to increase the educational level of practitioners so that a greater number of Ph.D.'s may be absorbed by the job market providing an alternative opportunity for those who might have originally contemplated an academic career.

Changes Required

This new group of students will not replace the traditional student body without substantial adaptations by institutions of higher education. They have different interests, concerns, and goals for their educational programs and are likely to request several major changes on the part of colleges and universities. First, the new students often bring very specific goals for their education. Vague promises that the instruction will have usefulness in the future will not be as acceptable to them as will clear relevance to the work they want to do or the problem they are attempting to solve. Because credentials are likely to be perceived as less valuable by the new student, they may have less patience with traditional, formal requirements. They are more likely to draw upon their own experience and to apply that experience to the problem solving processes presented by the faculty. Thus, the adult student is typically more practically oriented, better grounded in real life experience, and more critical of theory that cannot be related to practice.

A second demand of the new student is likely to occur in course scheduling. They are generally responsible for families, jobs, homes, and other community roles; consequently, they will expect courses to be offered at times and in places accessible to them. Preferable times may be evenings or weekends, and a one-day session each month may prove more feasible than weekly class meetings. They may also prefer courses to be located close to their home or work; travel to campus simply because classrooms are available may not be acceptable to them. Community colleges, some without any facilities at all, are leading this development by offering courses in churches, union halls, community centers, store fronts, and a wide variety of other locations. As higher education institutions appeal to new students, this practice is likely to become more common.

A third consideration is that new students will probably attend classes part time. They will not progress through the program with the same speed as the traditional student and in fact may take twice or three times as long. They will expect that the program offered off-campus or in the evening will be available for several years, will be able to be completed in a variety of sequences, will require somewhat less time in on-campus library facilities, and will give some consideration to their informal learning on the job and in the family.

A fourth consideration occurs in the area of financial support. For some mature students returning to degree programs, costs may be prohibitive. Although the family may have a sufficient income, it may not perceive that it has funds to commit for tuition, travel, books, and the other expenses attached to serious study. Normal sources of funding for students may also not be available since the new students do not meet the "poverty" criteria required for national student loans or institutional financial aid. Thus, financing their education is likely to require alternative sources of funding and new ways of determining financial need.

A final consideration in recruiting the new student is that of maintaining their interest and involvement. For most of them, education is a voluntary endeavor. They attend courses because they want to, not because it is required by law, parents, or job. Thus, they must be continually convinced that they are learning, that the knowledge is useful, and that their goals are being achieved. In addition, many must be convinced that they are enjoying themselves since they see the hedonistic life all around them and frequently reject the premise that education in its most valuable form involves suffering. Thus, instructors compete for their attention with many recreational and entertainment forms and find it necessary to remind themselves that the new students vote with their feet, that is, they simply do not reappear if the course is uninteresting, poorly organized, or irrelevant to their needs. The student dropout rate is massive in some classes, often totaling over 50% in the course of a semester.

The mature student will not automatically turn to higher education as the institution to meet their educational needs. There are many other organizations that currently offer courses and workshops for them. These include libraries, churches, museums, unions, businesses, clubs, voluntary organizations, the military, government agencies, insurance companies, banks, investment firms, consulting groups, proprietary schools, and professional associations. Although these agencies and groups do not offer academic credit, they are currently providing much in the way of educational service, and enroll well over half of all adult participants.[19]

These potential problems notwithstanding, it appears that one way in which educational institutions can recoup the loss of traditional students inflicted by demographic trends is to begin addressing the needs of the new adult students. Education throughout the life span is a logical reaction to demographic change and provides the institution with one way to meet the various needs that adults have for continuing learning. By recruiting these individuals into existing programs and by designing new instructional endeavors specifically for them, institutions of higher education have the opportunity to continue their growth and move to a new level of service to the community and the nation.

INSTRUCTION OF OLDER PEOPLE IN HIGHER EDUCATION

Persons beyond retirement age have not been major participants in educational programs offered by colleges and universities. However, they are one of the largest groups of potential new clientele for institutions of higher education and may have both the available time and resources to pursue such an undertaking. For the most part, they have been uninterested or unwilling to make the commitment to educational participation. This may be less true in the future. Since educational participation has been shown to be associated with higher levels of health and socioeconomic status, it can be expected that future groups will be more likely to participate. Each succeeding cohort of older people has more formal education, higher income, better health, and higher status occupations,[20] all characteristics that have been shown to be positively correlated with adult education participation.

Older people have a variety of interests and needs that can be met through education. Howard Y. McClusky[21] has identified the needs as 1) coping: the need for skills to address current problems and issues; 2) expressive: the need for growth and enjoyment; 3) influence: the need to affect one's own life and those of others; 4) contributive: the need to help others; and 5) transcendence: the need to accept physical aging and eventual death. Individuals obviously vary as to the intensity with which the needs affect them, but it is likely that many older people feel some of these weaknesses that could be addressed through well-planned instructional programs.

Education for older people then can be viewed as having several purposes. James E. Birren and Diane Woodruff[22] suggested that education for older persons can serve a remedial function to raise the older persons to an adequate level of functioning in personal, vocational, or social situations; that education can provide enrichment, allowing for the continuing growth and development of the individual in esthetic, psychological, and spiritual areas; and that education can be used as prevention, to develop the motivation and skills necessary to anticipate the problems of old age and to address them before they reach crisis proportions. K. Warner Schaie and Joyce Parr Schaie[23] suggested that educational purposes include an understanding of the changes that occur in the body and behavior as a result of aging: a comprehension of the technological and social changes that affect all of us; the development of new skills for coping with social and personal change; the refinement of old skills and the development of new ones for occupational purposes; and the development of new occupational roles. Thus, there are many purposes and values of education for older people.

Instructional Accommodations

In designing instruction for older people, there are some special adaptations that need to be made if the learning is to be as effective as possible. Although there is ample research to assure us that learning is possible for most people regardless of their age, the means by which people learn best may change somewhat in later life. Thus, the instructor of a group of older students will need to have some awareness of these changes and will be well advised to modify the traditional instructional methods to facilitate the most effective learning by this group.

The first adaptation that has been shown to be effective is to use student-centered instruction. This is often described as an andragogical approach, one designed for adults rather than children. The distinctions between andragogy and pedagogy may be summarized by suggesting that the pedagogical view of education emphasizes the transmission of knowledge from teacher to student. This philosophical orientation is not appropriate since adults have different perceptions and values for specific knowledge. Andragogy emphasizes an alternative position, that the development of learning skills and the continuing practice of those skills throughout the lifetime is the purpose of education.

Developed and refined by Malcolm Knowles,[24] andragogy emphasizes the relationship between the teacher and the learner and encourages the facilitation of a cooperative planning, instruction, and evaluation climate that is most supportive, conducive to learning, and best received by adults. Andragogy assumes that adults are volunteers for learning, i.e., they are not required by law or custom to participate in formal learning situations but do so because they find it of interest or value. Thus, they are able to choose to leave the learning setting at any time, especially when they find that they are not learning the type or level of content they desire.

The flexibility of the instructor is the key to the effective development of andragogical instruction. He or she must be able to share with the adult students the responsibility for the learning and must be conscious of the feelings that the learners have about both the content and the process.[25] The andragogical approach will not be preferred by every older person, but it is well accepted by the vast majority and can be effectively applied by the informed instructor.

Other instructional insights come from laboratory research on the learning skills and behaviors of older people. Although much research has been conducted in this area, implications will be drawn in only three areas—pacing, interference, and cautiousness. The studies have shown that pacing is extremely important when teaching older people. They perform less well on a learning task when it must be completed under the pressure of time.[26] Older people consistently learn more successfully when they are provided additional time both to take in the information and to retrieve the answer. Although they may perform less well than younger people on timed exercises, most of the learning deficit will disappear when the older learner can control the pace of learning. Thus, a slow, relaxed atmosphere with individualized pacing when possible is desired.

Interference can also be a major hindrance to older people's learning. This can occur when there is a conflict between knowledge already acquired and the knowledge to be learned, between two learning tasks undertaken at the same time, and when subsequent learning interferes with the material taught. The instructor can compensate for this potential problem by minimizing conflicts between new and current information, concentrating on one learning task at a time, and spacing the learning experiences so that they do not infringe upon each other.[27]

Cautiousness is another factor that may interfere with effective learning. In general, there appears to be an increase in the likelihood of nonresponse to questions with increasing age. This indicates that older people are less willing to guess when they are not sure; they are less likely to take a chance or to act impulsively. In a teaching setting, the result may be that participation is reduced, that new ideas will have to be explored carefully, and that the threats of performance evaluation in the classroom must be avoided. The instructor, then, will need to develop a supportive approach and to reduce criticism to a minimal level in order to encourage the older persons to overcome their cautiousness.

Changes in vision and hearing also provide the need for adaptation in teaching a group of older people. Since both visual and auditory acuity may decline in some persons from middle age, most older people experience some difficulty in situations in which lighting is poor or in which background noise is present. The instructor will need to be sure that lighting is especially good and not glaring; that high contrast is used in printed and chalkboard materials; and the speaker is visible, speaks loudly, and uses the lower frequencies of pitch in presenting materials; and that checks are made frequently to assure that the material is being received and understood by the older participants.

The development of instruction for older people will cause the need for substantial adjustments not only in the classroom but in administrative areas also. Since older people have not been major participants in educational programs in the past, active recruitment will need to be undertaken. This will probably be most effective when it is directed toward existing groups and organizations of older people since their membership is most likely to respond positively. Admission and registration procedures will need to be abbreviated or avoided to reduce confusion and provide easy entry for older students. Both academic and professional counseling will be needed by some older participants since their understanding of the educational system may be based upon experience of many decades ago. To assure that these are undertaken in an appropriate manner, advisory groups from the local area may be used to identify problem areas, raise the visibility of the program, and involve volunteer assistance.

Although there are many additional considerations when an educational institution begins an instructional program specifically for older persons or attempts to integrate them into existing programs, the rewards for both the individual student and the institution can be great. Examples can be seen in the burgeoning Elderhostel program that nationally is serving thousands of older students on hundreds of college campuses and in community colleges that are now enrolling thousands of older adults per semester in both new and existing courses. The enthusiasm is both infectious and exhilarating in these programs. The future is likely to see an increasing number of educational institutions developing instruction for older people, and larger percentages of the 24 million older persons participating in them. By itself, this will probably not solve the financial problems of higher education, but it does provide the elements for new statements of purpose and offers the potential for building an additional rationale for instructional programs that may be funded from alternative sources.

At the present time, most of us have little hesitation about investing in education early in life. It is generally considered a necessity for the development of social and personal skills required for successful living. What remains to be accepted is the resolve to invest in education of the value of continuing education through the life span, there would be no shortage of students or support for instructional programs. Perhaps this will occur in the future, but conscious effort will be needed to expand the awareness of its value and to help educational institutions reorient their purposes and programs. That is the goal toward which we must strive and the end that will provide the best means of revitalizing higher education.

INSTRUCTION IN GERONTOLOGY

The aging of the American population has encouraged many researchers to examine the causes and results of aging. Over the past 50 years a great amount of knowledge has accumulated that is now being used to help students understand the processes of aging and the implications for individuals and societies. This knowledge is increasingly available in texts and reports and is the subject of study in many institutions of higher education. Initially it was incorporated into courses in the traditional disciplines and professions, but in the past ten years, programs of gerontology instruction culminating in a degree, major, minor, certificate, or specialization have been developed.

Instruction in gerontology has emerged for a variety of reasons. The demographic changes described earlier certainly are a major cause, but others such as the increasing visibility and assertiveness of older persons and their organizations have also added impetus. Concerns about the quality of life for persons in all age ranges have led to the development of health, social service, recreation, education, and mental health programs offered by a multitude of agencies and institutions. This has created the need for personnel who are knowledgeable about aging and older people and are able to administer, plan, and conduct these programs. Thus, professional instruction has developed to prepare individuals for service positions and to sensitize policy makers to the needs of older people.

Instruction in gerontology is now relatively pervasive in higher education but is not easy to describe in its present state. Because some programs developed from a professional service orientation, while others came from a research base, and others from a liberal arts position, it is necessary to describe some categories of gerontology instruction today, rather than attempt to combine it into one overall description. We will use three categories for this purpose.

The first orientation of gerontology instruction is liberal education. It emphasizes the acquisition of a general understanding of the processes of aging process and the development of appropriate attitudes rather than the development of skills or behaviors. It is a broad, interdisciplinary approach to the field and provides the student with an overview of the historical, philosophical, scientific, and social context of aging. This orientation to gerontology is most frequently found at the undergraduate level and is generally structured so that courses are offered throughout the various departments of the institution. Frequently the students completing the program receive a minor or certificate in gerontology; less often a major or degree in the field is awarded. In general, administrative structures are modest and the program operates informally with each department contributing its perspective on aging.

The second approach is scientific gerontology education. Its general orientation is to describe and explain on an empirical basis the processes of aging. It emphasizes methodological rigor and results in a greater depth of knowledge than does the liberal approach. In essence, it is a continuing search for understanding the nature of aging, but a search that is oriented toward finding specific data and organizing them into understandable categories. Scientific gerontology instruction is most frequently offered at the doctoral level and seldom involves the awarding of a degree in gerontology. Rather, the degree would be in one of the disciplines and the course work would be taken within one department with a modest amount of interdisciplinary exposure. No administrative structures other than that of the host department are usually involved.

The third gerontology education orientation is referred to as professional education. This is the attempt to apply current knowledge to solve the practical problems of the older cohort. Persons completing the program of instruction expect to be considered professionals who base their practice on the best of theory and scientific knowledge. Professional gerontology instruction is generally offered at the master's degree level although it is occasionally found in undergraduate programs. It is more likely than other instruction to result in a degree in gerontology and to have a more formal administrative structure such as an institute, center, or department of gerontology.[28]

Extent of Gerontology Education

The expansion of gerontology instructional programs has come primarily in the social science and professional fields. Christopher R. Bolton[29] analyzed a national directory that included data on 219 programs of gerontology instruction in 1976. He reported that more than half of all credit courses in gerontology were offered by universities, that over 70% occurred within traditional departments, that academic majors were the most common designation although they amounted to less than 25% of the total credentials or outcomes, and that programs were approximately evenly divided between undergraduate and graduate offerings. There is much evidence that instructional programs in gerontology have continued to grow rapidly since that time and that the total may now be close to double what it was in 1976.

This may appear to be significant growth and an indication of the interest higher education has shown in aging. It does, however, leave much to be accomplished. Most gerontologists would assert that each person in the human services area should have some general knowledge about aging and the ways by which services to older people can be most effectively developed. This clearly is not happening today. In a recent survey of nearly 100 professional schools and departments on the west coast, Birren and Ira S. Hirschfield[30] reported that 70% of the professional departments and schools surveyed had no required course offering containing any gerontological content. Nursing and social work schools had the most gerontology instruction, but others such as public administration, medicine, adult education, counselor education, dentistry, and law had very little current instruction and few plans to develop it. From these data, gerontologists have argued that there exists a need to develop separate gerontology instructional programs and degrees apart from other professional areas since there is so little intention on their part to cover the knowledge and skill needed to provide service to older clients. The emerging gerontology degree programs are providing the beginnings of a professional field of gerontology.

Currently there are no standards for the development or evaluation of gerontology instructional programs. If accreditation is to exist, it will occur several years in the future as there are currently no generally accepted criteria for assessing the quality of gerontology programs. The Western Gerontological Society[31] has developed some proposed definitions and guidelines for gerontology instruction and has suggested quantitative measures of program content. The Association for Gerontology in Higher Education, in cooperation with the Gerontological Society,[32] has published the results of its study on curriculum guidelines for several types and levels of programs. These, however, are the only available sources of criteria for evaluating a program and neither has been available long enough to have been used in this manner.

The future of gerontology education is unclear at this time. Although growth has occurred rapidly in the past decade, some persons suggest that the number of degree programs may be reaching a peak. On the other hand, it seems reasonable to suggest that the expansion of gerontology courses within undergraduate programs in a variety of disciplines will continue for some time to come. It is likely that within another decade most undergraduate students will receive some instruction on the processes of aging during their postsecondary education. As the visibility of the older population increases, a parallel expansion will occur within the gerontology offerings of higher education.

Issues in Gerontology Instruction

There are several issues that will confront gerontology educators in the next few years. Most administrators and faculty agree that a wide diversity of program types, content emphases, administrative structures, credentials, and instructional outcomes currently exist. This diversity is likely to continue for several years until a consensus emerges about the most appropriate models for gerontology instruction. The question facing the field is not how to identify the one best model, but how to gain consensus on the several models—liberal education, professional education, and scientific education. These models will begin to answer such questions as: Under what conditions is gerontology education best taught in depth, in breadth? Should gerontology education be organized as a separate field of study or incorporated into existing professions and disciplines? Should the result of gerontology instruction be the development of skills or of knowledge? Decisions on these and other fundamental questions will need to be reached in the years ahead in order to clarify the direction(s) to be taken by instructional programs.

It is our belief that professional gerontology education will continue to develop and that occupational roles for gerontologists will expand. There are four major considerations facing professional gerontology education today whose resolution will in many ways determine the parameters of the field in the future. These are the determination of appropriate content for various emphases and levels of instruction, the identification of professional skills, the development of a job market for gerontologists, and the expansion of research on professional practice.

The most pressing issue in gerontology education today is the determination of which content should be taught to which students. A large amount of knowledge is available about the social, psychological, physical, biological, economic, political, religious, and service aspects of gerontology. It is no longer possible to teach a gerontology course and include a sample of everything that is known. Decisions on content must be based on student level and the purpose of the instruction. To date there is little agreement on which content is most appropriate for which levels, which texts are most useful for which emphases, or which instructional methodology will provide the desired outcomes. Continued consideration of the available options and the applicability of these to specific program needs will be required before we can be sure that we are teaching the most important content to each group of students.

One implication of this concern may be seen in the area of articulation. Currently, gerontology instruction is offered at the lower division, upper division, master's degree, and doctoral levels of instruction. There are a few articulation agreements among these levels and little assurance that a sophomore course provides an appropriate background for a master's degree course. The need exists for faculty to clarify the content and outcomes of their instruction and to convey this to others so that knowledge ladders can be built within the field.

The second issue involves identification of skills that a professional gerontologist should have. Since gerontology is multidisciplinary in its knowledge base, it is possible to select and develop a large number of skill outcomes. For instance, skills in interpersonal communication, counseling, administration, planning, program development, education, social service, evaluation, and supervision may be emphasized. It remains to be decided which, if any of these, are the most appropriate and at what level of sophistication the skills will be achieved. If gerontology is to fulfill its promise of becoming a profession, skills clarification and definition will be expected.

The third issue also faces the development of a professional focus in gerontology education. This relates to the clarification of the occupational roles for gerontologists. At the present time there are a variety of roles and employers utilizing the skills and knowledge of gerontology graduates. Additional insight and decisions are needed in order to define the several roles of a professional gerontologist. These need to be closely coordinated with gerontology instruction and should be defined so that they do not compete with other professional fields. These roles will be developed from an examination of the current and prospective services and policies being designed for older people. This is likely to develop occupational roles in several areas such as direct service, administration, health planning and coordination, and older worker management and retraining. Time and effort will need to be devoted to clarifying these roles, determining the education necessary for them, and legitimizing them through collective agreement or legislation. This process is beginning now as new jobs are created and gerontology knowledge is identified as a prerequisite. Increased specification will be required in order to assure that the relationship between the instruction and the practice is precise.

Finally, a future challenge to gerontology education will occur in the development of research paradigms that will document the impact of education gerontologists on the lives of older people. Since professional gerontology education is designed expressly to assist older people in improving the quality of their lives, it will be necessary to show its impact in community and institutional settings. We must be able to support our beliefs that gerontology education is of value by identifying the changes that occur in the lives of older people because of the increased quality of services gerontologists provide and the improved public policies that result from our graduates' efforts.

SUMMARY AND CONCLUSION

The changing demographic and social structure of American society is exerting substantial pressure on institutions of higher education. As the number of traditional age students declines, colleges and universities are faced with reduced enrollments and a rapid increase in the age and tenure density of the faculty. Unless some currently unforeseen force intervenes, it is likely that many institutions of higher education will face a crisis in the coming decade—that of closing their doors or substantially redirecting their activities.

This redirection provides an exciting opportunity for colleges and universities to reexamine their purpose and objectives and to establish new goals for the future. So long as the social and demographic changes are ignored, the future will lead to increased competition, reduced standards, and declining prosperity. By seeking new missions, new student audiences, and faculty renewal, we can encourage continued growth and public support.

There are at least four areas where opportunities are currently present; these are the expansion of educational programs to include new students, the development of auxilliary services to older persons, the cultivation of gerontology instruction, and the renewal of faculty.

The magnitude of the demographic changes make it mandatory for educational institutions to adapt their programs for new student groups. Middle-aged and older persons are two large groups that can be of extreme importance to colleges and universities. Development of new programs of study, continuing education opportunities, and professional upgrading will make higher education more relevant to these groups and will not only increase their enrollment but will increase the level of community support when expanded funding from public sources is required. They have been ignored too long and a conscious, planned, and public strategy must be developed to involve them. This will obviously require modification of admission and advisement approaches. These adults will not tolerate the inefficiency and red tape that traditional students have been forced to suffer. They will demand more efficient and more courteous service before they will undertake classroom participation.

Second, colleges and universities have the opportunity to develop additional services and activities that will benefit older people and their families. This may be as simple as conducting preparation for retirement programs for individuals in their communities, or it may involve the development and application of sophisticated policy analysis and research designed to impact the public policy process through legislative hearings and project evaluation. Many colleges and universities are now involved in some of these ancillary activities, e.g., information and referral services, Elderhostel instruction, nutrition programs, activity centers, emeriti programs, counseling services, and housing for the elderly. The closer relationship between most institutions of higher education and the community will become increasingly common and mutually supportive as time passes. In those cases where this does not occur, the college or university will need to rely on the highest of academic visibility and respectability in order to stand outside the continuing scrutiny of the community.

The third opportunity lies in the development of instruction in gerontology. As the number of older people grows, increasing interest will be directed toward understanding this older group. Professional and vocational training may be initiated at all levels of instruction. This may occur as a separate degree or certificate program or as an emphasis within such degree programs as social work, medicine, nursing, counseling, clinical psychology, business administration, education, recreation, occupational therapy, physical therapy, public health, dentistry, and optometry. Research training in aging is also likely to expand as federal agencies and philanthropic foundations direct more of their resources toward understanding the process of aging. This is likely to occur in many of the disciplines and will begin the redirection of research toward greater concern for later life.

Finally, educational institutions have the opportunity to design programs of renewal of their faculty and curricula in order to achieve continued vitalization of the institution. The university has been a leader over the decades in providing sabbaticals for faculty growth and renewal. They will need to be expanded to include both internal and external programs for faculty retraining and collective review of the curricular trends. If undertaken successfully, colleges and universities can look toward the future with increased hope and confidence. The opportunities are there, but as with all aging, they are confounded by problems and difficulties. It is easier to decry the difficulty than to confront it, but through hard work and perceptive planning, it is possible to predict a future as good as the past for institutions of higher education.

NOTES

1.   Malcolm G. Scully, "Carnegie Panel Says Enrollment Declines Will Create a 'New Academic Revolution,'" *The Chronicle of Higher Education*, XIX (January 28, 1980), p. 11.

2.   Scully, "Carnegie Panel," p. 1.

3.   Gail Thain Parker, *The Writing on the Wall* (New York: Simon and Schuster, 1979), p. 42.

4.   Ibid.

5.   David D. Henry, *Challenges Past: Challenges Present* (San Francisco: Jossey-Bass, 1975), p. 151.

6.   Ibid.

7.   Scully, "Carnegie Panel," p. 11.

8.   Parker, *Writing on the Wall*, p. 47.

9.   Scully, "Carnegie Panel," p. 11.

10.   Ibid.

11.   Parker, *Writing on the Wall*, p. 46.

12.   Wilbert J. McKeachie, "Perspectives from Psychology: Financial Incentives Are Ineffective for Faculty," in *Academic Rewards in Higher Education*, ed. by D. R. Lewis and W. E. Becker, Jr. (Cambridge, MA: Ballinger Publishing Co., 1979), p. 14.

13.   Richard Chait and Andrew T. Ford, "Affirmative Action, Tenure, and Unionization," in *Lifelong Learners: A New Clientele for Higher Education*, ed. by Dyckman W. Vermilye (San Francisco: Jossey-Bass, 1974), p. 127.

14.   "U.S. Median Age Tops Thirty for Second Time in History," *Los Angeles Times*, sec. 1 (June 22, 1980), p. 1 and p. 11.

15.   J. W. C. Johnstone and R. J. Rivera, *Volunteers for Learning* (Chicago: Aldine Press, 1965), p. 96.

16.   J. O. Hooper and G. B. March, "A Study of Older Students Attending University Classes," *Educational Gerontology*, III (October-December 1978), p. 327.

17.   John C. Flanagan, *Identifying Opportunities for Improving the Quality of Life of Older Age Groups* (Palo Alto, CA: American Institutes for Research, 1979).

18.   Ibid., p. 20.

19.   National Center for Education Statistics, *Participation in Adult Education, Final Report, 1972* (Washington, DC: U.S. Department of Health, Education and Welfare, 1976).

20.   Erdman Palmore, "The Future Status of the Aged," *The Gerontologist*, XVI (August 1976), p. 297-302.

21.   Howard Y. McClusky, "Education for Aging: The Scope of the Field and Perspectives for the Future," in *Education for the Aging*, ed. by S. M. Grabowski and W. D. Mason (Syracuse, NY: ERIC Clearinghouse on Adult Education, n.d.), pp. 332-38.

22.   James E. Birren and Diana Woodruff, "Human Development Over the Life Span Through Education," in *Life Span Developmental Psychology*, ed. by Paul Baltes and K. Warner Schaie (New York: Academic Press, 1973), pp. 318-23.

23.   K. Warner Schaie and Joyce Parr Schaie, "Intellectual Development," in *The Future American College*, ed. by A. W. Chickering (San Francisco: Jossey-Bass, in press).

24.   Malcolm S. Knowles, *The Modern Practice of Adult Education* (New York: Association Press, 1970), p. 37.

25.   Sheldon L. Meyer, "Andragogy and the Adult Learner," *Educational Gerontology*, II (April-June 1977), p. 117.

26.   R. E. Canestrari, Jr., "Paced and Self-Paced Learning in Young and Elderly Adults," *Journal of Gerontology*, XVIII (April 1963), p. 167.

27.   D. Arenberg and E. A. Robertson, "The Older Individual as a Learner," in *Education for the Aging*, ed. by S. M. Grabowski and W. D. Mason (Syracuse, NY: ERIC Clearinghouse on Adult Education, n.d.).

28.   David A. Peterson and Christopher R. Bolton, *Gerontology Instruction in Higher Education* (New York: Springer Publishing, 1980), pp. 60-71.

29.   Christopher R. Bolton, *Gerontology Education in the United States: A Research Report* (Omaha, NE: University of Nebraska, 1978).

30.   James E. Birren and Ira S. Hirschfield, "The Emergence of Gerontology in Higher Education in America," in *Gerontology in Higher Education*, ed. by Harvey L. Sterns, et al. (Belmont, CA: Wadsworth Publishing Co., 1979), p. 3.

31.   Western Gerontological Society Education Committee, "Draft Standards and Guidelines," *Generations*, III (Summer 1978), pp. 43-51.

32.   Harold Johnson, et al., "Foundations for Gerontological Education," *The Gerontologist*, XX (June 1980).

BIBLIOGRAPHY

Arenberg, D., and Robertson, E. A. "The Older Individual as a Learner," in *Education for the Aging*. Ed. by S. M. Grabowski and W. D. Mason. Syracuse, NY: ERIC Clearinghouse on Adult Education, n.d.

Birren, J. E., and Hirschfield, I. S. "The Emergence of Gerontology in Higher Education in America," in *Gerontology in Higher Education*. Ed. by Harvey L. Sterns, et al. Belmont, CA: Wadsworth Publishing Co., 1979.

Birren, J. E., and Woodruff, D. "Human Development Over the Life Span Through Education," in *Life Span Developmental Psychology*. Ed. by P. Baltes and K. W. Schaie. New York: Academic Press, 1973.

Bolton, C. R. *Gerontology Education in the United States: A Research Report*. Omaha, NE: University of Nebraska, 1978.

Canestrari, R. E., Jr. "Paced and Self-Paced Learning in Young and Elderly Adults." *Journal of Gerontology*, 18 (April 1963), pp. 165-68.

Chait, R., and Ford, A. T. "Affirmative Action, Tenure, and Unionization," in *Lifelong Learners: A New Clientele for Higher Education*. Ed. by D. W. Vermilye. San Francisco: Jossey-Bass, 1974.

Flanagan, J. C. *Identifying Opportunities for Improving the Quality of Life of Older Age Groups*. Palo Alto, CA: American Institutes for Research, 1979.

Henry, D. D. *Challenges Past: Challenges Present*. San Francisco: Jossey-Bass, 1975.

Hooper, J. O., and March, G. B. "A Study of Older Students Attending University Classes." *Educational Gerontology*, 3 (October-December 1978), pp. 321-30.

Johnson, H., et al. "Foundations for Gerontological Education." *The Gerontologist*, 20 (June 1980).

Johnson, J. W. C., and Rivera, R. J. *Volunteers for Learning*. Chicago: Aldine Press, 1965.

Knowles, M. S. *The Modern Practice of Adult Education*. New York: Association Press, 1970.

McClusky, H. Y. "Education for Aging: The Scope of the Field and Perspectives for the Future," in *Education for the Aging*. Ed. by S. M. Grabowski and W. D. Mason. Syracuse, NY: ERIC Clearinghouse on Adult Education, n.d.

McKeachie, W. J. "Perspectives from Psychology: Financial Incentives Are Ineffective for Faculty," in *Academic Rewards in Higher Education*. Ed. by D. R. Lewis and W. E. Becker, Jr. Cambridge, MA: Ballinger Publishing, 1979.

Meyer, S. L. "Andragogy and the Adult Learner." *Educational Gerontology*, 2 (April-June 1977), pp. 115-22.

National Center for Education Statistics. *Participation in Adult Education, Final Report, 1972*. Washington, DC: U.S. Department of Health, Education and Welfare, 1976.

Palmore, E. "The Future Status of the Aged." *The Gerontologist*, 16 (August 1976), pp. 297-302.

Parker, G. T. *The Writing on the Wall*. New York: Simon and Schuster, 1979.

Peterson, D. A., and Bolton, C. R. *Gerontology Instruction in Higher Education*. New York: Springer Publishing, 1980.

Schaie, K. W., and Schaie, J. P. "Intellectual Development," in *The Future American College*. Ed. by A. W. Chickering. San Francisco: Jossey-Bass, in press.

Scully, M. G. "Carnegie Panel Says Enrollment Declines Will Create a 'New Academic Revolution.'" *The Chronicle of Higher Education*, 19 (January 28, 1980), p. 11.

"U.S. Median Age Tops Thirty for Second Time in History." *Los Angeles Times*, sec. 1 (June 22, 1980), p. 1 and p. 11.

Western Gerontological Society Education Committee. "Draft Standards and Guidelines." *Generations*, 3 (Summer 1978), pp. 43-51.

PROVIDING FOR A LEARNING SOCIETY—
CONTINUING EDUCATION*

by
Rosalind K. Loring

Dean, School of Continuing Education
University of Southern California

Continuing education is the structured learning experience planned for adults with the goal of producing change in the learner's knowledge, attitudes, values, skills, appreciation, awareness, and/or general capabilities and understanding. In the United States that means other than basic literacy; in fact, we typically intend postsecondary school level for both the student and program content. Thus the term covers education for credit and noncredit; career and leisure; pre-service and in-service; community needs and personal desires; and a multiplicity of methods of instruction and relationships between teacher and student as well as alternatives in location and timing. It consists of courses and organized educational activities other than those taken by full-time students in a continuous learning pattern of attendance in educational institutions. The latter criteria refer to those who define themselves not primarily as student but as worker, parent, community leader, veteran, etc.

In a brief paper it is impossible to cover so wide a field completely. Thus, this paper concentrates on purposes, funding, philosophy, and the span of continuing education in funding. A greater, yet concise, examination is given to data and trends as well as to the influence of government. Finally, the importance of institutional policies and procedures and local institutional options, issues related to adult higher education students, and a brief look at changing faculty scenarios are presented.

COLLEGE AND UNIVERSITY EXTENSION
AND CONTINUING EDUCATION

Universities have been involved in continuing education longer than any other educational institution. Starting with Harper at the University of Chicago in 1892 and Van Hise at the University of Wisconsin, a history of making ideas into reality can be traced back to antecedents like the Lyceum and Chautauqua movements of the nineteenth century. Extending the resources of the university to more people through new applications has been the organizing principle.

*Sections of this paper are adapted from an unpublished manuscript, *The Continuing Education Universe—USA*, presented by Rosalind K. Loring as an address at the Salzburg Seminar on Continuing Education, Session 185, August 1978.

If we examine the private University of Southern California's College of Continuing Education and the public University of California, Los Angeles, Extension Division, we will find amazing similarity in revenue sources, pricing policies, and the fact that both are self-supporting. In fact, continuing education in higher education across the nation receives no or low subsidies in contrast to the regular youth-oriented programs. This principle is virtually universal and rests on at least two premises. First, education for the adult community is above and beyond the original purposes of most institutions—a service for which adults are expected to pay. Second, adults are stereotyped as being a group able to pay, but of course, there are subgroups that cannot. I will return to these policy issues later. It is known that tuition and fees range from $10 to over $1,000 for a single course. A splendid example of institutional goals carried into action and of a national leader in the field is Michigan State University (MSU), which has earned a reputation for excellence in continuing education using multiple delivery systems. MSU has achieved statewide coverage consistent with its ambitious and comprehensive goals:

> These activities reflect the basic philosophy that a state university should serve all the people. They are designed to help people learn to do their jobs better, to lead more useful lives, to challenge active minds, to employ leisure time more wisely, and to become better citizens in addition to assisting in attaining of advanced degrees. Some programs serve people indirectly by helping to improve government agencies, social service and welfare organizations and special interest groups in such fields as health, labor, business and environment.[1]

There is no single model for university and college continuing education. Associated with the same campus can easily be a mixture of degree, certificate, and nondegree programs; formal and informal instruction; traditional and nontraditional curricula; on-campus and off-campus locations for learning; credit, noncredit, and continuing education units; and lower division, upper division, graduate, postgraduate, and continuing professional education.

Several universities and colleges have gained a reputation for introducing new methodology or for using familiar procedures in a noteworthy manner:

- New York's Empire State College was a pioneer with its external degrees.

- C. W. Post College was among the first to promote the "weekend college."

- Adelphi University gained notice for its "College on Wheels" offerings on commuter trains.

- The University of Mid-America has brought attention to the use of media across several states in cooperation with a number of institutions.

- Dartmouth College has promoted its alumni institutes for intensive summer studies among friends and families.

- Thanks to the Kellogg Foundation, there are the residential continuing education conference centers across the land.

- There is the Program Afloat for College Education where professors from six institutions join with the Navy in sailing the seas and teaching classes.

- The University of Maryland, University of Southern California, Boston University, and others have extended their courses to locations around the globe.

- Alongside general extension, Agricultural Extension operates out of our land-grant colleges and universities in every state.

This list could go on and on, but the message would still be one of responsiveness to institutional understanding of student needs. Not all institutions respond in the same manner. Undeniable institutional stratification exist in America with universities ranking first, four-year colleges second, and community colleges next in terms of academic reputation, admission requirements, and theoretical versus practical curricular orientations. But how could there be diversity without differences? While housed in institutions, Extension and Continuing Education Divisions are typically separated administratively from the regular, youth-oriented, day programs. This bifurcation allows for autonomy in roles. For example, many universities with selective admissions to their regular programs have an evening program that admits students who would not have access otherwise and who then have an opportunity to demonstrate their academic capabilities.

While continuing education at universities usually adheres to a voluntary student philosophy, many are undergoing changes to keep up with the times. For example, in a number of occupational fields there is growing pressure to move continuing education for professionals from a voluntary to a mandatory activity. The former recommendations of professional associations are being replaced by state requirements for continuing education. Several states are not satisfied that credentials for entry into a profession and the initial award of a license are permanently sufficient. Several states legally demand proof of continuing education from architects, certified public accountants, dentists, engineers, lawyers, licensed practical nurses, registered nurses, nursing home administrators, optometrists, pharmacists, physical therapists, physicians, podiatrists, psychologists, real estate personnel, and veterinarians. These 16 professions are being regulated in the public interest.

> The most heavily regulated profession is optometry, followed by nursing home administrators, podiatrists, CPA's and physicians, while the least regulated professions are engineers, architects, physical therapists and dentists.[2]

Yet this is an area that has sparked controversy for it is an arena where state mandates, professional prerogative, public rights, and institutional priorities collide. The quality of the resolution is critical. Decisions have an impact on the field and the nation since there are over 500 occupational and professional licenses issued in our nation. While a steady supply of students may be welcome, the attendant responsibilities are awesome, and there is growing concern about the desirability of mandatory education of adults.

Approximately 1,250 universities and four-year colleges offer noncredit continuing education for a total of about 4,650,000 registrations (not individuals). A forthcoming study will document credit offerings and will presumably show a figure higher than 1,250 since a number of four-year colleges and universities offer only credit classes through evening and off-campus classes. Despite the magnitude of noncredit registrations, the most recent growth in enrollments documents the perception by adult students that credits, degrees, and certificates are still the mainstays of socioeconomic mobility.

ENROLLMENT PATTERNS

It is common knowledge that the best source of continuing education statistics is the U.S. National Center for Education Statistics (NCES). Therefore, much of the content of this section relies on NCES documentation to depict the facts and trends in enrollment. Comparisons of change in youth and adult matriculation are dramatic.

In 1972, 29 percent of those age 18 and over enrolled in college were over 24 years old. By 1978, the proportion had risen to 33 percent. Enrollment of 18-to-23-year-olds peaked in 1976 at 115 percent of the number enrolled in 1972, but enrollment of older students grew at a much faster rate. In 1977, enrollment of persons over age 24 was 162 percent of the 1972 figure, dropping to 152 percent in 1978. Most of the increase in enrollment of both traditional college age groups and older students can be attributed to increased participation of women.[3]

A first variable in these patterns is cogently expressed by the trends in post-baccalaureate degrees, though it should be remembered that the increase of women in all postsecondary education is the most significant of all groups.

The numbers of master's degrees conferred by institutions of higher education grew at a steady rate, reaching a high of 317,164 in 1977 before dropping slightly in 1978, while the number of doctor's degrees awarded peaked at 34,777 in 1973. At both levels, the proportion of women earning degrees rose steadily throughout the decade, reaching 48 percent of master's and doubling to 26 percent of doctor's degrees in 1978. In the 1980's the number of master's degrees awarded is projected to level off, with degrees awarded to men decreasing and those awarded to women increasing. Women are expected to represent over one-half of the master's degree recipients in 1980.[4]

Secondly, age group variation in enrollment presents a view of the life patterns of society. Work and study patterns of course have an impact, as do family responsibilities. It is interesting to note the length of time spent in learning by a growing segment of Americans.

[Thus] a look at the number and age structure of continuing education participants suggests their unique character when compared to those of full-time postsecondary students. The number of continuing education participants in 1978 was over 18 million, almost 40 percent greater than the number of full-time high school or college students 17 years old and over. Among the 17-to-24-year-old age group, continuing education participants comprised about 11 percent of the population and full-time high school and college students approximately 31 percent. In the next age group, 25-to-34-year-olds, the pattern was reversed, with continuing education participants representing 20 percent and full-time students, less than 4 percent of the total. Thirteen percent of 35-to-54-year-olds and almost 7 percent of 55-to-64-year-olds participated in continuing education activities, compared to under 1 percent in both age groups enrolled full time in school. Although participation declined with age, about 2 percent of persons 65 years old and over participated while under a tenth of a percent were enrolled full time.[5]

A third interesting but distressing variable is the enrollment patterns in relation to racial/ethnic distributions.

Although female representation appeared more than equitable, disparities in racial/ethnic representation were evident in continuing education participation. A look at trends in participation . . . suggests further that the disparities have increased over time. The two largest minority groups were significantly underrepresented in relation to the population counts. The underrepresentation of Blacks and Hispanics was greater in continuing education than in higher education generally.[6]

It should be noted here that many efforts by the federal government to provide education for the ethnic minority groups have been carried out under the rubric of training and under the provision of agencies other than educational institutions. Primarily, therefore, these efforts are occupational and still lack the benefits of a wider, liberalizing education of citizenship issues and other multidimensional learning.

Educational attainment levels constitute a fourth significant variable as the NCES statistics clearly portray.

That continuing education participants represent a rather homogenous group is further substantiated by educational attainment levels reported in the 1978 survey. Continuing education participants were almost twice as likely as the total adult population to have higher education experience, 57 percent compared to 30 percent. Almost 33 percent of continuing education participants had completed at least 4 years of college in comparison to 14 percent of the total adult population.[7]

Income, occupational, and geographical distributions are other demographic variables that are instructive for the continuing education specialist since participation in programs is closely tied to these factors.

The income and occupational distributions of participants were reflected to some extent in metropolitan participation rates. Central city areas with higher concentrations of the poor and unemployed had lower continuing education participation rates than suburban areas. Rural farm areas had the lowest rates, consistent with the low participation of agricultural workers. Regional differences were also apparent; the Northeast and South were lower than the National rate, while the West was considerably higher. It is noteworthy that participation in Western non-metropolitan areas was as high as rates in the metropolitan areas located in other regions.[8]

It is certain that the changes in the legal status of students and the new age of majority, as well as the contractual rights of students have broad implications for the 1980s. As William A. Kaplin points out in *The Law of Higher Education*,[9] students are now legally "persons" with their own enforceable rights. Higher education is no longer termed a privilege under the discretion of the state nor does "in loco parentis" serve to characterize student higher education institution relationships in the 1980s. The age of majority is established by state law, most states having lowered the age to 18. Thus, regular students can now enter into contracts without a co-signer, can consent to their own medical treatment, can purchase alcoholic beverages, and can maintain a legal residence. The traditional 17- to 24-year-old student now has become an adult in a legal as well as a pragmatic sense. Many are part-time students who work and are looking for educational experiences closer to the continuing education model than the more rigid traditional academic pattern. At the present time, for example, continuing education students have no opportunity to participate in institutional governance.[10]

Therefore, enrollment pattern analysis including the basic all-university profile and its variation by trends in postbaccalaureate degree levels, cohort structure comparison, racial/ethnic distributions, educational attainment levels, and income and occupational distributions provide an array of data that can be consumed by the adult educator who wishes to program to meet oncoming needs, etc.

INFLUENCES OF GOVERNMENT

The federal government both stimulates and regulates by providing incentives and by passing laws. A task force has identified three concerns of national policy for postsecondary education:

1. The responsibility to preserve an open society and the conditions necessary for a free competition of ideas.

2. The responsibility to overcome inequities facing specific individuals and groups.

3. The responsibility to support research, development, and other "strategic interventions" necessary for effective service which no other level of government can make.[11]

It can be stated with certainty that federal involvement is substantial. It is known that the federal government is a direct provider of continuing education through Cooperative Extension, the military, etc. But there is no consensus on federal activities in continuing education; the goals are unrelated and the definitions are unstable. The present structure favors competition among institutions for government subsidized students and government grants. Increasingly the federal government funds individuals and institutions and funnels money through the states. The proliferation of regulations and forms to fill out have driven many participants and providers to the brink of despair. At the same time, national priorities, equity, and balanced development are items that can only be federally addressed. The fact is federal roles in continuing education are relatively new, increasingly funded, and still evolving.

However, the recent federal and state elections indicate the potential of retreat on the part of the government in support of the new groups who seek to enter some form of postsecondary education. The continuation of programs that have sought to address demographic change may be endangered. If that proves to be true, institutions will most certainly need to reexamine their policies and their resources deployment.

Despite what we hear about local control and campus automony, state policies influence institutional policies. In other words, not all public institutions look for the same sources of financial support. Generally, the higher the level of education, the more expensive it is, and the greater the number of support sources involved. There is one exception to the spreading of costs among tuitions plus federal and state subsidies. State policies reinforce the historical principle of the less compulsory the education, the more the student is expected to bear the full cost of education. The voluntary nature of most of continuing education has led state policy makers to subscribe to a pay-as-you-go rationale for withholding state subsidy. The far-reaching implications will be discussed later under institutional level policies.

The means for state control reside not just in its legal authority, but in the allocation of state and federal funds. While there is little direct state funding of continuing education programming, such programs in public institutions are indirectly affected by conditions in local institutions. For example, if the subsidized portion of the institution is not fully funded, the pressures are also experienced by continuing education. Furthermore, in addition to distributing its own money, each state usually distributes federal funds. This disbursement of money from several sources has led states with limited resources to encourage efforts to economize at the local level. One consequence has been a number of efforts for coordination (a condition considered to be synonymous with efficiency). At neither the federal nor the institutional levels is coordination so eagerly sought. There are many styles of coordination ranging from voluntary to involuntary and formal to informal, but local institutions tend to view coordination as control.

The basic problem for states has been that while coordination is theoretically feasible in the public sector, the private sector presents different issues. In most states, voluntary efforts are under way to bring together public and private providers to draft statewide plans. The state can exercise more control over public organizations than over privates ones where, except for the most general areas, the state cannot mandate binding agreements concerning the definition and scope of educational activities. In the public sector, the phrase "delineation of functions" is often heard with the intent to avoid duplication and overlap in educational programming. Considering institutional type, location, plus costs to the students and state, questions cover vertical articulation by grade level, and horizontal articulation by academic discipline and geographic area. In practice, state financial and legal sanctions have been unable to induce much spirit of cooperation, though the form and the effort may well be there.

REALITIES OF INDIVIDUAL INSTITUTIONS

Educational institutions and other community organizations exist in the same geographical area. No single entity presumes it can satisfy all the continuing education requirements of a community. Each provider has corresponding strengths and weaknesses. The call to eliminate duplication and overlap ignores two facts of organizational life. First, with the belief "we can do it better" institutions and units within these institutions freely engage in duplication unless forbidden to do so. Second, the competitive spirit that aspires to excellence can be weakened by mandates unless top administrations devise and monitor workable systems. In the real world of segmental coexistence, entrapreneurial behavior allows a degree of competitively motivated coordination. Tradeoffs for voluntary communication and cooperation in one sphere may yield high returns in another if the capabilities of each provide a peer relationship.

Utilization and disbursement of institutional resources are also major indicators of the status of continuing education.[1][2] Typically lacking federal, state, and institutional support, continuing education operates within a market economy. It depends on maintaining and expanding enrollments for obtaining funds. Without doubt, the reality of self-support has led to responsiveness to adult needs and interests. At the same time, expensive programs may be withheld because of the lack of surplus investment capital and the consequent risk of taking a loss.

This situation is exacerbated at some public and private institutions that require the continuing education department to subsidize regular programs. In effect, "self-supporting" continuing education is sometimes also expected to generate profits to be spent elsewhere in the institution.

Of course management practices are affected by the constraints of self-support. Constant responding to demands for low-cost programs and to readily identifiable needs does not promote long-range planning. It is difficult enough to keep up with a volatile market, driven by changing people in a changing world, and those who cannot afford to pay for their continuing education are often omitted from institutional plans. This harsh reality is due to the lack of endowments, scholarships, and other forms of financial aid. Some institutions have been forced to avoid government and foundation grants that could be used for underrepresented groups. Their rationale is that such money is "soft" or short-term, and creates public expectations that cannot be met for long. Consequently, many challenges go unanswered since financing and programming capabilities are inextricably linked.

The root cause of many problems in continuing education can be traced to the inequalities in funding policies that subordinate adult programming to youth-oriented programming. While institutions are slow to abandon past internal policies, external pressures have forced a number of adaptations. The decline in 18- to 21-year-old enrollments, sharply rising expenses, and institutional political vulnerability have led to accommodations at many places.

In an influential 1974 report by the American Council on Education, *Financing Part-time Students*, we find the first pronouncement that adults are the new majority in postsecondary education. We also find documentation of the fact that adults are massively discriminated against in student financial aid policies.[13]

The former executive director of the National University Extension Association, Robert J. Pitchell, has noted that only four states have a needs-based student aid policy that allows adults to apply. At the institutional level, Pitchell notes 59% of all colleges and 67% of public colleges charge part-time students higher tuition than their full-time students.[14] At the federal level, 92% of the students benefiting from the Basic Educational Opportunity Grant are full-time because less than half-time students (the bulk of adults) are ineligible. It is not easy to explain why state, institutional, and federal policies are weighted against adult students. Adults are not a homogeneous group. Not all adults have jobs, and not all adults with jobs can afford continuing education.

The assumptions that place continuing education on unequal financial footing for institutional and individual assistance are also expressed in the low levels of student support services and compensation for part-time faculty. Non-instructional services common in the regular program, such as counseling, may be drastically reduced to keep costs as low as possible. It is not unusual to find 2 or 3 administrators responsible for 10,000 students. Extraordinary demands on program administrators' time detract from the personal attention that should be spent on scheduling, class selection, curriculum development, staffing, and community relations. The combination of self-supporting programming and self-supporting adults results in few amenities beyond instruction.

Still another piece of evidence relates to decisions regarding faculty employment. Because continuing education is more market sensitive than any other form of education, it is therefore conducted on business principles related to supply and demand, income and expenses, product and advertising, slim margin for error, and tight management of personnel and facilities. The resource situation is twofold. First, within any given community institutions differ in their ability to attract students with the resultant variations in income. Second, institutions internally allocate faculty resources differentially between regular and adult programs.

The resource situation is magnified by the use of outside part-time instructors, as researcher and educator Dr. John Lombardi suggests:

> A thesis that seemed reasonable is that the growth of part-time student enrollment was in large part subsidized by the low wages of part-time instructors.[15]

If continuing education is a peripheral activity in higher education, the underfunding of part-time students and part-time faculty are both a cause and an effect of that ascribed status. Across the country in colleges and universities there is one part-time for every three full-time instructors. In community colleges there are more part-time instructors than there are full-time instructors. As *The Chronicle of Higher Education*[16] and other media have cited, there are economic reasons for the dramatic rise in the number of part-time instructors:

- They can be brought in to teach at a rate per course that is less than that paid to full-time faculty members.

- They receive fewer fringe benefits than do their full-time counterparts.

- They can be hired only for the semesters or quarters they are needed.

In much the same manner, part-time instructors teach for many different reasons: affiliation with a well-known institution, opportunity to discuss new concepts and formulations, additional income, and exposure to the public. Another point: part-timers can and do bring a wealth of additional talent to the campus. Also, full-timers often do not possess the skills, knowledge, and experience appropriate and current in specialized continuing education offerings, whether credit or noncredit. The dilemma becomes more visible when part-timers press for higher pay and more rights with consequent rise in costs to students while institutions lose some of their flexibility in the selection of the best faculty for instructional purposes.

With the principle equal pay for equal work, wages, job security, and professional status are issues. In some cases, a full-time instructor teaching the same course in the regular program may receive $2,500 and the part-timer in continuing education may receive $1,000. There is debate over whether responsibilities are in fact equal in both cases. Frequently the part-timer does not fulfill the myriad of faculty duties such as performing research, holding office hours, serving on committees, etc. The financial goals of part-time teachers are pro rata pay, on-the-job security, and part-time tenure. It is argued that after a period of employment the instructor earns the right to expect a permanent part-time assignment.

The rapid change alluded to throughout this and other papers, only serves to remind us that change agents are subject to changes even as they cause and encourage movement in attitude, ability, and access. Any analysis of continuing education today must take into account the diversity that exists among personnel even as it exists among policies, roles, and relationships.

We have been analyzing the role of those who instruct in the educational experience; yet whether they are part-time or full-time in the institution, they are almost always only part-time as they participate in continuing education. Central to the quality and maintenance of the continuing education program are the full-time professionals who create, innovate, conceptualize, facilitate, evaluate, manage, coordinate, research, plan, etc. They possess academic credentials (degrees) yet they are typically called "non-faculty"; and while demonstrating managerial skills, they are only rarely part of an institution's management team. Continuing education specialists in most institutions are still striving to accomplish a separate but equal status. As institutions turn more to adults as the source of salvation or even of ballast, those personnel whose skills and knowledge have concentrated on adults and their educational needs and capacities find themselves in an ambiguous status. Faculty, who in earlier years disdained adults, are now claiming greater capabilities in providing for adults since the discipline (and therefore, the students) is "theirs." However, the processes of continuing education—needs assessment, interdisciplinary curriculum design, selection of methodology, counseling, marketing, and evaluation of program and process for adults have long been the expertise of continuing educators. Thus the issue of management location within the institution has become crucial; to centralize budget and functions or to decentralize to various academic units is still the debated and unresolved question. The answer, however, determines selection of staff and administrators and the power to determine the size and scope of programs.

A reading of the vast array of brochures, bulletins, and newsletters from the 3,000+ institutions of higher education that provide education of adult programs of even the smallest dimension reveals that *professional development* consumes about one-half of all programs. Within that number, *business* programs lead all others. Career changes— in fact, career counseling of all kinds—come next.

Further, as we focus on the needs and interests of an aging population, a primary change in programming is the necessity to become more attuned to the needs for learning throughout the life span. Moreover, the significance in job changes in the 1980s has to do with changes at different stages and facets of the life trajectory. A recent publication by The College Board[17] clearly points out the opportunities and challenges of additional education as adults cope with the transitions in their lives, both personal and occupational, occasioned by change.

THE FUTURE

To attain a "learning society" we will need to build truly educative communities. What happens at the institutional level is of the greatest importance to continuing education. Federal and state policies take on their full meaning only through local practices. The significant differences among communities are reflected in their institutional configurations. The forms and forces, and individuals and institutions exhibit synergistic patterns of interaction. Movements in any given sector reverberate in the others. Individual planning takes into account what is accessible. Institutional planning takes into account what is being done elsewhere.

In *No Limits to Learning*[18] the impact worldwide of planning that recognizes the interactions and interfacings of individual and national goals is documented with unique examples. In this country, continuing education programming is responsive to both actual and anticipated situations. Institutions are selective about needs and interests they try to meet. The manifold nature of continuing education allows it to be many things to many people.

NOTES

1. Continuing Education Service, *Annual Report 1973-1974* (East Lansing, MI: Michigan State University, 1974), p. 1.

2. Rosalind K. Loring, "New Trends in Professional Continuing Education" in *Professional Continuing Education Comes of Age*, ed. by Roger W. Axford [Proceedings of a conference on Professional Continuing Education, February 7-8, 1980; An unpublished manuscript] (Tempe, AZ: Arizona State University), p. 14.

3. *The Condition of Education, A Statistical Report*, National Center for Education Statistics (Washington, DC: U.S. Government Printing Office, 1980), p. 96.

4. Ibid., p. 100.

5. Ibid., p. 230.

6. Ibid., p. 321.

7. Ibid.

8. Ibid., p. 230.

9. William A. Kaplin, *The Law of Higher Education* (San Francisco: Jossey-Bass, 1978), pp. 175-82.

10. Ibid., p. 181.

11. *The Second Newman Report: National Policy and Higher Education Institutions*, Special Task Force to the Secretary of Health, Education and Welfare (Cambridge, MA: The Massachusetts Institute of Technology, 1974), p. 92.

12. For further information, see Rosalind K. Loring, "Dollars & Decisions," in *Power and Conflict*, ed. by Philip E. Frandson (Belmont, CA: Wadsworth Publishing Co., 1980).

13. Committee on the Financing of Higher Education for Adult Students, *Financing Part-time Students* (Washington, DC: American Council on Education, 1974).

14. Dyckman W. Vermilye, ed., *Lifelong Learners—A New Clientele for Higher Education* (San Francisco: Jossey-Bass, 1974), p. 44.

15. John Lombardi, *Part-time Faculty in Community Colleges* (Los Angeles, CA: ERIC Clearinghouse for Junior Colleges, 1975).

16. Jack Margarell, "Part-time Professors on the Increase," *The Chronicle of Higher Education*, 16 (January 1978), p. 6.

17.   Carol B. Aslanian and Henry M. Brickell, *Americans in Transition* (New York: College Entrance Examination Board, 1980).

18.   James W. Botkin, Mahdi Elmandjra, and Mircea Malitza, *No Limits to Learning* (New York: Pergamon Press, 1979).

BIBLIOGRAPHY

Aslanian, Carol B., and Brickell, Henry M. *Americans in Transition*. New York: College Entrance Examination Board, 1980.

Axford, Roger, ed. *Professional Continuing Education Comes of Age*. Proceedings of a Conference on Professional Continuing Education, February 7-8, 1980. [An unpublished manuscript] Tempe, AZ: Arizona State University.

Botkin, James W., Elmandjra, Mahdi, and Malitza, Mircea. *No Limits to Learning*. New York: Pergamon Press, 1979.

Committee on the Financing of Higher Education for Adult Students. *Financing Part-time Students*. Washington, DC: American Council on Education, 1974.

Condition of Education. A Statistical Report. National Center for Education Statistics. Washington, DC: U.S. Government Printing Office, 1980.

Continuing Education Service. *Annual Report, 1973-1974*. East Lansing, MI: Michigan State University, 1974.

Frandson, Philip E., ed. *Power and Conflict*. Belmont, CA: Wadsworth Publishing Co., 1980.

Kaplin, William A. *The Law of Higher Education*. San Francisco: Jossey-Bass, 1978.

Lombardi, John. *Part-time Faculty in Community Colleges*. Los Angeles, CA: ERIC Clearinghouse for Junior Colleges, 1975.

Loring, Rosalind K. "Dollars and Decisions," in *Power and Conflict*. Ed. by Philip E. Frandson. Belmont, CA: Wadsworth Publishing Co., 1980.

Loring, Rosalind K. "New Trends in Professional Continuing Education," in *Professional Continuing Education Comes of Age*. Ed. by Roger W. Axford. Proceedings of a Conference on Professional Continuing Education, February 7-8, 1980. [An unpublished manuscript] Tempe, AZ: Arizona State University, 1980.

Margerell, Jack. "Part-time Professors on the Increase." *The Chronicle of Higher Education*. January 16, 1978.

Second Newman Report: National Policy and Higher Education Institutions. Special Task Force to the Secretary of Health, Education and Welfare. Cambridge, MA: The Massachusetts Institute of Technology Press, 1974.

Vermilye, Dyckman W., ed. *Lifelong Learners—A New Clientele for Higher Education.* San Francisco: Jossey-Bass, 1974.

LIBERAL EDUCATION AND CAREERS

by
Sterling M. McMurrin

E. E. Ericksen Distinguished Professor
Professor of History
Professor of the Philosophy of Education
University of Utah

The severe decline over the past several years of the job market for certain categories of college and university graduates has in some segments of the society forced a reconsideration of the worth of nonprofessional higher education. A critical examination of the educational program and process is always useful, but there are signs now that this growing skepticism regarding higher education may not only throw doubt upon the value of colleges and universities and adversely affect the character of education, but may even strike a serious blow at the intellectual integrity of our culture in general. It is the culture of both the individual and the society in general that ultimately count, not the educational institutions. The institutions are means for the achievement of personal and social ends that define the worth of life and the character and quality of human experience. To the extent that they do not satisfy the needs and interests of the society that provides their substance and the individuals who come to them for instruction, they fail in their proper task. That the colleges and universities are indeed failing is becoming a rather common complaint. Whether this charge is justified is a question deserving careful consideration. It is a question concerning the meaning of education and the purposes of colleges and universities.

In our culture, where the intrinsic worth of the individual person is of central importance, education is properly directed first to the satisfaction of the basic needs and interests of the individual. But it has a crucial responsibility also for the strengthening and perpetuation of the culture. It is basic to our faith in democracy that whatever contributes effectively to the genuine well-being of the individual adds substantially to the quality and strength of our society and culture. The forces of education must be critical, creative, and productive, and must concern the entire range of human values—biological, economic, social, intellectual, moral, and spiritual.

But education is a task of the total society involving all its institutions. The proper function of the school is primarily, though not exclusively, intellectual. Its central purpose is the cultivation of the intellect, which involves the love and pursuit of knowledge, a passion for truth, respect for evidence and logical argument, and a disposition toward reason and reasonableness that makes irrational thought and behavior abhorrent.

Various skills, of course, are essential elements in the processes of schooling; those of literacy are absolutely necessary to education. But for the most part, skills are a matter of training; they are means to ends rather than end values in themselves. Much of the time and energy of the schools is devoted to the development and perfection of skills and even some university work preparatory to the highest level professions is, in a measure, training in skills rather than education in the sense of the basic meaning of a university.

It is in what is commonly called liberal education that the meaning of education is best exhibited, for it is here that knowledge is pursued not for the sake of skills nor for its uses toward other ends, but for its own sake. It is here that the mind is cultivated in those virtues that bring the powers of intellect to their highest reaches, where knowledge and truth and the degree of understanding of the world and experience they make possible are the supreme values.

Not only the sciences, but morals and art and religion as well, have a proper claim on liberal education. Here as much as anywhere else there is need for reliable knowledge, respect for evidence, and commitment to reasonableness and truth. Liberal education is not something that stands alone without a substantial base in matters of fact, or that is totally independent of moral sensitivity and artistic appreciation, or religious sentiment and commitment. That there is no theoretical possibility of a science of normative ethics comparable, for instance, to physics or chemistry, a science that will answer our questions of what we ought or ought not to do, that will tell us what is good or evil, right or wrong, does not mean that reliable knowledge and correct reasoning are not essential to wisdom in moral judgment and action. In effect the same may be said for rationality as against irrationality in art, although here the case may not be so obvious. Its importance is immeasurable when consideration is given not only to the intrinsic value of art but as well to its impact on all facets of the personality and on the total character of a society. And though religion is not a body of knowledge or an exercise in logic, but is, rather, an experience, a sentiment, or commitment, some degree of reasonableness in religion is a possibility. I say "possibility" because genuinely rational religion is not a common achievement. I have no disposition to argue here with those who hold against the idea of rationality in art and religion, or in morals. Rather, I want simply to point out that the cultivation of intellectual interests and capabilities, which is the proper function of a college or university and is basic to the meaning of liberal education, is not irrelevant to those facets of human experience and endeavor that are not essentially cognitive in character as are the natural and social sciences.

During the 1960s and 1970s in the United States there was a large investment, from both national and state resources, in the establishment of middle-level technical schools and colleges and the upgrading of existing institutions. This was a response to an advancing technology that was spreading rapidly into the economy of everyday life and also to the acute shortage of low- and especially middle-level technicians, those whose skills required a type of training that was generally not available in either the secondary schools or the conventional colleges and universities. Many community colleges have provided this training, and in some instances the technical schools have developed curricular functions more or less appropriate to community colleges. These institutions perform a most important service, whether judged by the needs of society or the value of job preparation. They deserve, and seem to be receiving, strong support.

Schools of this order are constantly confronted with a basic dilemma: that insofar as they adequately perform their primary function of preparing specific skills for jobs, they usually fall short of providing anything like an adequate education for their students; and when they move toward a more general curriculum, they are in danger of damaging their competence in skill training, for time, energy, and resources are limited. But we seem justified in insisting that the values of a liberal education should be made available to everyone, to those who enroll in technical schools for immediate job training, whatever the level of that training, as well as to those who commit themselves to four-year degrees from a liberal arts college or university. How to develop a curriculum that will overcome this dilemma is one of the large problems of American education. The technician trained in specific skills is as deserving of a basic education that will enable him to cultivate a profound appreciation of the arts and great literature, some grasp of the economic, social, and political forces that swirl around him, at least a minimum understanding of the nature of science, and an intelligent curiosity regarding the large philosophical problems that stretch the human mind, as is the graduate of a university educated quite specifically in an area of the fine or liberal arts. A concern for the great questions, an appreciation of the arts, or a serious attempt at understanding the self in the world are not values that should be the exclusive property simply of a highly educated elite. There are inevitable and necessary differences of degree in education, of course, as there are differences in capabilities, interests, and career aspirations; but in a truly democratic society ideally none should be denied access to some measure of a liberal education. Our great problem is that the irrational egalitarianism that has pervaded and distorted our sense of equality has for the most part produced a refusal to recognize difference, resulting in a deadening mediocrity that has cast a serious doubt on the very worth of a liberal education.

At best the meaning of liberal education is somewhat ambiguous. The term is difficult to define for it has meant different things at various times and places. In the earlier period of occidental education, a liberal education seems to have meant an education designed especially for a free person. It was the education in the arts and letters appropriate for a person of leisure and high social status. This meaning has been to some extent perpetuated into our own day and has contributed to the current negative attitude toward liberal learning, especially when that learning is associated chiefly with the literary arts. It seems to me that today in our society liberal education should be defined as that education that will free a person—free his mind from ignorance, superstition, and irrationality, his perception from the blinders of prejudice and predilection, his thought from fallacious reasoning, his understanding from the parochialisms of time and space. There is no set curriculum that will provide this kind of education for everyone. Flexibility in curriculum, in subject matter, and instructional methods is essential to accommodate to inevitable individual, social, and cultural differences and to provide for constant experimentation for educational improvement.

It is understandable but regrettable that the job market for liberal arts graduates has led to such a large measure of skepticism of the value of liberal learning and irresponsible criticism of the colleges and universities for their investment of faculty and student time and energy in nonprofessional instruction. Much of the criticism, from laymen, students, and educators alike, a criticism that threatens to seriously affect public confidence in higher education, is irresponsible first because it fails to appreciate the function of a university or liberal arts college, supposing their proper role to be simply to provide elemental job training and professional or paraprofessional preparation rather than to *educate* the student; and second, because it fails to comprehend the value of a liberal education for the successful pursuit of any career. This, of course, is aside from the great intrinsic worth of a liberal education without which both the individual and his society are severely deprived. And it often ignores the high-level preparation for careers in numerous professions that is commonly possible only in universities or in the best technical or professional schools of university stature. Where else except from our colleges and universities do we get our scientists, philosophers, doctors, lawyers, teachers, historians, and a multitude of others whose vocations are essential to the ongoing life of society?

With regard to the second matter, the failure to appreciate the worth of a liberal education for any career whatsoever, I will repeat a statement I made in a recently published essay in which I commented on what I called the antinomy of the useless and the useful in higher education:

> It seems strange, indeed, that anyone should suppose that a liberal education that is devoted to the cultivation of the intellectual life, giving attention to the ways of knowing, the structure of science, some knowledge of the structure of contemporary society and how our society came to be where it is, with an appreciation of literature and art and the great philosophic discussions, in its better forms an education which attempts to induct a person into the culture of which he is a part—it is strange that this would not be seen as an essential and necessary preparation for any life's work that calls for judgment, intelligent decision, a capacity for critical thought, an understanding of human relationships, and some grasp of what the world is like. Why such an education should not be seen as genuinely useful, not simply as an enrichment of the quality of personality and life, but as a factor in the pursuit of one's vocation, is one of the mysteries of our society's perverse temperament.[1]

Now in arguing for the "practical" worth of liberal education, I do not for a moment mean to place the extrinsic value of liberal education as a means for furthering or enhancing a career above its intrinsic value as the "enrichment of the quality of personality and life." What a genuinely liberal education may bring as a simple increment to the life of the individual and society is of worth beyond measure. It is an end in itself whatever may or may not be its value as an instrument for gaining other ends. Those who attack liberal education are attacking not only something essential to the world of work in an advanced and highly cultivated society; they are probably unknowingly attacking some of the basic values to which they are otherwise fully committed.

On this matter, as on the entire subject of education, I strongly urge the reading of *The Uses of a Liberal Education* by America's preeminent living philosopher, Professor Brand Blanshard. No one has written on the worth of liberal education more effectively or argued his position more reasonably or with more profound insight into the forms of human experience and the interests and needs they generate than has Professor Blanshard. Says Blanshard:

> What is significant about a person or a people is the invisible things about them, the place where they keep their treasure stored, the unseen sun behind the clouds that determines the orbit of their lives. And curiously enough, it is these unseen things that are most nearly eternal. The educators of the West were those restlessly active people, the Greeks. But not one ship or bridge, not one palace or fortress or temple that their impatient activity erected has come down to us except as a ruin; and the state they built so proudly was already a ruin two thousand years ago. Does anything of them remain? Yes, the Greek spirit remains. The thought of Plato remains, the art of Sophocles, the logic and ethics of Aristotle. Literature, it has been said, is the immortal part of history. No doubt there were hardheaded practical men in Athens who stopped before the door of Plato's Academy and asked what was the use of it all. They and their names have vanished; the little Academy became a thousand academies among nations then unborn. There is a moral, I think, in this history. It is the usefulness, the transcendent usefulness, of useless things.[2]

The root of the matter of the devaluation of liberal education is the materialistic emphasis of our culture, which inclines us toward an almost exclusively economic interpretation of the nature of man. It is the tendency to regard a human being primarily as a material producer and consumer and therefore to judge his education by his capacity for production and consumption, essentially on quantitative terms. Obviously, the student graduating from secondary school should and must pursue a course that will ensure a satisfying career, one that will provide a good living that will meet his economic and other needs and expectations. But it is unfortunate when he and his counselors, both at school and at home, fail to recognize those other needs, or to cultivate and encourage those other expectations, or see only narrow immediate skills or only the wage dollar sign when they consider the economic side of his vocation. Just as there is more to life than wages and salary, necessary and essential as these are, there should be more to education than simply training for a job or a lucrative position.

Fortunately, we are by no means engrossed in a total cynicism with respect to liberal education, and there is some indication that good results may eventually ensue from the current predicament of liberally educated graduates without a job market, good results for those of the future but no great comfort for the present jobless. Among other things, I have in mind the fact that some of the advanced professional schools are showing a preference for applicants with undergraduate arts and liberal arts majors. This is true, I believe, in the case of some of the strongest graduate schools of business, and it is true also that many major corporations are recognizing the worth of a liberal education for those seeking executive careers. Experimental work in retooling persons with liberal graduate degrees to qualify them for business careers apparently has revealed heretofore unrecognized strength in their type of education.

But retooling the liberally degreed is at best an emergency measure affecting only a few. The answer to the problem lies in both employers and educators taking a new and fresh look at the matter. For their part, the leaders in the professions, industry, business, and government should examine closely the advantages to their enterprises of employing persons who have at least the rudiments of a genuine education rather than simply training in a specialized discipline. They will find that those advantages are both numerous and important. They involve the capacity to think creatively, to adapt to changing circumstances, to judge and act intelligently, and, not least in importance, to bring to their work, whatever it may be, a measure of civility and intellectual refinement. And educators, especially those in the universities and liberal arts colleges, should raise again the question of what constitutes a genuine education and undertake the very difficult task of developing objectives and curricula that will make liberal education more clearly relevant to the facts of living and the task of "making" a living. It is not enough to argue that a liberal education has career as well as intrinsic values. The social sciences, humanities, and arts, for instance, should be pursued academically in such a way that their extrinsic worth will be ensured as their value for the sake of increased knowledge and the pursuit of truth is increased.

This is a difficult task in which we may not fully succeed. It means that the professional, industrial, and governmental leaders of our society must overcome their penchant for treating human beings simply as producers, consumers, and voters and begin to see them as persons who have intellectual, moral, artistic, and spiritual interests and aspirations as well as economic needs. And it means that educators must continue to take long, hard looks at their educational programs. Here at least two things, in my opinion, should be done. Abandon the notion that many academics still have that a "general" education is the equivalent of liberal education, an idea that has often produced a serious weakening of the curriculum and has robbed students of genuine depth in education; and second, update the common conception of what constitutes a liberal education. Even today, there are some for whom liberal education is simply a classical education. I personally feel a great loss in the diminished interest in classical languages and literature, but "classical" should not define "liberal." Sometimes even the sciences are omitted from the conception of liberal education, another serious error. But the main thing is to recognize that a genuine education, that is, a liberal education in the best sense of the word, is one that cultivates one's rational powers and contributes to an understanding of self and the world. Over the past century new things have come into the picture that affect the problem of understanding—evolution, relativity, depth psychology, new forms of social, political, and industrial organization, new patterns of international trade and finance, the possibility of nuclear war. And there are new aids to the mind in the quest for knowledge and understanding—computers and the remarkable instruments of communication that characterize the electronic age. All of these factors and countless more must be taken into consideration in defining liberal education and developing a liberal curriculum. The loss of Latin as a degree requirement does not mean the decline of liberal education if something more appropriate to an understanding of today's world replaces it. That something may come from the department of finance or management or from the school of engineering. We can no longer simply equate liberal education, which is the truly *basic* education, with the humanities. Important and basic as these are, the humanities as traditionally conceived in academic circles are not the totality of liberal education.

Finally, against those who persist in setting "career" education against liberal education, who argue, as some do, that the technical colleges thrive because the universities have failed, I will simply insist that the very notion of career education, as distinct from liberal education, is in a sense a misnomer. All real education is education for careers. It is a question of whether one is referring to genuine education or technical training and whether by career is meant a life's work that brings full satisfaction or simply a remunerative job or position.

We should not suppose that the schools and colleges and universities are the only route to good education. Education begins in the family and is a task of the total society with its multiple and varied institutions. But the schools at every level have the specialized task of cultivating the reason and pursuing knowledge, and these are the ground of a truly educated person. No doubt for a long time to come, for the vast majority the organized schools will be essential to the educative process. But it is the end product that counts, not the means to its achievement. And the end product, the education of the person, must continually be redefined. Some time ago, at the request of the National Education Association, I composed a brief description of an educated person that may bear repetition here:

> An educated man is at home with ideas. He is as comfortable with concepts as he is with objects. He readily infers the general from the particular, for his capacities for rational abstraction equal his powers of concrete perception.
>
> An educated man is one whose reason disciplines his attitudes and action, but in whom the emotions are alive and sensitive and in whom there is genuine moral awareness, artistic perceptiveness, and spiritual commitment.
>
> An educated man has some understanding of himself. He is aware of his own prejudices, is critical of his own assumptions, and knows his own limitations.
>
> An educated man is aware of the events that have brought the world to where he finds it. He knows the wellsprings of his own society and

culture and understands the essential unity of past, present, and future.

An educated man has a fine sense of the relation of the ideal to the real, of the possible to the actual. He is not satisfied with the world as it is, but he knows that it will never be what he would like it to be. He has hope for the future, but refuses to deny the tragedies of the present.

An educated man has a cultivated curiosity that leads him beyond the bounds of his own place and circumstance. Provincialism and parochialism have no place in his world, for they stifle thought and inhibit creativity.

Finally, an educated man is one who loves knowledge and will accept no substitutes and whose life is made meaningful through the never-ending process of the cultivation of his total intellectual resources.[3]

NOTES

1.   Sterling M. McMurrin, "The Antinomies of Higher Education," in *The Philosophy and Future of Graduate Education*, ed. by William K. Frankena (Ann Arbor, MI: University of Michigan Press, 1980), p. 116.

2.   Brand Blanshard, *The Uses of a Liberal Education*, ed. by Eugene Freeman (La Salle, IL: Open Court Publishing Co., 1973), p. 43.

3.   "What Is a Well-Educated Man?," *NEA Journal* (April 1962), p. 221. (Please update this statement by reading "person" for "man.")

SUMMARY AND RECOMMENDATIONS

by
Martha Boaz

We are living in a world that is increasingly complex and unpredictable. Many educators are examining the situation and exploring ways to go ahead, even under adverse circumstances, toward programs of excellence in education. The professional educators who have written papers for this book have studied the trends and prospects in their fields and have expressed their opinions about future developments. The opening article gives a background of some of the general trends, issues, problems, and possible future directions in the field of higher education. Articles on specific areas of professional education follow and include: law, medical fields (general medicine and pharmacy), architecture, engineering, business administration, public administration, higher education, librarianship, gerontology, and continuing education. There is also a general essay on liberal education and careers.

SUGGESTIONS AND RECOMMENDATIONS

In brief summary, suggestions are being made to combat problems and to go forward. These suggestions include: 1) using facilities on a year-round and a round-the-clock basis; 2) integrating the new electronic technology into academic life; 3) adjusting educational programs to make them more innovative, more flexible, and to include more nontraditional students; 4) examining programs eliminating weak ones, strengthening vital ones, and, at the same time, being fiscally responsible and administratively accountable; 5) requiring administrative/faculty/staff commitment to the educational and professional goals of the institution, with high expectations of performance and excellence from everyone; 6) promoting cooperative research arrangements between universities and between universities and industry; 7) emphasizing education for international relations and world understanding; 8) proceeding with courage, imagination, and concern towards educational programs that will answer personal, social, national, and international needs.

Two of the above recommendations are receiving national attention: the promotion of cooperative research arrangements between universities and business and the emphasis on education for international relations and world understanding. With reference to the first point, according to a recent report by the National Commission on Research, cooperative research programs between higher education and business should be encouraged. Such arrangements could strengthen research, encourage innovation, and provide better products and services for the public. Among benefits to the universities would be: 1) access to more technical resources from industry; 2) improved understanding among university researchers of innovation, development, and marketing through the "market connection"; 3) consistent and longer-term additional funds for research; 4) less administrative reporting detail than government-financed research; and 5) greater public credibility for service to society. Industry would also have benefits, including: 1) opportunity to influence university research; 2) looking ahead to new areas of research using experimental research programs of the university; 3) making jobs in industry more attractive to students; and 4) greater credibility in the eyes of the public.

The second subject of national interest, mentioned above, deals with the international components of our curricula and education for international relations, communication, and world understanding. This means a revision of educational programs from nineteenth century concepts to deal with twentieth century problems. Shirley Hufstedler, the former Secretary of Education, points out that we live in an interrelated global world, yet this is only marginally reflected in our school systems. She quotes a recent editorial: "America's young face a set of new national and international circumstances about which they have only the faintest of notions. They are globally speaking, blind, deaf, and dumb; and thus handicapped, they will soon determine the future direction of this nation."[2] Hufstedler continues, "The growing disparity between the realities of an interdependent world and the relative parochialism of our schools and colleges cannot help damaging the nation's capacity to decide its wisest future course."[3] The urgent need for examining current curricula offerings and educational programs in light of national and international problems, trends, directions, and opportunities is a matter that transcends ordinary curricula or financial matters. Kenneth Boulding has noted that no country can go it alone any longer; he says, "if the human race survives, it will have to change its ways of thinking more in the next 25 years than it has in the last 25,000."[4]

In light of statements such as these, it seems urgent that educators and administrators give serious thought to fresh intellectual vigor and responsibility on the national/international/transnational scene.

CONCLUSION

It is clear that educational institutions must examine the current needs of society and look ahead to the challenges of the future, investigating the needs for new information and changing values and designing educational programs for a changing interdependent society in an increasingly complex world.

When history is written, 30 years from now, the question may be asked, "Why didn't the 1980s society seize opportunity and shape the world and change it?"

NOTES

1. *The Chronicle of Higher Education*, (September 29, 1980), p. 7.

2. Shirley M. Hufstedler, "A World in Transition," *Change*, (May-June 1980), p. 8.

3. Ibid.

4. Ibid.

BIOGRAPHICAL SKETCHES OF THE AUTHORS

STEPHEN ABRAHAMSON, Ph.D., is director of the Division of Research and chairman of the Medical Education Department, School of Medicine at the University of Southern California. He has been active in international medical education, having served as educational consultant for the World Health Organization in many countries of the world, and is responsible for numerous publications in the field of medical education.

RUSSELL E. BIDLACK has been a member of the faculty of the University of Michigan's School of Library Science since 1953; he has served as the school's dean since 1969. His Ph.D. degree was awarded by the University of Michigan in 1954. His teaching interests have included cataloging and classification as well as library history and bibliography. His publications, numbering over 50 monographs and articles, relate to local history as well as to library education. His professional honors include the 1977 Beta Phi Mu Award for Distinguished Service to Education for Librarianship and the 1979 Melvil Dewey Medal·for Recent Creative Professional Achievement of a High Order.

JOHN A. BILES, professor of pharmacy (pharmaceutical chemistry) and dean of the University of Southern California School of Pharmacy, serves as consultant to the Bureau of Health Manpower Education, Health Resources Administration, on the National Advisory Council on Education for Health Professions (1970-1971). He is also consultant to the Bureau of Health Services Research and consultant to the Veterans Administration hospitals in San Diego and Los Angeles. He is a fellow of the Academy of Pharmaceutical Sciences, having served or chaired prominent committees of the Academy since 1967. He is a member of the American Public Health Association, the American Association of Colleges of Pharmacy, the American and California Pharmaceutical Associations, the American Society of Hospital Pharmacists, and the Board of Directors of Allergan Pharmaceuticals in Irvine.

JAMES E. BIRREN, Ph.D., (Psychology), is executive director of the Ethel Percy Andrus Gerontology Center, and dean of Leonard Davis School of Gerontology, University of Southern California. He has published over 150 journal articles, book chapters, and books including: *Handbook of the Psychology of Aging* (with K. W. Schaie); *Handbook of Mental Health and Aging* (with R. Bruce Sloane); and the *Psychology of Aging*. In 1978-1979, Dean Birren was a fellow in the Center for Advanced Study in the Behavioral Sciences at Stanford. He was formerly chief of the Section on Aging, National Institute of Mental Health, and director of the Aging Program, National Institute of Mental Health and Human Development. Among honors he has received are the Distinguished Scientific Contribution Award, APA; the Gerontological Society Award for Meritorious Research; and the CIBA Foundation Award for Research on Problems of Aging. His primary research and teaching interests include psychophysiology of aging, speed of behavior and aging, psychology of aging, and the psychology of adult development.

MARTHA BOAZ, Ph.D., is a research associate, Center for Study of the American Experience, Annenberg School of Communications and dean emeritus of the Graduate School of Library Science, University of Southern California. Prior to her long tenure as library school dean, she had held positions in school, college, and public libraries. She has also served as a consultant in various aspects of librarianship both in the United States and the Far East. She has been president of the Association of American Library Schools, the Library Education Division of the American Library Association, and the California Library Association. She has been author and editor of numerous books and articles, with special interests in library education, research methods, administration, and new developments in technology and information retrieval.

V. THOMAS DOCK received his Ph.D. degree in 1970 from the University of Northern Colorado. His major field of concentration was management information systems. Presently, he is associate dean for Administration and Budgets of the School of Business Administration at the University of Southern California. He has authored and coauthored six textbooks and several articles in the field of management information systems. He has been an officer and presently is a director of the American Institute for Decision Sciences. He also has participated in several of the professional programs sponsored by the organization. Tom has advised the managers of several national and foreign organizations concerning the development, implementation, and operation of management information systems.

MELVIN GERSTEIN is associate dean of the School of Engineering and professor of mechanical engineering at the University of Southern California. He obtained his Ph.D. at the University of Chicago. He worked on the Manhattan Project for NASA and for 12 years was scientific advisor to NATO in the field of aerospace research and development. An author of numerous papers in the field of combustion, he also teaches a course entitled Technology and Society for non-engineers and is a member of the Board of the Council for the Understanding of Technology in Human Affairs.

MARTIN LYON LEVINE is professor of law and professor of psychiatry and the behavioral sciences at the University of Southern California Law Center and Medical School. He was first chairman of USC's University Council/President's Advisory Council, and has also taught at Columbia Law School, George Washington University Medical School, and the University of California, San Diego. A graduate of Brandeis University and Yale Law School, he was selected by the American Council on Education and *Change* magazine as one of the 100 Outstanding Young Leaders in American Higher Education.

ROSALIND K. LORING is the dean of the College of Continuing Education at the University of Southern California. She has coauthored two books: *Breakthrough: Women into Management* (revised, 1974) and *New Life Options: The Working Woman's Resource Book* (1976). Among her numerous professional articles are "Matrix Management of Continuing Education" (*NUEA Spectator*, June 1976), "The Multi-Levels of Continuing Education: Federal, State, and Local Institutions" (*Convergence*, 1979), "Dollars and Decisions" (in Frandson's *Power and Conflict*, 1980), and "New Trends in Professional Continuing Education" (in Axford's *Proceedings of the Conference: Professional Continuing Education Comes of Age*, February 7-8, 1980). Currently, Dean Loring is a Trustee of the College Board and a member of the National Advisory Council on Extension and Continuing Education.

She is esteemed as a specialist in nontraditional education and is recognized as one of the top 25 contributors to her professional field.

STERLING M. McMURRIN is E. E. Ericksen Distinguished Professor, professor of history, professor of the philosophy of education, and adjunct professor of philosophy at the University of Utah. He has authored or edited several books and published numerous articles on philosophy, religion, and education. During the administration of President John F. Kennedy he was United States Commissioner of Education.

DAVID MARS is professor of public administration and associate dean for Undergraduate Programs in Public Affairs at the University of Southern California (USC). He served, 1968-1971, as director of the School of Public Administration and has served as acting dean of the Center for Public Affairs at USC. He has also taught at Rutgers, Connecticut, and Hawaii. He has published widely, primarily articles in such areas as state/local government, metropolitan affairs, organizational behavior, criminal justice, and intergovernmental relations.

DAVID A. PETERSON, Ph.D., is professor and director of the Leonard Davis School of Gerontology, Andrus Gerontology Center, University of Southern California. Previously he was director of the Gerontology Program and Center on Aging at the University of Nebraska at Omaha, and director of training at the University of Michigan's Institute of Gerontology. His publications and research are on the design of professional training in gerontology and instruction of older people. His doctorate was completed in 1969 in adult and continuing education at the University of Michigan.

DAVID STEA, who has a Ph.D. from Stanford University, is professor of Architecture and Urban Planning at the University of California in Los Angeles. He had also taught at the University of Oregon, at Brown University, and at Clark University. He is the author of several books and numerous articles. Among his honors and awards are First Award, Journal of Architectural Research International Competition, 1976; First Award, Monument Design Competition, West Chicago Historical Society, 1965; and Grand Prize, Architectural Models, New Mexico State Fair, 1958, 1960, and 1962.

LESLIE WILBUR, chairman and professor, Department of Higher and Postsecondary Education at the University of Southern California, holds degrees from the University of Illinois, the University of California, and the Ph.D. from the University of Southern California. His educational experience, prior to his current appointment, included teaching and administration at Bakersfield College and serving as president of Barstow College. Among his other services, Dr. Wilbur has been a consultant on community colleges, and has done research and published in several subject areas of the college and university fields.

INDEX